Introduction to Instructed Second Language Acquisition

D0221767

Introduction to Instructed Second Language Acquisition is the first book to present a cohesive view of the different theoretical and pedagogical perspectives that comprise instructed second language acquisition (ISLA), defined as any type of learning that occurs as a result of the manipulating the processes and conditions of second language acquisition. The book begins by considering the effectiveness of ISLA and the differences between ISLA and naturalistic L2 learning. It then goes on to discuss the theoretical, empirical, and pedagogical aspects of such key issues in ISLA as grammar learning; interaction in the classroom; focus on form, function, and meaning; vocabulary learning; pronunciation learning; pragmatics learning; learning contexts; and individual differences. This timely and important volume is ideally suited for the graduate-level ISLA course, and provides valuable insights for any SLA scholar interested in the processes involved in second language learning in classroom settings.

Shawn Loewen is Associate Professor in the Second Language Studies program at Michigan State University.

Introduction to Instructed Second Language Acquisition

Shawn Loewen

Michigan State University

Routledge
Taylor & Francis Group

NEW YORK AND LONDON

First published 2015
by Routledge
711 Third Avenue, New York, NY 10017

and by Routledge
2 Park Square, Milton Park, Abingdon, Oxon, OX14 4RN

Routledge is an imprint of the Taylor & Francis Group, an informa business

Library of Congress Cataloging-in-Publication Data

Loewen, Shawn.
  Introduction to instructed second language acquisition / Shawn Loewen.
    pages cm
  Includes bibliographical references and index.
  1. Second language acquisition—Study and teaching.   I. Title.
  P118.2.L65   2015
  418.0071—dc 3   2014006484

ISBN: 978-0-415-52953-2 (hbk)
ISBN: 978-0-415-52954-9 (pbk)
ISBN: 978-0-203-11781-1 (ebk)

Typeset in Minion
by Apex CoVantage, LLC

For Pamela

Contents

Preface   ix

Acknowledgments   xi

1 Introduction   1

2 The Nature of Second Language Knowledge   18

3 Interaction in the Second Language Classroom   38

4 Focus on Form   57

5 The Acquisition of Grammar   76

6 The Acquisition of Vocabulary   95

7 The Acquisition of Pronunciation   115

8 The Acquisition of Pragmatics   128

9 Contexts of Instructed Second Language Acquisition   143

10 Individual Differences and Instructed Second
   Language Acquisition   162

11 Conclusion   179

    References   185
    Index   203

Preface

The idea for this book came out of the Introduction to Second Language Acquisition (SLA) courses that I have taught, primarily for master's students, but also for beginning doctoral students. In these courses, many students have been more pedagogically oriented, with the result that they find it difficult to begin the course with a heavy theoretical focus, which is the starting point for several introductory SLA textbooks. Consequently, we often all breathe a sigh of relief when we reach the more classroom oriented component of the course.

In addition, the field of SLA has burgeoned in recent decades, and it appears that this trend will continue unabated for the foreseeable future. As a consequence, sub-disciplines within SLA have expanded such that they now justify fuller and more focused attention. The term Instructed Second Language Acquisition (ISLA) is becoming more commonly used to refer to the subdomain of SLA that investigates the effects of manipulating various aspects of the L2 learning endeavor, from L2 input, to language processing, to contexts of learning. However, in spite of the term's popularity, there has not been, to my knowledge, a book that attempts provide a broad overview of ISLA. In some cases, books have covered one or two areas, but through this book, it is my intention to provide a more comprehensive account of ISLA, in order to see both the commonalities and differences that arise when researchers investigate, for example, the acquisition of grammar or pragmatics in traditional classroom or study abroad contexts.

I have tried to maintain a balance of theory, research and pedagogy in order to make the book accessible to individuals who may have some experience of second language (L2) teaching and/ or learning, but may have less knowledge of (or interest in) the more abstract aspects of acquisition. However, it is not my intention for this book to be primarily a pedagogical resource, but rather my goal is to use the familiar context of the classroom to highlight the processes that underlay the acquisition processes that occur therein. To that end, each chapter begins with a definition of the topic at hand, followed by an account of several of the more important theoretical issues related to the topic. Next, each chapter reviews important research related to the topic. In some cases, there are meta-analyses that synthesize the research, and in other cases, I have chosen individual research studies that illustrate important concepts. Next, the more practical aspects of the topic in terms of the L2 classroom are considered, and finally, each chapter concludes with activities that can be used with students in an Introduction to ISLA course.

I am keenly aware that this book provides primarily one account of ISLA, and before the end of book, you may realize that I approach language acquisition from a cognitive-interactionist perspective. It is not my intention to suggest that other approaches to SLA and ISLA are not valid or interesting; however, I write from my own perspective, which is, I believe, also a perspective in which much ISLA research has been conducted. Nevertheless, I hope other works will offer different perspectives on the multi-faceted nature of L2 acquisition in instructed contexts.

In the end, I found writing this book an exciting, challenging and daunting enterprise. It was exciting to consider a broader perspective than I often take in my own narrower research agenda. It was also rewarding to attempt to make connections across areas of ISLA and to consider how we might best assist learners engaged in the hard work of L2 learning. On the other hand, this book presented a considerable challenge as I realized the need to distill in an understandable and accessible manner the breadth of theory and research that has focused on L2 learning. It is my hope that this book will prove as rewarding and thought provoking for you as it has for me.

Acknowledgments

I am greatly indebted to numerous individuals for their assistance in various aspects of writing this book. I would like to thank my ISLA seminar students for their stimulating discussions on many of these topics: Dominik Wolff, Cristen Vernon, Ayman Mohamed, Virginia David, Scott Sterling, and Ji-Hyun Park. In addition, several colleagues graciously provided comments on previous drafts: Susan M. Gass, Patti Spinner, Jacob Reed, Masatoshi Sato, and Aline Godfroid. My editor, Leah Babb-Rosenfeld, was always supportive and patient. For additional inspiration and encouragement along the way I have to thank Ken Frank and Dean Smoll. And finally, for their forbearance throughout this long process, I am indebted to my children, Austin, Patrick, and Winona, and especially my wife Pamela, who made many sacrifices to see this book to completion. Unfortunately, any and all shortcomings are my own responsibility.

1

Introduction

The academic discipline of instructed second language acquisition (ISLA), at its most basic, attempts to answer two questions: (1) is instruction beneficial for second language (L2) learning, and (2) if so, how can the effectiveness of instruction be optimized? Because of this instructional perspective, ISLA has been used to refer to aspects of second language acquisition (SLA) theory and research that pertain directly to the L2 classroom. ISLA has focused, in particular, on the cognitive and psycholinguistic processes of L2 development which are arguably similar for all learners. In addition, the social aspects of L2 acquisition have been investigated, although perhaps to a lesser extent. Numerous research studies have investigated various facets of ISLA, and several books have provided a collection of studies (e.g., Housen & Pierrard, 2005) or a synthesized view of individual components of ISLA, such as grammar (e.g., Ellis, 1990). Even so, although Ortega (2013, p. 5) refers to ISLA as a 'burgeoning subdomain' of SLA, few works have attempted to go beyond individual research studies or specific linguistic areas to consider the broader scope of ISLA in an effort to bring together various issues and strands of research. This book endeavors to present a fuller examination of a range of topics and concerns related to ISLA. To that end, the current chapter considers the defining features and limits of ISLA. In addition, this chapter considers the foremost assumption of ISLA that L2 instruction matters and can be beneficial for L2 learning. Although most L2 teachers and students may consider such an assumption to be self-evident (otherwise why spend so much time in the classroom?), they would surely agree that L2 instruction is not always successful and students do not always learn what is taught in the L2 classroom. Some SLA researchers (e.g., Krashen, 1982, 2003) would contend, in fact, that L2 learners acquire very little in the classroom that enables them to use the L2 for spontaneous communicative purposes; rather, these researchers propose that learners acquire a second language in a similar way to their first language, by being exposed to the language from its speakers and from other sources of input such as books, movies, and music. Even though views about the overall ineffectiveness of L2 instruction are in the minority in the field of SLA, it is nevertheless important to ask, and investigate, if instruction really makes a difference for L2 acquisition.

WHAT IS ISLA?

Before addressing the effectiveness of instruction, however, it is important to consider the scope of ISLA. The term ISLA has been used in many cases as a rather loose description to refer to research that is focused on the L2 class-room; however, there is often little attempt to consider in detail the characteristics and definition of ISLA. For example, several recent SLA articles have included *instructed SLA* or *instructed second language learning* in their titles (e.g., Henry, Culman, & VanPatten, 2009; Mackey, 2006), although there is no discussion of what constitutes instructed SLA. Rather the definition of ISLA appears to be taken for granted, a not uncommon phenomenon perhaps because of the general familiarity and perceptions that both laypeople and applied linguists have regarding the L2 classroom. Nevertheless, in order to clarify and understand the nature and scope of ISLA, it is important to consider its defining features. Several researchers and theorists have presented more systematic definitions and operationalizations of the term. Ellis (1990), in his book entitled *Instructed Second Language Acquisition*, states simply that he is 'concentrating on the research that has addressed how **classroom** second language acquisition takes place' (original emphasis: p. vii). Ellis (2005) further states that 'instruction can be viewed as an attempt to intervene in the process of language learning' (p. 9). In a more recent definition, Loewen (2013, p. 2716) states that ISLA investigates L2 learning or acquisition that occurs as a result of teaching; he also states that 'the defining feature of L2 instruction is that there is an attempt by teachers, or instructional materials, to guide and facilitate the process of L2 acquisition'. An even more detailed definition of instruction is provided by Housen and Pierrard (2005) in their edited volume of research studies investigating various aspects of ISLA. They define ISLA as 'any systematic attempt to enable or facilitate language learning by manipulating the mechanisms of learning and/or the conditions under which these occur' (p. 2). Based on these previous works, the definition of ISLA upon which this book is premised is as follows: Instructed Second Language Acquisition is a theoretically and empirically based field of academic inquiry that aims to understand how the systematic manipulation of the mechanisms of learning and/or the conditions under which they occur enable or facilitate the development and acquisition of a language other than one's first.

Before considering in more detail the instructed component of ISLA, it is also important to consider the other terms in the acronym: *second, language,* and *acquisition.* The term *second* refers to any language other than one's first language. In most cases, it is clear what a learner's second language is because he or she started learning it well after their first language was fully established. For example, in the United States, many students begin studying a second language at the age of 13 or 14, by which time their knowledge of English is essentially complete. There are, however, instances where the difference between a person's first and second language is less clear. In multilingual societies or in bilingual families, children may be exposed to two or more languages from birth, and these languages may develop in tandem. In general, such contexts are studied more in the field of bilingualism than in ISLA, in part because much of the language development in these contexts is uninstructed. Finally, it is acknowledged that many people study more than one additional language and thus may be involved in third or fourth language acquisition. However, for convenience sake, the fields of SLA and ISLA have retained the term *second* with the understanding that it may refer to multiple additional languages.

Language is another term that needs some consideration. In general, language can be considered a system of form-meaning mappings that is used for communication. It has traditionally been thought of as containing various subcomponents, such as grammar, vocabulary, and pronunciation (or morphosyntax, lexis, and phonology to use more technical terminology) (Housen & Pierrard, 2005). In addition, pragmatics, the study of language use in social contexts, has recently received attention. Because of the importance of each of these areas of language, and the existence of unique learning and instructional challenges associated with them, each of these areas will be explored in more depth in their respective, subsequent chapters.

Finally, it is necessary to consider *acquisition.* At first, the meaning of acquisition may also seem self-evident, but on further reflection, acquisition is also a complex concept. Furthermore, difficulties in definition are compounded by the use of terms such as *learning* and *development* to refer to similar constructs. In many cases, the terms *acquisition* and *learning* have been used synonymously, but some researchers, particularly Stephen Krashen (1982, 2003) in the acquisition-learning hypothesis of his Monitor Model of SLA, have made significant distinctions between the two terms, with *learning* referring to the accumulation of metalinguistic, declarative knowledge about the L2, and *acquisition* referring to gaining the implicit L2 knowledge that results in learners' ability to use the L2 for communication. Although these processes and types of knowledge are important to distinguish, in keeping with current ISLA usage, the terms *learning* and *acquisition* will not be used in this book to convey these distinctions; instead, terms such as *implicit* and *explicit knowledge* or *declarative* and *procedural knowledge* will be used, while *learning* and *acquisition* will be used interchangeably. Another term that is sometimes used to refer to acquisition is *development*. In fact, Loewen and Reinders (2011) define acquisition as 'the process of L2 development' (p. 6). There are slightly different connotations between acquisition and development, with the former emphasizing the end product of learning, while the latter underscores the process of learning. Yet in both cases, there is the notion of an increase in L2 knowledge and/or proficiency, and it is this idea that will serve as a general definition of acquisition.

In order to highlight the instructed nature of ISLA, it is helpful to consider ISLA in relation to other related, but distinct areas, including uninstructed L2 acquisition (sometimes also called naturalistic L2 acquisition), the more general discipline of SLA, as well as L2 pedagogy. The distinction between instructed and uninstructed L2 acquisition might be thought of as merely the difference between learners being inside or outside of the classroom, with the classroom providing teaching and more formal opportunities for learning (Ellis, 1990). And yet the definitions of ISLA in the previous paragraph do not focus so much on the location of instruction as on the manipulation of the L2 learning process. Thus, according to the current definition, it is possible for instructed L2 acquisition to occur outside the classroom, for example, if learners are participating in study abroad programs or are using textbooks or computer-assisted language learning materials for self-selected, individual study program.

In an effort to more fully understand the contexts with which ISLA is concerned, it is helpful to consider its two prerequisites, namely instruction and acquisition, or more specifically, attempted acquisition. Without these two conditions, ISLA does not exist. With the previously discussed definitions of instruction and acquisition in mind, it is possible to place the terms on intersecting scales, as in Figure 1.1, to help identify the scope of ISLA. When considering acquisition, it is true that it does not always occur even though there is effort on the part of learners and teachers, and indeed the reasons for such failure are a main concern of both ISLA and SLA. However, an assumption of ISLA is that learners are making an effort to acquire the L2; if acquisition is not a goal of an encounter with the L2, then such a situation would fall outside of the realm of both SLA and ISLA. For example, Quadrants 3 and 4 in Figure 1.1 represent contexts in which there is no attempt at acquisition by an individual. This lack of effort may exist even though the person is surrounded by the L2— as in the case of expatriates who live in a larger L2 society but interact mostly with other L1 speakers (Quadrant 3). Additionally, it is possible that there is no attempt at acquisition because of the unlikely possibility that an individual is completely unengaged with the instructional process even though he or she is within the four walls of a classroom (Quadrant 4). ISLA is not concerned with such situations because there is no attempted acquisition.

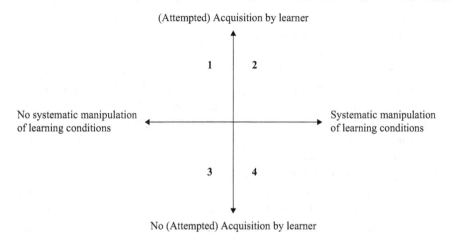

FIGURE 1.1 Defining Instructed Second Language Acquisition

In addition to attempted acquisition by the learner, there must be some systematic attempt to manipulate the conditions for learning, and here is the primary way in which instructed and uninstructed SLA differ. If there is no attempt to manipulate the conditions for learning, then there is no instruction, and any learning is uninstructed in nature (Quadrant 1). For example, individuals may simply be immersed in an L2 environment, and they may acquire the language incidentally as they go about their daily lives, even though they may not have the time or make the effort to engage in any type of more formal or systematic study. In contrast, other individuals may take advantage of their presence in the L2 context to more actively and systematically pursue learning the language. These latter cases would approach, and perhaps blur, the boundary between instructed and uninstructed SLA.

Although individuals may engage in autonomous study of an L2, the prototypical context of ISLA is the L2 classroom, in which there is generally both systematic manipulation of the learning conditions and attempted acquisition. This manipulation can happen in at least two ways: first, the linguistic input itself can be transformed. For example, a teacher might take an authentic Internet news article and simplify the vocabulary and grammar before presenting it to the class. Alternatively, a textbook passage might be written to include numerous examples of a specific grammatical structure. In these ways, the input that the learners receive has been altered in some way in hopes of facilitating the L2 learning process. A second type of manipulation is altering the way in which learners engage with the input. In the previous example of the Internet news article, the teacher may decide to provide the authentic, unaltered version, but she might ask students to read it multiple times, each time focusing on a specific comprehension issue or linguistic feature. In many cases in the L2 classroom, both the input and the processes of learner engagement with that input are manipulated. An example of this combination is found in processing instruction (VanPatten, 2007) which will be discussed in Chapter 5.

An issue to keep in mind when considering the manipulation of learning conditions is who is doing the manipulating. Typically, this manipulation is done by teachers, either in traditional classroom contexts or in private tutoring situations. Teachers may draw on their own experiences and training in order to design lessons that they expect to be beneficial for their students. Of course, teachers' training and intuitions may or may not reflect current ISLA theory about optimal L2 learning conditions. In addition to drawing on their own experiences, teachers often rely greatly on textbooks and their authors to provide manipulated linguistic input, such as grammar and vocabulary, as well as the ways in which learners are anticipated to engage with that input through a variety of activities (Richards, 2007). Again, such resources may or may not utilize up-to-date ISLA concepts. It is also possible for learners themselves to manipulate the conditions for learning; however, such instances have not been a primary focus of ISLA research. Thus, while it is acknowledged that self-study can involve manipulation by individual learners, this book will be concerned mostly with manipulation that is done by teachers or other resources. The questions that ISLA seeks to address, as stated earlier, pertain to the effectiveness of manipulating the learning conditions, and what types of manipulations are most effective.

In sum, Quadrant 1 represents contexts in which there is no systematic manipulation of learning conditions, but there is an attempt to acquire the L2. This is referred to as uninstructed or naturalistic L2 acquisition. Quadrant 2 combines systematic manipulation of learning conditions and attempted acquisition, and represents the general area of inquiry for ISLA. In contrast, in Quadrant 3 there is no manipulation of input and no attempt to acquire the L2, while finally Quadrant 4 represents contexts with manipulation of input, but no attempt at acquisition.

Of course, these constructs are represented on continuums, which means that the boundaries between the quadrants are indistinct. The quintessential example of ISLA is an L2 classroom in an organized educational context with clear instructional materials; however, some L2 classrooms, particularly those embracing communicative language teaching, may not contain much systematic manipulation of L2 input or processes. In addition, study abroad programs may make minimal adjustments to the environments in which learners find themselves. Nevertheless, these contexts still have the goal of L2 acquisition, and the effects of only a slight manipulation of the conditions of L2 learning are of interest to ISLA researchers and theorists.

One question that arises when considering instructed and uninstructed L2 acquisition is if the cognitive processes of acquisition are similar in both instances, with differences only in the nature of the instructional context (typically inside versus outside the classroom); types of input (authentic versus manipulated); types of processing (naturalistic versus manipulated); and amount of time spent in the learning process (considerable versus minimal). In general, it is assumed that the cognitive processes are the same. Ellis (1989) states that 'the same acquisitional mechanisms operate, irrespective of setting' (p. 307). Other scholars have also argued that the psycholinguistic processes and developmental stages of L2 acquisition are the same regardless of whether the learning context is instructed or naturalistic (Bardovi-Harlig, 2000; Gass, 1989; Howard, 2005; Krashen, 2003). If this is the case, then the distinction between instructed and uninstructed SLA is one of degrees not one of kind. In other words, an individual being exposed to the L2 while living in the L2 environment will undergo the same cognitive processes in acquisition as would an individual inside the classroom. In fact, some research suggests that both instructed and uninstructed learners proceed through the same natural sequences of acquisition (Ellis, 2005). However, research in general suggests that instruction can improve the rate of acquisition, and instructed learners may progress more quickly. Furthermore, instruction may be necessary to achieve higher levels of ultimate attainment and to avoid fossilization (Housen & Pierrard, 2005).

SLA THEORY

Having considered the characteristics of instructed acquisition in comparison to uninstructed acquisition, it is also important to consider the similarities and differences between ISLA and SLA as disciplines of academic study. First and foremost, it should be said that the field of ISLA is fully encapsulated by SLA (Ortega, 2013). It is difficult to think of any concepts or issues that occur in the former but not in the latter. That being said, it is clear that some areas of concern in SLA are not a focus of ISLA.

Theories are normally charged with explaining the entirety of a phenomenon, such as L2 acquisition in general (VanPatten & Williams, 2007). Thus SLA theories are broader in scope than ISLA because they must account for L2 acquisition, whether it occurs as a result of instruction or mere exposure to authentic input. While ISLA is concerned primarily with the classroom, SLA encompasses larger and more theoretical aspects of L2 acquisition as well, and while all SLA theories presumably have some implication for instruction, some are more pedagogically focused than others. For example, some SLA theories are concerned with cognitive structures and processes that have little to do with instruction because the processes are presumed to be unconscious and thus not amenable to teaching or manipulation. For instance, usage-based accounts of L2 learning suggest that learners unconsciously register linguistic patterns in the input, and these patterns are strengthened when learners encounter multiple examples in the input (N. Ellis, 2007a). While researchers and teachers can manipulate the input to increase exemplars of a specific linguistic structure, it is not possible to affect the cognitive processes that strengthen these connections in the brain; consequently, such theories are generally beyond the concern of ISLA. Nevertheless, although some aspects of SLA may not pertain to ISLA, the entirety of ISLA is rooted in various aspects of multiple SLA theories, models and approaches (VanPatten & Williams, 2007).

In an attempt to elucidate the relationships between SLA theories and the L2 classroom, Lourdes Ortega (2007) has taken some of the main SLA theories and considered how they view the role of instruction in the L2 acquisition process. She proposes three different possibilities for the relationship between SLA theory and ISLA: (1) no effect for instruction, (2) limited effects for instruction, and (3) beneficial effects for instruction. In the first category, Ortega places four theories for which she argues that 'instruction can play no substantial role in learning of L2 grammar' (p. 240); these are Universal Grammar Theory, Processability Theory, Autonomous Induction Theory, and the Concept-Oriented Approach. It is worth considering two of the theories because of their broader impact. Universal Grammar (UG) is a generativist theory of language acquisition that originated to account for first language acquisition, and has come to be used in SLA as well. UG views language use as based on an innate, abstract linguistic system that is unconscious (White, 2007). Acquisition occurs, in somewhat simplistic terms, when the unconscious linguistic system receives input, and extracts rules and patterns that conform to universal linguistic constraints. There is considerable debate about the details of generativist theories. For example one issue is how much of the innate, unconscious linguistic system is available for L2 learners. Nonetheless, the important point for ISLA is that generativists view acquisition as an unconscious process that cannot be manipulated. So for example, from a generativist perspective, teaching learners explicit grammatical rules, such as 'add –ed to form English regular past tense' will not affect their unconscious linguistic system, even though such a rule might add to their general knowledge about the English language.

Although generativist perspectives might propose no effect for instruction (Doughty, 2003), they may still provide information that is informative for the L2 classroom. For example, generativist approaches can provide evidence regarding the natural orders of acquisition, as well as information about the learnability of certain L2 features. Generativist approaches may provide predictions about what morphosyntactic features might be easier or more difficult for learners, considering the parameters of their L1 and the L2 that they are studying. Such information may guide teachers in deciding which linguistic features to highlight in the classroom.

Another theory to consider in Ortega's category of no impact for instruction is Processability Theory (Pienemann, 1998, 2007). In brief, Processability Theory maintains that the cognitive processing of language occurs relatively automatically and unconsciously. Input is processed in specific ways, with processing at the initial stages of learning limited to small chunks of language and developing to larger units, such as noun phrases and clauses. Processability theory argues that little can be done to alter these cognitive processes; therefore, classroom instruction has little impact in terms of processing. Nonetheless, if researchers and teachers are aware of these constraints, they may better understand learner development and adjust their expectations for language acquisition accordingly. Thus, in the case of both UG and Processability Theory, although they may not have direct implications or suggestions for the classroom, there are insights that can be gained about the acquisition process that can be helpful to raise teachers' awareness regarding their learners' L2 development.

The second position that Ortega describes for theory in relation to pedagogy is that 'instruction can play an important, if only complementary, role in facilitating L2 acquisition' (p. 241). In this category, she places the Associative-Cognitive CREED and Vygotskian Sociocultural Theory. These theories, she states 'offer general principles for optimal instruction—for example, that L2 input brought into classrooms needs to be as abundant, rich, and authentic as possible' (pp. 241–242). Associate-Cognitive CREED (N. Ellis, 2007a) refers to a group of connectionist and usage-based theories that suggest that acquisition occurs subconsciously as the cognitive system is exposed to various patterns in the input. The more exposure to specific structures, the more those connections are strengthened. Because learning is subconscious, instruction has little effect on the processes of acquisition; nonetheless, classroom instruction can bring about optimal conditions for the working of these processes, conditions which may not be found in uninstructed contexts. Finally, Vygotskian Sociocultural Theory (Lantolf & Thorne, 2007) suggests that learning is a socially mediated process in which more expert individuals help scaffold novice individuals into higher levels of performance. Ortega argues that Sociocultural Theory holds a complementary role for instruction because it can provide an environment in which learners may receive assistance from teachers and peers, as well as participate in negotiated interaction.

In the third position, Ortega says that three theories 'take a firm position that instruction can optimize natural learning processes and may even be necessary when the goal is truly advanced levels of proficiency' (p. 242). These three theories are Skill Acquisition Theory, Input Processing, and the Interaction approach. Because these are the three main theories that address the classroom, these are the ones that will be explored in detail throughout the rest of this book.

SLA RESEARCH METHODOLOGY

In addition to some SLA theoretical perspectives that are not directly relevant to ISLA, there are also research methodology issues that fall outside the realm of ISLA. In this regard, there are two issues. The first relates to the vein of enquiry within SLA about the empirical and methodological issues surrounding conducting research. These concerns are seen in research methods textbooks and overviews (e.g., Mackey & Gass, 2012), as well as in the debates about the construct validity and reliability of specific research methods (Doughty, 2003). For example, the debate about think-aloud protocols, in which participants speak their thoughts aloud as they conduct specific tasks, clearly falls within the scope of SLA because it is a methodology employed in SLA research (Bowles, 2010); however, it is not directly relevant for ISLA because it is a research method, not a pedagogical one. Another example is the measurement of different types of L2 knowledge that learners possess (Ellis, Loewen, Elder, Erlam, Philp, & Reinders, 2009). As will be discussed in the next chapter, learners may have explicit knowledge of L2 rules; however, such knowledge does not necessarily imply that they have the implicit L2 knowledge necessary to use those L2 rules during spontaneous communication. In order to empirically investigate the effects of different types of instruction on different types of L2 knowledge, it is important to have tests that can measure those types of knowledge. ISLA is not directly concerned with the development and validation of measures of L2 knowledge, but such measures have the potential to impact classroom instruction because they reveal what types of instruction are beneficial for different types of knowledge (Doughty, 2003; Norris & Ortega, 2000).

The second issue related to research methodology concerns the implications and generalizability of research, particularly when comparing different types of instructional contexts or when investigating instruction in a laboratory context. Because of the complexities of the L2 classroom, some researchers argue that laboratory-based studies that isolate specific aspects of the L2 instruction and acquisition process provide limited insight for the L2 classroom (Lyster & Saito, 2010). For example, L2 interaction may be qualitatively and quantitatively different in the classroom compared to the laboratory (Foster, 1998). However, at least one study (Gass, Mackey, & Ross-Feldman, 2005) has found no differences in the amount and types of interaction that occurred when participants conducted interactive tasks in a classroom context versus a laboratory one. In contrast, Li (2010), in a meta-analysis of corrective feedback studies, found that corrective feedback was more effective in laboratory-based studies than in ones conducted in the L2 classroom. Investigation of such methodological issues can provide information about the relevance of laboratory-based studies for the classroom.

While these methodological issues do not fit directly into the purview of ISLA, they do nonetheless have an impact because they affect the conclusions that ISLA researchers make about the effects of classroom instruction. Many research studies investigating the effectiveness of L2 instruction employ a quasi-experimental design consisting of a pretest, treatment, and one or more posttests. The treatment takes the form of whatever instructional variable is being investigated, such as corrective feedback or explicit instruction. By comparing learners' scores on the pretest with those on the posttests, researchers can infer if the treatment had any effect on L2 learning. Additionally, quasi-experimental studies usually have several groups of learners, some who receive the treatment and some who do not. In this way, researchers can better confirm that it is the treatment itself, and not some other variable, that is responsible for any learning that occurs. In these ways, methodological issues support the endeavors of those investigating ISLA because quality research methods are needed to ensure that valid conclusions about ISLA are drawn from the data provided by the research studies (Plonsky, 2013). Nevertheless, because methodological issues do not relate directly to instruction, they will not generally be addressed in this book.

SECOND LANGUAGE PEDAGOGY

Finally, in addition to some aspects of theory and methodology falling outside the direct interests of ISLA, there are also some aspects of classroom pedagogy that are not directly related to ISLA. For example, there are issues of classroom pedagogy such as classroom management (Horwitz, 2005), and strategies for teaching large classes, ethnically diverse classes and economically disadvantaged students (Burnett, 2011), that are relevant to numerous educational contexts, not just the L2 classroom. These general pedagogic concerns are not usually investigated in ISLA research (Wright, 2005), and although they certainly have implications for the L2 classroom, they will not be addressed in this volume.

Another issue relates to aspects of L2 pedagogy that are not theoretically or empirically well-supported. Some teaching methods, such as Total Physical Response, Suggestopedia, and the Silent Way, are relatively well-known, but have received little support from SLA theory and are not all that common in the classroom (Jin & Cortazzi, 2011). Additionally, there are pedagogical techniques that are no longer considered theoretically valid, such as the repetitive drills of audiolingualism based on the behaviorist assumption of habit formation. However, as theories rise and fall, so do pedagogical techniques. For example, although some theorists suggest dispensing with explicit grammatical instruction (e.g., Krashen, 2003), others argue that it is important and relevant (R. Sheen, 2005). Obviously ISLA is concerned with sorting out these claims, and thus is interested in most aspects of L2 pedagogy.

THE EFFECTIVENESS OF L2 INSTRUCTION

Having compared and contrasted ISLA with related areas that do not fall directly within its purview, it is now important to consider what does constitute its focus. As such, we return to the primary question of ISLA: is instruction beneficial for L2 acquisition? If the answer is no, then it begs the question of what to do about the fact that probably more students study an L2 inside the classroom than outside of it (Housen & Pierrard, 2005). If the answer is yes, or maybe, then the logical follow-up question is what characteristics or conditions maximize its effectiveness. In order to assess the effects of instruction, it is necessary to consider the goal of instruction. In other words, what yardstick should be used to determine if instruction is successful or not? Many researchers, teachers, and learners propose that, in general, the goal of L2 instruction and learning is to develop communicative competence in learners so that they may use the L2 for spontaneous communication (Jin & Cortazzi, 2011; Littlewood, 2011; Ur, 2011). Of course, some L2 learners may have other goals for studying an L2, such as fulfilling an educational requirement, visiting exotic places on study abroad (Kinginger, 2011), or increasing their explicit knowledge of the linguistic properties of the L2 (DeKeyser, 2007a). In these instances, learners may view the ability to communicate in the L2 as a secondary goal. Nevertheless, it is generally assumed that the underlying objective of most teachers and students involved in L2 classroom learning is that the learners will be able to use the language to communicate. There is little doubt that providing explicit, declarative information about the L2 can bring about increased knowledge of the L2, just as instruction benefits the learning of any type of factual information, such as history dates or mathematical formulas. The larger controversy regarding the effectiveness of L2 instruction pertains to whether or not classroom instruction can help learners develop L2 knowledge that results in communicative ability (DeKeyser, 2007a; Ellis, 2005; Krashen, 2003).

One of the most well-known critics of the effectiveness of explicit L2 instruction is Stephen Krashen, whose Monitor Theory argues that instruction is beneficial only for learned knowledge, which he defines as explicit, declarative knowledge about the rules of the L2. Krashen (1982, 2003) argues that such learned knowledge is not helpful for spontaneous, communicative language use, except in very limited instances when easy grammar rules might enable learners to monitor their own output, notice errors in their own production, and produce self-corrections. The reason that instruction is not beneficial for acquisition, according to Krashen, is that the internal processes of language development are not amenable to external manipulation. For example, his natural order hypothesis states that acquisition follows developmental sequences in which some linguistic structures, such as English regular plural –s, are acquired earlier than other structures, such as English regular past tense –ed. Because of this natural order, Krashen and others argue that instruction will not alter this sequence, and teaching late acquired structures early in the pedagogical syllabus will not facilitate their acquisition before earlier acquired structures. Krashen's recommendation for the L2 classroom, then, is for teachers to provide profuse amounts of comprehensible input, which he termed $i + 1$. This input, which is intended to be one step beyond learners' current linguistic ability, would allow learners' natural language learning processes to function. Although Krashen's Monitor Theory was widely influential in the late 1980s and early 1990s, its prominence waned as research and theoretical perspectives superseded it. Nevertheless, the basic idea of several of Krashen's hypotheses are still being researched and debated today (VanPatten & Williams, 2007). In addition, as recently as 2003, Krashen restated his view that explicit L2 instruction, particularly grammar instruction, is not effective, and he endeavors to disprove a number of research studies that claim to prove otherwise.

In contrast to the few voices arguing to the contrary, there are several SLA theories (Ortega, 2013) and numerous research studies that argue that instruction can be valuable for L2 acquisition, although there are differences of opinion regarding which types of instruction are most beneficial for which areas of language. As seen in the previous section, the Interaction Approach, Input Processing Theory, and Skill Acquisition Theory all propose specific ways in which instruction can be beneficial. Although these theories will be explored in more detail in subsequent chapters, a brief account of their theoretical perspectives will provide some insight into the role that they theorize for classroom instruction.

The Interaction Approach argues that encountering and negotiating language forms during the course of meaningful interaction allows learners to notice the language forms, thereby enabling them to incorporate these forms into their interlanguage system. To quote Michael H. Long (1996): 'negotiation for meaning, especially negotiation work that triggers interactional adjustments by the native speaker or more competent interlocutor, facilitates acquisition because it connects input, internal learner capacities, particularly selective attention, and output in productive ways' (pp. 451–452).

Input Processing theory (VanPatten, 2005) proposes that learners process language in specific ways that are influenced by a learner's L1. These processing strategies may be unhelpful in processing the L2. Through processing instruction in the classroom, teachers can make learners aware of these unproductive strategies, and provide structured input activities which force learners to process the L2 in more productive ways. For example, English L1 speakers tend to rely on word order and the First Noun Principle to determine the subject of a sentence; however, in many other languages, word order is flexible and other cues, such as morphology, are used to indicate the subject. Input processing argues that making learners aware of these strategies, and providing opportunities to practice new processing skills will result in language development.

Finally, from a Skill Acquisition Theory perspective, learners begin with declarative knowledge about the L2 which becomes proceduralized through practice, enabling learners to use their knowledge in more automatized ways. Thus, providing practice opportunities in the classroom is a key tenet of Skill Acquisition Theory (DeKeyser, 2007c).

In addition to theoretical perspectives concerning the efficacy of instruction, there have been numerous empirical studies weighing in on this issue. As early as 1983, Michael H. Long asked if second language instruction made a difference. His conclusion after reviewing 12 studies was that yes, it does. More recently, multiple meta-analyses, which statistically synthesize numerous individual research studies, have concluded that instruction, or various aspects thereof, can have a positive influence on L2 development. One of the first such meta-analyses was Norris and Ortega's (2000) in which they examined 49 ISLA research studies. Their conclusions were that instruction, particularly explicit instruction, was effective, and that the results of instruction were durable. However, they did caution that the instruments used to measure L2 development in the research studies may have favored the use of explicit knowledge and explicit instruction.

More recent meta-analyses have investigated specific aspects of ISLA such as conversational interaction (Mackey & Goo, 2007), the interaction between type of instruction and type of language feature (Spada & Tomita, 2010) and comprehension-based versus production-based grammar instruction (Shintani, Li, & Ellis, 2013). All of these meta-analyses have found that instruction can be effective. In fact, Spada and Tomita (2010) claim that 'there is a general consensus that instruction is beneficial for second language development' (p. 263).

THE SCOPE OF ISLA

The bedrock assumption of ISLA is that instruction can be beneficial for L2 acquisition. Once that assumption has been made, then it remains to consider if certain factors are better than others in bringing about L2 development. As early as 1998, Craig Chaudron said that 'the ultimate objective of classroom research is to identify those characteristics of classrooms which lead to the learning of the instructional content' (1988, p. 1).

Indeed, examining various aspects of instruction that are more or less effective for L2 learning will comprise the remaining chapters of this book. The first consideration relates to the nature of L2 knowledge and what the goal of instruction should be. In order to gauge if instruction is effective, it is important to answer the question 'effective for what?' Chapter 2 will consider two possible goals of L2 instruction: (1) explicit, declarative knowledge of grammatical rules and other linguistic areas, and (2) implicit, proceduralized knowledge that enables spontaneous communication in the L2. After considering the goals of L2 instruction, the book begins to explore various ways in which these goals have been approached. In other words, if the goal of instruction is a specific type of L2 knowledge, what can SLA theory and research tell us about the best ways to achieve those goals? Chapter 3 considers the role of communication and interaction in the development of L2 knowledge. It investigates whether a classroom rich in L2 input and L2 interaction can bring about L2 knowledge and skills. Particular attention will be given to the theoretical support provided by the Interaction Approach, and its manifestation in the classroom in the form of communicative language teaching and task-based language learning. Chapter 4 explores what has been termed focus on form in which learners' attention is drawn to specific linguistic forms within a larger meaning-focused context. Considerable research has examined various types of focus on form (Long, 1996) and their effectiveness. After exploring the two broader theoretical approaches of the Interaction Approach and focus on form towards developing communicative competence, the focus of the book shifts to consider how instruction might influence specific linguistic areas. Chapter 5 tackles grammar, which has been the object of much theoretical speculation, empirical investigation, and pedagogical intervention. This chapter will explore the theoretical issues that pertain specifically to the instruction of grammar in the L2 classroom, such as Input Processing and explicit grammar instruction. Chapter 6 brings the focus to vocabulary, another linguistic area that has received considerable attention in ISLA research. This chapter considers the role of both explicit instruction and implicit learning of vocabulary and how such instruction affects the resulting types of vocabulary knowledge. Chapter 7 considers the less researched area of pronunciation. Again, the unique challenges of pronunciation instruction will be explored in relation to theories of phonological learning. The last chapter to address linguistic areas, Chapter 8, examines the role of pragmatics instruction in the classroom. Can pragmatics be taught in the classroom, and what has research shown about such efforts? After looking at these specific linguistic areas, the book considers the more contextual as well as individual aspects of classroom instruction, respectively. Chapter 9 considers the larger instructional contexts in which L2 learning occurs, such as L2 immersion classes and content-based instruction. This chapter also moves outside the walls of the classroom to consider the role of study abroad, as well as the impact that technology can have on L2 acquisition. Chapter 10 considers how learner differences can impact classroom instruction, exploring such issues as motivation and aptitude. Finally, Chapter 11 attempts to bring some unification to the variety of issues that have been discussed throughout the book. For example, it is true that grammar has received the bulk of attention in SLA/ISLA research (Ellis, 1990; Nassaji & Fotos, 2011; Ortega, 2007); however, an integrated view of ISLA cannot overlook other areas of language.

Because of the interwoven nature of the topics of ISLA, there will be some overlap as well as artificial divisions among the chapters. For example, the acquisition of grammar has been a primary concern of explicit grammar instruction, communicative language learning, and focus on form; however, these approaches will be dealt with in separate chapters. Similarly the role of context is applicable to the learning of various linguistic areas; however, content-based instruction and study abroad contexts will be examined in their own chapter. In spite of such commonalities, each chapter will focus on the primary features of the topic at hand, and use those as the guide for locating various issues within the book. For example, an examination of the role of individual differences, such as anxiety and working memory, on the efficacy of recasts for learning grammar is placed in the individual differences chapter and not the focus on form or grammar chapters. In sum, the purpose of this book is to provide information about what is known about L2 learning in the classroom, based on theory and research. The fact that these theories are tied to specific pedagogical techniques can be helpful for teachers, but the goal is not to provide an inventory of teaching techniques, but rather to consider the interplay between classroom activities and what is known about ISLA. The main theme is how ISLA theory and research underpin and support classroom L2 learning.

DISCUSSION QUESTIONS

1. The following quote comes from a research study investigating the impact that reading research studies had on teachers' beliefs about oral corrective feedback. In this quote, the teacher being interviewed expresses his frustration with the link between research and teaching. What is your response to the teacher's statement? In your opinion, what should be the relationship between theory and research on the one hand, and L2 pedagogy on the other? How should research influence teaching? How should teaching influence research?

   In education, there should be a right answer . . . what works best in the classroom. There's a right answer. Right? . . . My problem with research [studies] is that they tend to be contradictory . . . You should be able to come to a conclusion that says this will make you a better teacher. This style will be optimal in the classroom. (Kamiya & Loewen, 2013:7)

2. The overall assessment of this chapter is that L2 instruction makes a differ-
    ence in L2 acquisition. What evidence from your own experiences can you
    use to support or challenge this claim? Are there specific areas of language
    that you think are especially resistant to instruction? Why do you think this
    is the case, and what could be done to overcome these obstacles?

ADDITIONAL READING

Doughty, C. J., & Long, M. H. (Eds.). (2003). *The handbook of second language acquisition*.
    Malden, MA: Blackwell Publishing.
Ellis, R. (2008). *The study of second language acquisition* (2nd ed.). Oxford: Oxford University
    Press.
Gass, S. M., & Mackey, A. (2012). *The Routledge handbook of second language acquisition*.
    London: Routledge.
Housen, A., & Pierrard, M. (2005). *Investigations in instructed second language acquisition*.
    Berlin: Mouton de Gruyter.
Loewen, S., & Reinders, H. (2011). *Key concepts in second language acquisition*. New York:
    Palgrave.
Ortega, L. (2009). *Understanding second language acquisition*. London: Hodder Education.
VanPatten, B., & Williams, J. (Eds.). (2007). *Theories in second language acquisition: An
    Introduction*. Mahwah, NJ: Lawrence Erlbaum.

2

The Nature of Second Language Knowledge

The previous chapter concluded that L2 instruction can be beneficial, but it did not explore in detail the question of 'beneficial for what?' The current chapter considers the goal of L2 instruction. What is it that learners ought to know as a result of instructed L2 learning? In earlier and more traditional views, the goal of L2 instruction has often been seen as the acquisition of linguistic knowledge, especially about the morphosyntactic and lexical components of the language. As a result, numerous L2 students have spent countless hours memorizing linguistic information, such as Spanish verb conjugations or Russian noun declensions. However, not everyone views explicit linguistic knowledge as the primary goal of L2 instruction. Many L2 researchers, teachers and learners feel that the ability to use the L2 to communicate with other speakers of the language is just as important, if not more important, than knowing a set of grammatical rules (e.g., DeKeyser, 2007a; Littlewood, 2011). In general, teachers want their students to possess the ability to use the language to communicate (Scheffler & Cincała, 2010), and learners also often place a high priority on using the L2 in real-life contexts.

Of course, there are some instances where the goal of L2 instruction is not primarily communicative competence. For example, L2 reading courses, in which the objective is for learners to become proficient only in reading the L2, are sometimes offered in academic contexts. Alternatively, there are courses that focus more on the cultural characteristics of the societies in which the L2 is spoken. There may be some linguistic component to such courses, but the aim is more to familiarize learners with the L2 context, perhaps before a short visit to that region, than to enable them to communicate in the L2. In spite of these exceptions, however, an important goal of many learners is to be able to use the L2 for communication in some meaningful way.

In the late 1970s and early 1980s, changes in L2 instruction and the development of SLA theory began to suggest that knowledge of grammatical rules did not necessarily result in the ability to communicate in the L2, and that teaching linguistic rules, particularly without providing learners the opportunity to practice using the L2, might not be the best way to enable learners to communicate in the L2. In 1980, Canale and Swain introduced the term communicative competence to encompass what it takes to be able to use the L2 effectively for communication. They proposed that communicative competence consisted of four different competences:

1. Linguistic competence, which entails knowledge of the L2 morphosyntax, lexis, and phonology.
2. Sociolinguistic competence, which consists of learners' ability to use the language appropriately in various social contexts.
3. Discourse competence, which is comprised of learners' knowledge of how to produce coherent and cohesive written and oral language.
4. Strategic competence, which consists of learners' ability to deal with communication difficulties.

In large part, ISLA research has focused on the linguistic component of communicative competence, a fact that is reflected throughout this book; however, sociolinguistic competence has also begun to receive more attention as research into pragmatics continues to grow (Bardovi-Harlig, 2013). Discourse competence has been investigated primarily in the context of L2 writing (e.g., Polio, 2012), which may be viewed as a complementary area of research to ISLA. Finally, strategic competence comes into play in interactionist approaches to SLA, particularly in relation to learners' negotiation of meaning (Long, 1996). Based on these elements, communicative competence can be seen as consisting of an L2 learner's ability to use language accurately, fluently, and appropriately in meaning-focused contexts.

But what enables learners to develop communicative competence? To answer that question, this chapter will examine several theories about the nature of L2 knowledge, how it is acquired, and how it is stored in the brain. Much of this chapter will address issues related to grammar because that has been the traditional domain of much ISLA research, particularly as it relates to the nature of L2 knowledge. However, in an attempt to broaden the scope of this area of research, the nature of lexical, phonological, and pragmatics knowledge will be explored as well.

THEORETICAL CONCERNS

A primary theoretical concern for this chapter is the description of the nature of learners' L2 cognitive linguistic systems. If the goal of L2 instruction is to produce learners who can use the L2 in communication, then it is important to know what types of knowledge enable them to do so. Several SLA theories take similar positions about the nature of linguistic knowledge, namely that there is a distinction between knowledge that consists of information about the language versus knowledge that allows learners to use language for spontaneous communication (e.g., DeKeyser, 2007c; R. Ellis, 2005). Although this division is important in SLA, broader research suggests that a distinction between declarative and nondeclarative memory exists for most areas of human knowledge (Squire, 2009). For language, declarative memory consists of the knowledge that learners are aware of and can describe; in contrast, nondeclarative memory is the knowledge that learners use unconsciously when they are communicating in the language. It is the exploration of these two types of knowledge, sometimes referred to as explicit and implicit L2 knowledge, or alternatively as declarative and procedural knowledge, that we turn to next.

The Nature of L2 Knowledge

Explicit and implicit L2 knowledge. From a cognitive perspective, one way of describing the knowledge that learners possess about the L2 is as explicit and implicit knowledge (Ellis et al., 2009; Rebuschat, 2013). The primary difference between the two types of knowledge is awareness. Explicit L2 knowledge has been described as knowledge that learners are aware of and can retrieve consciously from memory. It is 'knowledge about' language. Learners know that they possess this information, and they can verbalize it in the form of an L2 rule or a description of L2 usage (Ur, 2011). In some cases, learners may use metalinguistic terminology to do so, although explicit knowledge is not necessarily comprised of technical terminology, and it may be stated in lay terms (Basturkmen, Loewen, & Ellis, 2002; Gutiérrez, 2013). For example, learners could express their explicit knowledge of the grammatical rule for the formation of first-person, present, simple tense Spanish verbs by saying that 'the first-person singular morpheme –o is added to the base form of the verb.' A nontechnical way of expressing such knowledge could be 'I use –o at the end of a word when I want to say that I usually do something or am doing it at the moment.' In both cases, learners possess explicit grammatical knowledge of the linguistic rule.

In contrast, implicit L2 knowledge has been called 'knowledge of' language rather than 'knowledge about' language. Implicit knowledge is considered to be unconscious. In other words, learners do not necessarily know that they know it, and they are not able to verbalize it (R. Ellis, 2005; Ellis et al., 2009; Rebuschat, 2013; Sonbul & Schmitt, 2012; Ur, 2011). Implicit knowledge is the type of knowledge that first language speakers have about their L1 that enables them to focus on the messages that they want to communicate rather than on the language forms that are needed to convey those messages. Implicit knowledge is tacit, and learners may describe such knowledge as intuition or feeling. For example, native speakers of English, when presented with the following four sentences, will most likely say that the first three are grammatical but the fourth one is not, even though it seems to follow the same pattern as the grammatically acceptable Sentence 3. When asked to explain the reasoning for their judgments, L1 speakers will most likely respond 'I don't know. Sentence 4 just sounds wrong.' In such instances, L1 speakers are drawing on their implicit linguistic knowledge to make judgments about the grammaticality of sentences, and they very well may not have the ability to state why sentences are grammatical or ungrammatical unless they have had some additional training in grammar or linguistics.

1. She gave the book to him.
2. She gave him the book.
3. She donated the book to the library.
4. *She donated the library the book.

The previous example illustrates that the presence of implicit knowledge does not imply the existence of explicit linguistic knowledge (Ur, 2011). It is possible for L2 learners to be unaware of linguistic knowledge that they possess, although this situation is probably more likely for naturalistic learners rather than instructed learners. Conversely, L2 speakers may have considerable explicit L2 knowledge without corresponding levels of implicit knowledge. Moreover, instructed L2 learners often have higher levels of explicit and metalinguistic knowledge than do L1 speakers (Alderson & Hudson, 2013).

In terms of cognitive processing, learners need to use attentional resources to retrieve explicit knowledge from memory, with the consequence that using explicit knowledge is cognitively effortful, and the time taken to access explicit knowledge is such that it does not allow for quick and uninterrupted language production (R. Ellis, 2009). By contrast, learners can access implicit knowledge quickly and unconsciously, allowing it to be used for unplanned language production. Although it is argued that implicit knowledge is the primary type of knowledge necessary for spontaneous communication (Ur, 2011), it is also acknowledged that language production typically utilizes a combination of implicit and explicit knowledge (Bialystok, 1982; R. Ellis, 2009).

Declarative and procedural knowledge. Skill Acquisition Theory, a general psychological theory of learning, is another theory that deals with the mental representations of knowledge (e.g., DeKeyser, 2007c; Segalowitz, 2003). Skill Acquisition Theory is not specific to language, and it proposes that developing communicative competence in an L2 may follow the same trajectory as learning other skills, such as playing a musical instrument or playing a sport. Similar to the previous cognitive approach to L2 knowledge, Skill Acquisition

Theory makes a distinction between two types of knowledge; however, instead of referring to them as explicit and implicit knowledge, they are called declarative and procedural knowledge. In many ways these two terms correspond to explicit and implicit knowledge, respectively. Declarative knowledge is knowledge that learners are aware of and can verbalize. In contrast, procedural knowledge is automatized and available for use without awareness. However, one difference between the constructs of explicit and implicit knowledge on the one hand, and declarative and procedural knowledge on the other pertains to the relationship that is proposed to exist between the two respective types of knowledge. Explicit and implicit knowledge are often viewed as modular, meaning that they are stored in two different places in the brain and do not intermingle (R. Ellis, 2009). In contrast, declarative and procedural knowledge are often viewed as a continuum, with declarative knowledge being able to be proceduralized or automatized through practice (DeKeyser, 2007c). These relationships will be considered further when exploring the interface hypothesis.

The investigation of explicit and implicit L2 knowledge has been framed largely in terms of grammar and grammatical rules; nevertheless, it is important to consider if, and how, these constructs relate to other areas of language such as vocabulary, pronunciation, and pragmatics. For example, Sonbul and Schmitt (2012) assert that there are reasons to consider that the explicit-implicit knowledge distinction is different for vocabulary and grammar. One of the distinctions to draw on here is the difference between rule-learning and item-learning (Hulstijn & DeGraaf, 1994; Sonbul & Schmitt, 2012). It is rule-learning that the previous discussion has been concerned with because the rules of grammar are what allow learners to generate utterances that have never been produced before. Rule-learning involves the acquisition of the systematic patterns that language follows. For example, the English past-tense rule for regular verbs requires *–ed* to be added to the end of the base form of the verb. Knowledge of that rule enables learners to use that rule whenever they want to form a sentence about the past. In contrast, item-learning involves the memorization of specific, individual pieces of information. To continue with the example of English past tense, there are irregular verb forms, such as *were*, *broke*, and *taught*, that do not follow the regular rule for past-tense formation. These irregular verbs must be learned as individual items since there are no rules that can be applied to derive these forms.

Both rule-learning and item-learning can result in explicit knowledge that learners are consciously aware of and can verbalize. It is also possible for both types of learning to result in implicit and procedural knowledge that individuals can draw on when communicating without consciously thinking about that knowledge. However, because item-learning relies heavily on memorization, which generally involves intentional, explicit learning, it is more often associated with explicit knowledge, while rule-learning may be more affected by implicit learning processes when the patterns in the input are acquired by the cognitive system. Vocabulary acquisition relies heavily on item-learning as learners are involved in making explicit form-meaning connections between the meaning of the word and its phonological or orthographic form. Thus, much knowledge of vocabulary may be considered to be explicit (Sonbul & Schmitt, 2012).

However, not all aspects of vocabulary knowledge are necessarily explicit. Some aspects of vocabulary may be implicit (R. Ellis, 2004; Sonbul & Schmitt, 2012). In his consideration of what it means to know a word, Nation (2001) states that vocabulary knowledge does not consist exclusively of explicit information, such as the meaning, pronunciation, and spelling of a word. There are also aspects of vocabulary knowledge that may be implicit. For example, knowledge of the contexts in which words are likely to occur may be implicit. Learners may know that certain words, such as *contribute* and *precipitation,* are more likely to appear in formal contexts while other words, such as *give* and *rain,* may be more common in informal contexts, even though the meanings of the words are similar. Such knowledge may be implicit, having been picked up from exposure to numerous formal and informal contexts. On the other hand, it is also possible for such knowledge to be explicit and to have been learned explicitly. An example of the teaching of explicit knowledge about the context in which words are likely to be found is the English academic word list (Coxhead, 2000), which identifies roughly 550 English words that are commonly used in academic contexts and are thus useful for L2 learners at the university level. While L1 and L2 speakers may have implicit knowledge, perhaps described as intuitions, about the contexts in which specific words are more likely to occur, the academic word list makes this knowledge explicit.

Similarly, knowledge of how frequently words occur in the input may also be implicit. Learners may get a feeling for which words are more or less common, again based upon their contact with the language. Such implicit knowledge may apply to individual words or multi-word phrases. Of course, the relative frequency of words may be learned explicitly in the classroom, but even if such knowledge is not taught, learners may still develop intuitions based on exposure. There has been little research into the area of implicit lexical knowledge; nevertheless, there is growing acknowledgment that lexical knowledge may be comprised of both explicit and implicit knowledge (Sonbul & Schmitt, 2012).

In another area of language, pronunciation, the distinction between implicit and explicit knowledge can also be investigated. Much pronunciation knowledge may be implicit, and rely heavily on knowledge of L1 phonology. Thus learners may transfer their L1 knowledge automatically to their L2. Of course, it is possible for L2 learners to have explicit knowledge about phonology and such knowledge may even be taught explicitly in the classroom (e.g., Kissling,

2013). For example, many English L1 learners of Spanish are aware that a trilled /r/ phoneme exists in Spanish but not in English. In beginning Spanish classes, there may be some explicit teaching of this phoneme, and learners may have an awareness of whether or not they can perceive and produce this phoneme. In addition to the knowledge of individual segmental sounds, learners may also possess knowledge of intonation and other prosodic features. Again, this knowledge may be largely implicit, particularly because L2 pronunciation is not the subject of much explicit instruction in the L2 classroom. However, L2 learners may have difficulty picking up such knowledge implicitly due to the prevalence of L1 transfer.

Finally there is pragmatics, a relatively recent but growing area of ISLA interest (Bardovi-Harlig, 2013). The knowledge of what linguistic forms to use when speaking to specific individuals in specific contexts is perhaps one area of language that is taught and learned more explicitly in the L1 (Pearson, 2006). While children are generally not corrected grammatically when learning their L1, they may be corrected pragmatically more often. Children may also be taught explicitly what is appropriate or inappropriate in a specific context. For example, English-speaking parents may ask their child *what's the magic word* when they want him or her to use *please* when making a request. Because pragmatics is not frequently taught in the L2 classroom, it may be that learners transfer their implicit L1 knowledge to L2 contexts. It is possible for learners, particularly those in contexts in which the L2 is the language of the wider society, to acquire implicit L2 pragmatics knowledge (Hulstijn, 2002). However, learners may also acquire explicit pragmatics knowledge, particularly if L2 pragmatic norms are taught explicitly in the classroom (Bardovi-Harlig, 2013).

The Acquisition of L2 Knowledge

If there is some consensus across theories that learners possess two different types of knowledge, then it remains to consider how these types of knowledge might be gained, particularly as they relate to the purported goal of ISLA, namely the development of learners with high levels of communicative competence. In general, it is assumed that explicit and implicit knowledge are closely related to explicit and implicit learning, respectively, with the understanding that the two types of learning are separate processes, the results of which are stored in different parts of the brain (N. Ellis, 2007b). Thus, implicit learning, which occurs without intention or awareness, results in implicit knowledge, while in contrast, explicit learning, which is generally intentional and overt, results in explicit knowledge (Krashen, 2003; Macaro & Masterman, 2006; Rebuschat, 2013).

In more traditional approaches, learners, teachers, and researchers have sometimes viewed L2 learning as an accumulation of explicit knowledge about the grammatical rules and vocabulary of the L2 (Littlewood, 2011). This perception is demonstrated in the L2 classroom by lessons that focus on specific rules, with the intent that learners will use the rules as building blocks to create complete knowledge of the L2. The assumption is that once learners know all the rules, that is, once they have explicit knowledge of all the rules, they will know the language. In the classroom, it is relatively easy to teach explicit knowledge. Explicit grammar instruction works well because it results in explicit, declarative knowledge about the language (Doughty, 2003). The grammatical rules of an L2 are relatively clear, and they can be explicitly presented to learners. Teachers can then assess how well leaners are able to reproduce the rules that have been learned. Additionally, learners feel that they are learning something because they are able to articulate the L2 rules that have been presented to them. For example, if L2 learners are taught the present-tense verb conjugations for Spanish or French, they will most likely be able to provide them when called to do so on a grammar test. However, a problem arises when teachers and learners assume that explicit knowledge is going to allow them to use the L2 easily for communication. In other words, if learners know that they should place –o at the end of a Spanish verb when talking about what they do habitually or are doing at the moment, then the assumption may be that this knowledge will help them use that form when speaking with someone. But as many L2 learners, teachers and researchers will attest, being aware of a grammatical rule does not necessarily mean that it can be used in communication (R. Ellis, 2005, 2009).

As has been discussed, the ability to produce language relatively easily for communicative purposes draws heavily on implicit knowledge. Given that implicit knowledge is essential for successful L2 communication, one may think that implicit knowledge should simply be taught in the L2 classroom. However, implicit knowledge is hard to teach; in fact, some (e.g., Krashen, 2003) would argue that it cannot be taught. Rather implicit knowledge takes considerable time to develop as learners are exposed to L2 input (Hulstijn, 2002). Implicit knowledge builds up gradually as learners' cognitive systems register the patterns that are present in the input. Implicit learning is the way children learn their L1 during the first years of their lives. By the time children are 6 or 7, they are generally fluent L1 speakers; however, most L2 learners do not have five or six years to devote to full-time language learning. Additionally, the development of implicit knowledge requires exposure to vast amounts of L2 input, something that is unlikely to occur in many instructional contexts where learners' only contact with the L2 may be limited to 5 to 10 hours a week. Finally, the development of implicit knowledge takes large amounts of practice (DeKeyser, 2007b), and providing learners with numerous opportunities to practice using the L2 can be difficult, particularly with large classes and a full curriculum.

Another problem with the development of implicit knowledge is that learners might not feel as though they are learning anything because they cannot consciously verbalize what they have learned (Gatbonton & Segalowitz, 2005). Learners may therefore be unsatisfied with attempts to develop implicit knowledge, even if teachers emphasize that it is possible to learn an L2 without learning explicit grammar rules. Finally, the assessment of implicit knowledge is challenging and time-consuming. Learners need to demonstrate the ability to produce language relatively spontaneously in a context that focuses primarily on the meaning of the language and not the grammatical rules, something that is again challenging to make happen in many instructional contexts.

Because of these issues, it is possible that L2 learners might be better served by a combination of implicit and explicit instruction. For instance, because the development of implicit knowledge is so time consuming, it may be a more efficient use of instructional time to provide explicit instruction. Moreover, many adults have become highly efficient at explicit learning because their cognitive systems and reasoning skills are more developed than those of children. In addition, adults have spent considerable time involved in explicit learning during their formal education. Finally, although spontaneous L2 production is supported primarily by implicit or procedural knowledge, explicit L2 knowledge can play a considerable role in contexts where learners have time to monitor their production, such as in writing or careful speech. Therefore, in order to for adults to turn these factors to their benefit, L2 classroom instruction might be better comprised of explicit instruction, supplemented with implicit learning opportunities (Hulstijn, 2002).

The fact that explicit knowledge is relatively easy to learn but difficult to use for spontaneous L2 production, and that, conversely, implicit knowledge is relatively difficult to learn but important for L2 production is, I feel, one of the most important issues in ISLA and L2 pedagogy. It is essential for L2 learners and teachers to be aware of the different types of knowledge and the roles that they play in L2 acquisition and production. The implication is that the teaching of explicit language rules will not, by itself, result in students who are able to communicate easily or well in the language. If a primary goal of L2 instruction remains the development of implicit knowledge in order for learners to be able to use the L2 fluently in spontaneous communication, then it is incumbent upon ISLA researchers to consider how best to achieve that goal.

Interface hypothesis. Because implicit knowledge is difficult to teach in comparison to explicit knowledge, the question of whether or not explicit knowledge can become implicit knowledge has been addressed in the interface hypothesis (N. Ellis, 2005). In other words, can learners gain explicit knowledge in the classroom, and then assume that it will turn into implicit knowledge? Or can implicit knowledge be gained only implicitly, while explicit knowledge remains explicit? These questions are addressed in the following three positions in the interface hypothesis: noninterface, weak interface, and strong interface.

The noninterface position proposes that explicit knowledge cannot become implicit; the two are distinct and separate (R. Ellis, 2009; Krashen, 2003). This proposed inability for explicit knowledge to become implicit has implications for the classroom. If teaching explicit grammar rules results only in explicit knowledge that is primarily good for enabling learners to apply the rules in situations that allow for considerable time to monitor their production, then there is little point in teaching these rules, if the desired goal of instruction is the ability to communicate freely in the L2. Instead, proponents of the non-interface position argue that rich and plentiful input that engages learners in communication is the optimal pedagogical choice for the L2 classroom.

In contrast, the weak interface position argues that although the two types of knowledge are still distinct, there is a relationship between the two types of knowledge and they work together during L2 production (N. Ellis, 2007). Additionally, the weak interface proposes that explicit knowledge is also help-ful for monitoring L2 production and increasing the likelihood that learners will notice the explicitly taught forms in the input.

Finally, the strong interface position is based on the assumption that explicit knowledge can and does become implicit. The main theoretical sup-port for the strong interface hypothesis comes from Skill Acquisition Theory, which describes the process of declarative knowledge becoming procedur-alized (DeKeyser, 2007b, 2007c; Segalowitz, 2003). Skill Acquisition Theory proposes three stages in the process of transforming linguistic knowledge into spontaneous and fluent L2 production. The first stage is the acquisition of declarative knowledge, which has been characterized as 'knowledge that.' Examples of declarative knowledge include knowing that English regular past tense is formed by adding −ed to the base form of the verb, or that the first tone in Mandarin starts high in pitch and stays high. The next stage is procedural knowledge, or 'knowledge how.' In this stage learners have developed their declarative knowledge into a form that allows them to use that knowledge for language production—knowing how to form English regular past tense or produce Mandarin tones. The final stage of this process is automatization, in which learners gain the ability to use procedural knowledge in a fluent and spontaneous way. In order for learners to progress from the declarative stage, through the procedural stage, to the automatized one, they require time and large amounts of practice in using the L2 (Mora & Valls-Ferrer, 2012; Mura-noi, 2007). Furthermore, the requisite elements need to occur in the proper order for skill acquisition to develop. Learners must have declarative knowl-edge before they can begin the procedualization process. In turn, learners must possess proceduralized knowledge before it can become automatized (DeKeyser, 2007a).

In summary, the interface hypothesis presents three different perspectives regarding the relationship between explicit or declarative knowledge on the one hand, and implicit or procedural knowledge on the other. However, it has been suggested that these three positions may not be categorical and applicable equally to all linguistic areas (Han & Finneran, 2013). It may be the case that some linguistic features may be constrained by a noninterface condition, while other linguistic features may be subject to weaker or stronger interface effects. Additional research is needed to further understand these relationships and processes.

The Measurement of L2 Knowledge

In order to examine the relationship between explicit and implicit knowledge and to determine if L2 instruction is beneficial, it is necessary to have instruments that provide reliable and valid measures of implicit and explicit knowledge. If communicative competence is the purported goal of L2 instruction, then learners' implicit or procedural knowledge must be assessed because this knowledge is largely responsible for communicative competence. In addition, the extent of learners' explicit knowledge is of interest if researchers are to further explore the relationship between implicit and explicit knowledge. It may be possible to measure changes in learners' explicit and implicit knowledge of linguistic structures over time, and to infer that those changes are due to differential increases in the types of knowledge that learners possess. However, it is difficult to measure L2 knowledge, especially implicit knowledge; consequently, researchers have invested much time and effort establishing what instruments may be better measures of either type of knowledge.

To measure explicit knowledge, researchers have relied on explicit, direct tests of the L2 knowledge in question. For instance, after learners have been instructed on the rules of a specific grammatical form, for example, English regular past tense, they may then be tested on their ability to verbalize the rule, as well as apply it in various contexts. Learners might be asked to make grammaticality judgments about sentences containing obligatory occasions for past tense verbs, or they may be asked to provide the correct past tense forms on fill-in-the-blank tests. If learners possess explicit knowledge of the rule, they should be able to perform well on such tests, especially if they are given unlimited time to access their explicit knowledge.

In contrast, the measurement of implicit knowledge ideally requires samples of learners' spontaneous oral production. Thus, in order to assess implicit knowledge of English past tense, learners could be asked about their activities from the previous weekend. If learners possess implicit knowledge, they should be fairly accurate in their use of past tense while narrating their activities; however, a lack of implicit knowledge would be evident by their omission or incorrect use of past-tense verbs. By comparison, native speakers of English, who by definition have implicit knowledge of their L1, would use the past tense in such contexts without consciously thinking about its use; rather, native speakers would focus on the semantic content of their language production. However, measuring implicit knowledge in this way presents several difficulties. First, learners may be able to use their explicit knowledge of the rules to monitor their spontaneous production, particularly if they are allowed ample time to complete the task. Learners might consciously remind themselves to use the past tense, and they may even be able to pause mid-sentence to think about the correct form. Another difficulty in using spontaneous oral production as an indication of learners' implicit knowledge is that learners might avoid using certain structures; however, the absence of a specific structure does not necessarily indicate a lack of knowledge. Instead, the absence of overt production might simply mean that learners did not feel it was necessary to use the target structure. In order to circumvent such ambiguous situations, researchers have attempted to design tests that obligate learners to use the target structures, although requiring learners to use specific structures in free production is difficult. As a result, researchers have also employed other types of tests that result in more constrained production, but nevertheless attempt to encourage learners' use of implicit knowledge.

Multiple researchers (e.g., R. Ellis, 2005; Ellis et al., 2009; Rebuschat, 2013) have been involved in systematically investigating ways in which both explicit and implicit knowledge might be assessed. The fact that implicit knowledge is accessed quickly with little cognitive effort, while the retrieval of explicit knowledge involves more time and effort, has led researchers to design tests that measure language use in both time pressured and unpressured contexts. The assumption is that time pressure will predispose learners to draw on their implicit knowledge, while a lack of time pressure may encourage the use of explicit knowledge. However, as researchers acknowledge, it is probably not possible to obtain pure measures of either type of knowledge. Learners may have sufficient ability to draw on their explicit knowledge even if a test allows them little time to reflect. For instance, learners may be able quickly access a grammatical rule even if they are being asked to judge the grammaticality of a sentence in a very limited amount of time. Likewise, a lack of time pressure does not necessitate the use of explicit knowledge. For example, even with unlimited time, learners may make immediate, intuitive judgments about the grammaticality of sentences without taking the time to access explicit knowledge for their responses.

The importance for ISLA of having methods of measuring both implicit and explicit L2 knowledge is seen in the claims that can be made about the effects of various types of instruction. Valid and reliable tests of both types of knowledge enable researchers to compare the effects of various types of implicit and explicit instruction; however, a lack of such instruments, particularly for the measurement of implicit knowledge, may bias the interpretation of ISLA research. An important example of this consequence comes from an early meta-analysis of the benefits of implicit and explicit L2 instruction. In 2000, John Norris and Lourdes Ortega statistically analyzed the results of 49 independent, quasi-experimental studies investigating the effectiveness of L2 instruction. They categorized instruction as either explicit – that is involving any type of rule explanation – or implicit, lacking rule presentation or other directions for learners to attend to specific linguistic forms. In addition to gauging the effectiveness of instruction, Norris and Ortega questioned if the instruments used to measure L2 knowledge influenced the results of their analysis. They categorized the instruments as follows: metalinguistic judgments, selected response, constrained constructed response, and free constructed response. The results of the meta-analysis indicated that, overall, explicit instruction was more effective than implicit instruction for L2 development. However, results also indicated that effectiveness depended on the types of outcome measures used to assess development; studies employing instruments in which learners' performance would benefit from the presence of explicit knowledge (i.e., selected response and constrained constructed response) showed greater effects than did studies using free constructed responses, in which explicit knowledge would be expected to play less of a role. As a consequence, Norris and Ortega, as well as other researchers (e.g., Doughty, 2003) suggest caution in interpreting the meta-analysis results as favoring explicit instruction because it could be the case that the instruments used to measure L2 development were biased towards instruction that resulted in explicit knowledge. Thus, the claims that can be made about the efficacy of instruction may depend on how learning and knowledge are measured. Other studies have also stressed the importance of testing both explicit and implicit knowledge of L2 grammar (Spada & Tomita, 2010) and vocabulary (Sonbul & Schmitt, 2012), with the result that it is now fairly common for quasi-experimental research studies to employ tests that favor both types of knowledge, respectively (e.g., Andringa et al., 2011). In this way, the effects of instruction can be measured in terms of both explicit and implicit knowledge.

EMPIRICAL EVIDENCE

Having covered various theoretical aspects of the nature of L2 knowledge, it is important to consider some of the research that has been conducted to investigate these issues. Some of the most central questions that have been researched in relation to implicit and explicit L2 knowledge concern the effects of different types of instruction on their development. To that end, a number of representative studies addressing the issues are discussed.

The Relationship between Instruction and Knowledge

Explicit knowledge resulting from explicit instruction. Of some interest to ISLA researchers is the question of whether explicit instruction leads to the acquisition of explicit knowledge in L2 learners. Although such acquisition is generally assumed to occur (Doughty, 2003), it is possible that some types of explicit instruction are more effective than others. Several studies have investigated the development of explicit knowledge as a result of explicit instruction. One method of doing so is to compare groups of learners who have been exposed to the L2 in different instructional contexts. For example, Bowles (2011) investigated the L2 knowledge of three groups of Spanish speakers: native speakers, instructed learners from intermediate level university Spanish classes, and heritage learners who had grown up in a Spanish-English bilingual context but had received less than two years of formal Spanish instruction. Bowles administered several different tests of L2 knowledge that biased in favor of either explicit or implicit knowledge, and she found that the instructed L2 learners scored higher than the heritage learners on measures of explicit knowledge, but the heritage learners scored higher on the implicit measures. Bowles contends that the L2 learners, who had spent substantial time in the L2 classroom, had received considerable amounts of explicit instruction, which resulted in their superior performance on the explicit knowledge tests. In contrast, the heritage learners had been exposed to considerable amounts of communicative input, and they had received less explicit instruction. The implication of this study, then, is that explicit instruction can result in explicit knowledge.

Another way to investigate the relationship between type of instruction and type of knowledge is to perform quasi-experimental studies in which several different groups are pretested on specific structures, are then given different types of instruction, and finally are given one or more posttests. The results of the test scores can then be compared. In one such study addressing vocabulary learning, Sonbul and Schmitt (2012) investigated the effects of both implicit and explicit instruction on the knowledge of vocabulary collocations from the medical field. Thirty-five L1 English speakers and 43 advanced L2 English speakers were divided into three groups and provided with one of three types of treatment: (a) enriched input, in which a reading passage was embedded with five collocations, (b) enhanced input, in which five additional collocations were highlighted in bold red font, and (c) direct input, in which five collocations were taught in isolation in a PowerPoint presentation. Sonbul and Schmitt found that both L1 and L2 speakers in all three groups made durable gains on the explicit knowledge tests; in contrast, there was no effect for any of the treatment conditions on the test of implicit knowledge. These results suggest that explicit instruction, as well as implicit instruction, can lead to the development of explicit vocabulary knowledge.

Finally, in a meta-analysis of 41 studies published between 1990 and 2006, Spada & Tomita (2010) investigated the effects of explicit and implicit instruction on the acquisition of simple and complex English grammatical features. Instruction was considered explicit when it involved the explanation of grammar rules, while implicit instruction, which included input flood, interaction and recasts, did not provide grammatical explanations or any attempt to draw learners' attention to the targeted grammatical features. The measures of L2 knowledge were divided into two types: controlled and free constructed tasks. Controlled tasks, which encouraged the use of explicit knowledge, included grammaticality judgment tests, multiple choice questions, and sentence combination or reconstruction tasks. Free constructed tasks, which predisposed learners to use implicit knowledge, included free writing tasks, picture description tasks and information gap tasks. The results of the meta-analysis showed that explicit instruction was better than implicit instruction for both simple and complex grammatical features, although implicit instruction did yield some benefits as well. Moreover, explicit instruction was found to have a large impact on learners' performance on both controlled and free tasks, which measured explicit and implicit knowledge respectively. Spada and Tomita conclude that the fact that explicit instruction was found to be beneficial for both explicit and implicit types of knowledge suggests support for the strong interface position in which declarative knowledge can become procedural knowledge through practice. As a caveat, however, Spada and Tomita caution that such an assumption rests on the ability of the tests used in the various studies to provide valid and reliable measures of both implicit and explicit knowledge.

Implicit knowledge resulting from explicit instruction. One of the most important questions in ISLA research regards the role of explicit instruction in the development of implicit knowledge. Because explicit instruction is easier to provide in the classroom than implicit instruction, the ideal situation would be if explicit instruction was effective for the acquisition of both explicit and implicit L2 knowledge. As has been seen, explicit instruction can result in the acquisition of explicit knowledge. Now we consider some research studies that have investigated its effects on the development of implicit knowledge.

The studies in the previous section provide some insight into the question of explicit instruction resulting in implicit knowledge. In particular, Spada and Tomita's (2010) meta-analysis found effects for explicit instruction on both explicit and implicit knowledge. However, Sonbul and Schmitt (2012) found no evidence of explicit instruction resulting in implicit knowledge of vocabulary collocations. Other studies that have investigated this issue include Ellis, Loewen, and Erlam's (2006) study of lower intermediate ESL learners in New Zealand. Ellis et al. provided either explicit or implicit corrective feedback on learners' incorrect use of past tense during two 30-minute communicative tasks. To assess acquisition, Ellis et al. administered three separate tests. The oral imitation test, in which learners heard both grammatical and ungrammatical English sentences and had to repeat the sentences in correct English, was a test of implicit knowledge, while an untimed grammaticality judgment test and a metalinguistic knowledge test were tests of explicit knowledge. In addition to pretesting, the learners were tested immediately after the treatment as well as 12 days later. Ellis et al. found that explicit corrective feedback led to gains in accuracy scores on measures of both implicit and explicit knowledge on delayed posttests. Ellis et al. took these results to indicate that explicit instruction could result in the development of implicit knowledge.

In another study, White & Ranta (2002) examined the relationship between metalinguistic task knowledge and oral production among 11- to 12-year-old ESL students in Quebec. In their experiment, one group engaged in communicative activities, while the other group received explicit instruction regarding the rules of English possessive determiners. During the first 40-minute lesson, the explicit instruction group received two types of metalinguistic information about the use of *his* and *her*: (1) learners were taught a rule of thumb (i.e., ask yourself 'whose __ is it?'), and (2) their attention was directed to the contrast between the possessive determiner agreement rules in English and in their L1, French. In the study, the explicit instruction group improved on both a metalinguistic test and an oral production test, suggesting, White and Ranta claim, that there is an interface between metalinguistic knowledge and L2 knowledge used for spontaneous production.

Given the results of these studies, it is possible to infer that explicit instruction can be beneficial for the acquisition of implicit knowledge; however, it remains for additional research to confirm the generalizability of these findings and to investigate any moderating variables that may increase or decrease the effectiveness of explicit instruction.

Implicit knowledge resulting from implicit instruction. In addition to exploring the effects of explicit instruction, there has also been some investigation into implicit instruction, particularly as relates to the development of implicit knowledge. For example Rebuschat and Williams (2012) investigated the ability of 35 L1 English speakers to acquire knowledge of a semiartificial language through mere exposure to input. Participants were exposed to 128 sentences, half of which had plausible semantic meaning and half of which did not. Participants had to judge the plausibility of the sentences. All sentences conformed to the syntax of the semi-artificial language. To test implicit learning, participants were given 64 new sentences, half of which followed the syntax of the semiartificial language and half of which did not. Learners had to make grammaticality judgments about the test sentences. Rebuschat and Williams' results showed that learners were able to acquire L2 syntax rules incidentally – that is to say, some learners were able to use the syntax rules to make accurate grammaticality judgments about sentences that had not been

included in the treatment sessions. However, an analysis of verbal reports provided by the learners indicated that learning was limited to learners who were
aware that they had learned the rules. Rebuschat and Williams conclude that
implicit learning may be possible for adult L2 learners; however, such learning
may need to be accompanied by conscious knowledge.

Another study, which found positive effects for implicit instruction, is Li's
(2010) meta-analysis of 33 studies of corrective feedback. This study will be
examined in more detail in Chapter 4, but the relevant finding for the effects of
implicit instruction was that although explicit feedback was found to be more
beneficial in the short term (i.e., on immediate posttests), implicit feedback
was more effective long term (i.e., on delayed posttests). Li suggests that these
different effects for the two types of feedback may be the result of implicit
feedback contributing to implicit knowledge, which takes longer to develop
but is more durable. Thus, the effects of implicit instruction would not necessarily be seen immediately after its provision.

In summary, there is evidence to suggest that both explicit and implicit L2
knowledge can be developed by a variety of means. Explicit instruction may
benefit the development of both types of knowledge, while implicit instruction also appears to be effective. However, not all studies found significant
effects, and these results need to be confirmed with additional research studies. In addition, the subsequent chapters in this book will present additional
research that investigates the relationships between types of instruction and
types of L2 knowledge.

PEDAGOGICAL IMPLICATIONS

The theoretical and empirical evidence regarding the nature and acquisition
of L2 knowledge has several implications for the classroom, although in large
part these will be discussed in subsequent chapters. One important implication, though, is that teachers and students should be clear about the goals
of instruction because different objectives may necessitate different types of
classroom instruction. Implicit instruction may contribute to the development of implicit knowledge, but because implicit learning is time consuming,
it may be necessary to support implicit learning with explicit instruction and
focus on form (N. Ellis, 2007). Even Krashen (2003), a strong proponent of
implicit instruction and L2 exposure for the development of implicit knowledge, concedes a role for explicit instruction, primarily to provide information
to adult learners who may be more suited to learning explicitly. Moreover,
there is evidence to suggest that explicit knowledge can result in gains in
implicit knowledge. Thus, it would seem that a combination of explicit and
implicit instruction may be best for the L2 classroom. These issues related to
specific types of instruction will be explored further in the following chapters.

SUMMARY

Included below is a summary of some of the main points from this chapter.

- L2 knowledge consists of two distinct types, with have been referred to as explicit and implicit, or as declarative and procedural.
- Explicit knowledge is conscious and verbalizable, but it does not necessarily contribute greatly to communicative competence.
- Implicit knowledge is unconscious and underlies communicative competence, but it is time-consuming and difficult to acquire.
- Teachers and learners should be clear on their goals in studying an L2 because these goals should dictate the best types of instruction.
- Explicit instruction may not always result in the type of implicit knowledge that is useful for spontaneous communication.

ACTIVITIES

1. Here are two activities from Ellis et al. (2009) that have been used to assess implicit and explicit knowledge. How successful do you think these activities are in providing valid and reliable measures of different types of L2 knowledge? Is it possible to use implicit knowledge in the explicit test? Is it possible to use explicit knowledge in the implicit test? If so, how? If not, why not?

Implicit L2 Knowledge Test: Oral Narrative

Directions: Please read the following story. After your read it, the paper will be taken away, and you will be asked to retell the story in as much detail as possible.

Every morning Mr. Lee gets up at 6:30 a.m., walks to the dairy in Ponsonby Road and buys a newspaper. He has toast and tea for breakfast and reads the newspaper. Then, if he feels like it, he goes to work, but often he stays at home and sits in the sun. On these days Mrs. Lee complains. But he always smiles and says, 'I want to take life easy. I want to enjoy myself.' Yesterday Mr. Lee's life changed forever. Mrs. Lee's life changed too. This is what happened.

Mr. Lee found a wallet. It contained $55, some credit cards, and two lottery tickets. Mr. Lee checked the lottery tickets' numbers in the newspaper. He couldn't believe it. He had the winning ticket. It was worth $6 million.

Mr. Lee didn't know what to do. After all it wasn't really his ticket. 'Do I keep the money for myself? or Do I give the ticket back to the wallet's owner?' he asked Mrs. Lee.

After a while he knew what to do. He took the bus to the address of the wallet's owner. He knocked on the door. An old woman opened the door.

'Do you know a Mr. Martin?' asked Mr. Lee.

'Just a minute. He is my daughter's husband,' said the old woman.

Mr. Martin came to the door. Mr. Lee showed him the ticket and the newspaper.

'This is your ticket,' said Mr. Lee, 'I want you to have it back'.

Mr. Martin couldn't believe that he had won $6 million.

'I want to thank you for being so honest,' he said. 'I want to give you a reward. Do you think that a million dollars is enough?'

Mr. Lee accepted the million dollars. His life changed. He no longer needed to work. In fact he and Mrs. Lee lived happily ever after.

Explicit L2 Knowledge Test: Grammaticality Judgment Test

Directions: Please decide whether you think each sentence is grammatically correct or incorrect. You may take as much time as you need.

1. I haven't seen him for a long time.

   Correct   Incorrect

2. I think that he is nicer and more intelligent than all the other students.

   Correct   Incorrect

3. The teacher explained the problem to the students.

   Correct   Incorrect

4. Liao says he wants buying a car next week.

   Correct   Incorrect

5. Martin completed his assignment and print it out.

   Correct   Incorrect

6. I must to brush my teeth.

   Correct   Incorrect

2a. Lyster (2004) investigated the effects of corrective feedback on the ability of English speaking learners to assign grammatical gender in French. He used the following four tests to assess the learners' ability. What types of knowledge would learners most likely use to complete these tasks? Do the tests provide measures of both implicit and explicit knowledge?

   1. A written binary-choice test in which learners had to circle the correct article to accompany the noun that was provided.
   2. A text-completion test with two components. In Part 1, learners had to choose the correct article for 30 target nouns included in a reading

passage. In Part 2, learners were required to write a recipe based on a list of ingredients provided for them. Learners had to produce the correct article for each noun.

3. An oral object-identification test in which learners were shown drawings of objects and provided with the lexical item without the article. Learners had to provide the singular form of the noun along with the accompanying article.

4. A picture-description test in which learners were asked to describe a series of pictures in as much detail as possible.

2b. Investigate one or two additional ISLA studies that assessed the types of knowledge that learners' gained from instruction. What types of instruments did the researchers use to assess implicit and explicit knowledge? How effective do you think these instruments were in measuring what they claimed to measure?

ADDITIONAL READING

Ellis, N. C. (1994). *Implicit and explicit learning of languages.* London: Academic Press.

Ellis, R., Loewen, S., Elder, C., Erlam, R., Philp, J., & Reinders, H. (2009). *Implicit and explicit knowledge in second language learning, testing and teaching.* Bristol: Multilingual Matters.

Reber, A. S. (1993). *Implicit learning and tacit knowledge: An essay on the cognitive unconscious.* Oxford: Oxford University Press.

Sanz, C., & Loew, R. (2011). *Implicit and explicit language learning: Conditions, processes, and knowledge in SLA & bilingualism.* Washington, DC: Georgetown University Press.

3

Interaction in the Second Language Classroom

If a primary aim of instructed SLA is the development of implicit or procedural knowledge for communicative competence in L2 learners, it then remains to consider the most effective methods to achieve that goal. It might seem logical that communicating and interacting in the L2 classroom can help learners achieve this goal; however, the role of interaction in ISLA has been controversial (R. Sheen, 2005; Swan, 2005). Some early theoretical perspectives on ISLA, based on behaviorism, advocated the formation of good production habits through numerous repetitive drills and the avoidance of linguistic errors. In general, these mechanical drills did not provide opportunities for learners to engage in meaningful communication; in fact, free oral production was not encouraged because learners might make linguistic errors, which would reinforce bad L2 habits (Jin & Cortazzi, 2011). Another early perspective on L2 learning, sometimes referred to as a traditional approach, proposed that communicative competence could be achieved through explicit L2 instruction and step-by-step accumulation of knowledge of grammar rules and vocabulary. This point of view supported grammar translation activities in which learners used their explicit knowledge of grammatical rules and lexical items to translate sentences from the L2 to the L1 or vice versa (Jin & Cortazzi, 2011; Nassaji & Fotos, 2011). However, as has been discussed, the assumption that explicit instruction by itself will result in implicit, proceduralized knowledge is contentious. In many cases, explicit instruction results primarily in explicit knowledge of the information that was taught. Consequently, there has been an effort to introduce into the classroom types of instruction that are more likely to lead to implicit knowledge and communicative competence. One of these methods is meaning-focused interaction.

An early theoretical argument in favor of communication in the classroom was proposed by Krashen's Monitor Model, particularly the learning-acquisition hypothesis which stated that the ability to use language for spontaneous communication developed through implicit learning mechanisms (Krashen, 1982, 2003). Subsequently, the Interaction Approach has provided a theoretical rationale for the inclusion of meaning-focused communication in the L2 classroom (Gass, 1997; Long, 1991, 1996).

In some cases, it is possible for communication in the L2 to occur outside the classroom in uninstructed L2 acquisition, and indeed some strong versions of communicative language teaching propose that interaction inside the classroom should approximate interaction outside the classroom. However, not surprisingly such opinions are in the minority in ISLA, given that the primary concern of ISLA researchers is how best to facilitate acquisition by manipulating the processes of and conditions for learning. For example, authentic L2 interaction outside the classroom may not be the most conducive for acquisition; it may be beyond learners' ability to comprehend and it may provide limited opportunities for output. Furthermore, many L2 learners, particularly those in foreign language contexts, do not have *Latino too* many opportunities to communicate in the L2. Consequently, the classroom may be the only context in which many learners are able to engage in L2 communication; accordingly, a primary concern of researchers has been to determine the characteristics of interaction in the classroom that are most beneficial for L2 acquisition and the development of communicative competence.

THEORETICAL CONCERNS

Components of Interaction

When considering interaction in the classroom, it is important to explore its various components. In this regard, the Interaction Approach to ISLA has spent considerable effort investigating this issue, focusing in particular on input, negotiation for meaning, and output (Gass & Mackey, 2007; Mackey & Gass, 2005). The interaction hypothesis (Gass, 1997; Long, 1991, 1996; Pica, 1994) has developed since the early 1990s, and although it is not an all-encompassing theory accounting for all aspects of L2 acquisition, it has been described as a developing theoretical approach, encompassing multiple processes associated with L2 learning (Gass & Mackey, 2007). The primary assertion of the interaction hypothesis is that as learners engage in meaningful interaction, they will have opportunities to negotiate for meaning; that is, when communication breakdown occurs due to linguistic difficulties, learners will work to resolve the misunderstandings by focusing on the linguistic trouble sources. This negotiation for meaning draws learners' attention to linguistic items that are problematic for them, thereby facilitating the mechanisms of L2 acquisition. The example below, from a communicative task involving the description of a railway station, illustrates negotiation for meaning occurring when one learner is uncertain about a specific lexical item. Through the interaction, the learners are able to confirm the appropriate word for the context.

Example of negotiation for meaning

S1:   Platform two door is closed.
S2:   You mean the gate is closed?
S1:   Gates? Yeah, the gates are closed. Yeah, yeah, the gate is like door.
S2:   Yeah, closed. The gate is closed. You too?

—(Bitchener, 2004, pp. 81–82)

The goal of the Interaction Approach is for learners to develop implicit knowledge of linguistic forms that will enable them to engage in meaningful communication. In order to achieve this goal, the Interaction Approach attempts to account for acquisition by examining the input that learners receive, the interaction that they engage in, and the output they produce (Gass & Mackey, 2007). These three constructs will be discussed in turn.

   Input. Input is essential for L2 acquisition. No theory of ISLA proposes that an L2 can be learned without input. However, there is less agreement regarding the types of input that are most useful for acquisition. One distinction that researchers have made about input is in terms of positive evidence and negative evidence (Long, 1996). Positive evidence consists of examples of linguistic structures and forms that are permissible in the language. Any exposure to the L2, whether through native speakers' conversations, teachers' classroom instructions, song lyrics, or Internet webpages, provides learners with models of what can be said or written in the L2. Thus, it could be said that all target-like input constitutes positive evidence. In contrast, negative evidence consists of information about what is not possible or grammatical in the L2. Such information may come when learners experience a communication breakdown or receive corrective feedback. In these cases, learners obtain information that something they have said is not an accurate part of the L2. Although the role and importance of positive evidence is clear, the value of negative evidence is less agreed upon. L1 learners generally do not receive much corrective feedback during the L1 learning process, and L2 corrective feedback has been argued to ineffective or even harmful for learning (Truscott, 1999). Further exploration of the effects of negative evidence will occur in Chapter 4 because it often involves more explicit attention to language items.

   Although researchers agree that input in the form of positive evidence is indispensable for acquisition, they do not all agree on what types of input are best. For one thing, input in and of itself is not particularly useful until it enters learners' cognitive systems, a process called intake. Thus, intake is defined as that part of the input that is noticed, comprehended, and taken in to the cognitive system. There is some consensus that one benefit of classroom instruction is that input can be modified in order to increase the likelihood of it becoming intake. Authentic input found outside of the classroom may not be the most beneficial for L2 acquisition, in part because not all authentic input is comprehensible to learners.

Comprehensible input is argued to be important for acquisition. In particular, Krashen (1982, 2003) maintains in his input hypothesis that input is made comprehensible to learners when it contains only a few elements that are unknown to them, which they can figure out based on the situational and linguistic contexts. Situational contexts help make input comprehensible by referring to things that are understandable due to learners' familiarity with their immediate surroundings. Alternatively, linguistic context makes input comprehensible by providing language that is slightly more advanced than a learner's current interlanguage state; Krashen refers to this type of input as $i + 1$. Knowing the majority of linguistic items in the input helps learners comprehend the limited number of unknown elements. Based on his input hypothesis, Krashen suggests that teachers in the classroom should provide a language-rich environment in which learners can encounter L2 input in numerous and communicative ways. In this regard, Krashen, and other proponents of a strong version of communicative language teaching, are trying to approximate naturalistic interaction inside the classroom, albeit with considerably greater quantity and richer quality of input than learners might experience in everyday communication outside of the classroom.

Negotiation for meaning. One response to Krashen's comprehensible input hypothesis came from Long (1991, 1996) who argued that linguistic and situational context were not enough to make input comprehensible. Instead, a more important component for L2 comprehension and development is interactionally modified input, which is the result of learners negotiating for meaning when there is a breakdown in communication.

Interaction, then, becomes a core construct for communication in the classroom, and multiple studies have examined how interaction, and especially negotiation for meaning, occurs in the classroom. The examples below, taken from communicative tasks in a Spanish L2 context (Gass et al., 2005) illustrate three principal ways in which negotiation for meaning can occur. The specific negotiation strategy is bolded in each example. Confirmation checks involve learners in verifying the meaning of their interlocutor's previous utterance. In addition to the statements like the one in Example 1, learners might also say something like, *Do you mean X?* Another example is a clarification request in which learners seek out extra information to clear up their misunderstanding, as in Example 2 or the phrase *What do you mean?* The third option involves speakers attempting to avert misunderstanding through the use of comprehension checks to ensure that their interlocutor has understood their intended message, as seen in Example 3. In addition, a speaker may use a comprehension check, such as *Do you know what I mean?*, to verify that their partner understands what is being said.

Example 1: Confirmation Check (Gass et al., 2005, p. 585)

Learner 1:   En mi dibujo hay un pájaro.
              In my drawing there is a bird.
Learner 2:   **¿Solamente un?** Tengo, uh, cinco pájaros con un hombre, en sus hombros.
              Only one? *I have, uh, five birds with a man, on his shoulders.*
Learner 1:   Oh, oh, sí, sí.
              Oh, oh, yes, yes.

Example 2: Clarification Request

Learner 1:   ¿Qué es importante a ella?
              What is important to her?
Learner 2:   **¿Cómo?**
              What?
Learner 1:   ¿Qué es importante a la amiga? ¿Es solamente el costo?
              What is important to the friend? Is it just the cost?

Example 3: Comprehension Check

Learner 1:   La avenida siete va en una dirección hacia el norte desde la calle siete hasta la calle ocho.
              ¿Quires que repita?
              Avenue Seven goes in one direction towards the north from Street Seven to Street Eight.
              Do you want me to repeat?
Learner 2:   Por favor.
              Please.

These types of negotiating for meaning can potentially help learners notice gaps between their own linguistic errors that result in communication breakdowns and the target-like forms that convey learners' intended meanings.

   Output. Finally, it is important to consider the role of output, which is the language that learners produce. Some theorists (e.g., Krashen, 1982, 2003) see output as merely the byproduct of acquisition and ascribe it little if any role in the acquisition process. However, Swain's (1995, 2005) comprehensible output hypothesis argues that output is an important part of the L2 acquisition process. Swain and other researchers observed that L2 learners in Canadian immersion contexts had high levels of fluency, but they were consistently inaccurate in their production of some of even the most frequent of linguistic structures. Swain noted that although learners received extensive amounts of input, they had relatively few opportunities to produce output, a fact she suggested was responsible for learners' low levels of accuracy. Swain argued that learners were able to process language semantically because their primary need in the classroom was to comprehend the language; however, there was no need for learners to pay close attention to all of the grammatical forms in the input since many were redundant or did not contain information that was critical to the meaning of the input. Consequently, Swain concluded that learners need to be pushed to produce output during meaning-focused classroom interaction because it forces them to process the morphosyntactic elements of language as they attempt production, rather than just focusing on the semantic elements as they comprehend the input. For example, if learners want to describe what they did over the weekend, they will need to produce linguistic forms such as past tense. In contrast, if learners are listening to their peers discuss their weekend activities, they do not need to process the past tense grammatical markers because the context can provide the information regarding the time of the action.

Learner output can also be used for testing hypotheses that learners have about the L2 (Muranoi, 2007; Swain, 1995). If learners try out a form in their output and receive disconfirmation as to its accuracy, either through communication breakdown or corrective feedback, learners can reevaluate their hypothesis. Alternatively, learners may accept their hypothesis in the absence of any disconfirming evidence. In these ways, output is seen not as something that is merely the result of learning, but rather as something that can contribute to L2 development. Thus, the Interaction Approach generally sees a facilitative role for output in the process of L2 learning.

In sum, the Interaction Approach advocates for the importance of input, interaction, and output. Much of the research in this area has focused on the activities or tasks that learners and their interlocutors engage in to facilitate communication. Communication does not happen in a vacuum; learners must talk about something, and providing input for communicative activities allows researchers and teachers to affect task interaction. An important pedagogical outgrowth of the Interaction Approach is seen in task-based language learning and teaching, which uses a variety of tasks to achieve different types of interaction in the L2 classroom. In addition to investigating input, negotiation, and output, advocates of task-based learning are interested in other variables that affect interaction.

Variables Affecting Interaction

In keeping with the goals of ISLA, namely optimizing instruction for L2 acquisition, interaction researchers have been theorizing and investigating the optimal conditions for learning during communicative activities. To do this they have examined at least three sets of variables: (a) characteristics of the task itself, (b) characteristics of the interlocutors, and (c) characteristics of the interactional context.

Task characteristics. A major variable that has been explored in interaction research is how the structure of meaning-focused activities can result in different types of interaction and thus potentially differentially affect L2 learning. Often, such types of activities are referred to as tasks. A task is considered to be a communicative activity that has the following features: (a) it resembles a real-world activity, (b) it has a primary focus on meaning, (c) it has a non-linguistic outcome, and (d) learners are expected to use their own linguistic resources (Ellis, 2003). A specific example of a task can be seen in an activity that involves providing learners with a bus schedule and asking them to find the best route for a bus to take from points A to B to arrive at a specific time. This activity meets the criteria for a task because: (a) it is something that people do outside of the classroom in real life, (b) the primary focus is on meaning and discussing possible bus routes, (c) the goal of deciding on an appropriate bus route is non-linguistic in nature, and (d) learners are not provided with any specific linguistic forms that they must use. In this case, the task provides a context for meaning-focused interaction; however, within the parameters of such a task, there are several features that may be altered in various ways.

An initial, important decision pertains to how the information in the task is presented to the learners (Pica, Kanagy, & Falodun, 1993). For example, different parts of the task information can be given to different learners in a two-way information gap task, so that learners have to exchange information with each other in order to complete the task. In the case of the bus task, each learner could be given only part of the timetable, and learners would have to share information to construct it in its entirety. In contrast, in a one-way information gap task, one learner has all of the information and must convey it to the other individuals in the group. Finally, it is possible for there to be no information gap, with all learners receiving the same information (Doughty & Pica, 1986).

Another variable characteristic relates to the outcome of the task (Ellis, 2003). Tasks with convergent goals require learners to agree on a specific outcome. Alternatively, divergent tasks require learners only to express their own opinions, and it does not matter if learners are in agreement. In the bus task, a convergent goal would require learners to agree on the best bus route, but a divergent task would allow learners to express their own opinions without coming to a consensus. Generally, involving learners in two-way information gap tasks in which they are required to agree upon the outcome is better for bringing about more interaction and negotiation of meaning (Ellis, 2003; Yilmaz, 2011).

In general, task-based learning engages learners in tasks that do not have a specific linguistic focus (Foster, 2009), although it is possible for tasks to have a linguistic focus, even though such a focus is not in keeping with a strong version of task-based learning. If the other criteria for tasks are met, and the focus on language is relatively implicit, then it may be possible to maintain the benefits of tasks while incorporating a linguistic target. These are called focused tasks (Nobuyoshi & Ellis, 1993; Shintani, 2013), and they attempt to create obligatory occasions for the use of specific structures. Researchers have made a distinction between tasks in which the use of certain linguistic structures is essential, useful, or merely natural (Loschky & Bley-Vroman, 1993; Keck et al., 2006). Because learners are good at avoiding specific structures, it is often difficult to devise tasks in which the use of a specific structure is essential; however, the utility of specific features is easier to ensure. For example, it could be that in the bus route task, the task designers are trying to create obligatory occasions for the use of future tense (e.g., *The bus is going to stop at Main Street. The bus will arrive at 1 p.m.*). In addition, focused tasks may be seeded with specific linguistic structures in the input, so that the tasks provide some examples for the learners to draw on (Ellis, 2003). Unfocused tasks, on the other hand, have no predetermined linguistic focus and learners can use whatever linguistic resources they have at their disposal. Unfocused tasks are more in keeping with the goals of maintaining a focus on meaning and communication; however, tasks that integrate specific linguistic structures into meaning-focused interaction is a primary concern of focus on form, and will be explored in Chapter 4.

Interlocutor characteristics. In addition to task characteristics, there a number of issues related to the individuals who participate in the tasks that affect interaction. For example, task-based interaction has often been associated with group work; however, it is possible to perform tasks as a whole class, as well as in small groups and pairs. Some research has investigated how group size affects interaction, particularly when interaction occurs in dyads versus larger groups (Pica & Doughty, 1985).

Another important consideration is the task interlocutor, the individual with whom the learner is interacting. Studies have investigated a number of different types of interlocutors, including native speakers and teachers, as well as L2 learners of equal, higher, and lower proficiencies (Leeser, 2004; Sato & Ballinger, 2012). Often these studies are conducted in laboratory situations because of the difficulties of collecting such data in classrooms (e.g., Fernandez Dobao, 2012). For example, native speakers are not often found in the classroom apart from possibly the teacher. In many cases, these studies will examine the amount of language that is produced, as well as the frequency of negotiation for meaning.

One issue to consider in peer interaction is L1 use. In many foreign language contexts in which most learners in class share the same L1, there is concern that learners will use the L1 to complete the tasks, and thus negate the positive effects of L2 interaction. When the L1 is used, learners do not receive L2 input; furthermore, there may be no negotiation of meaning, nor are learners pushed to produce L2 output.

Another variable in peer interaction is pair dynamics and the role that learners play during the task (Kim & McDonough, 2008; Storch, 2002). Possible roles include dominant, passive, expert, and novice. These roles are important for the affordances they provide for acquisition. Pairs in which one learner takes a dominant role and the other takes a passive one may not engage in much interaction if one person is doing most of the talking and task activities, while the other individual contributes very little. Likewise, learners who both take a dominant role may not spend much time interacting because each individual is doing their own thing and not listening to the other. In contrast, learners involved in expert/novice relationships may have beneficial interaction in which the novice learners are helped to increase their communicative abilities during the task. Similarly, a novice/novice dynamic may allow both learners to work together to try to solve their interactional difficulties.

Contextual characteristics. Although L2 learners generally interact in the classroom, ISLA researchers have also investigated interaction in laboratory contexts due to the challenges of collecting data and controlling confounding variables inside the classroom. However, there has been controversy regarding the generalizability of ISLA research conducted in laboratory contexts because it is felt that laboratory conditions may alter the ways in which interaction occurs. In laboratory conditions, learners may be more likely to have a positive orientation to the tasks due to the halo effect of being involved in a research study. In addition, the uncommon situation of being in a laboratory-based study can heighten learners' awareness of the activities that they are involved in. Furthermore, if learners are aware that the study is investigating L2 acquisition, even in a broad sense, they may be more likely to pay attention to language and linguistic accuracy which can clearly affect meaning-focused interaction (Loewen & Nabei, 2007).

Another context that is receiving increased attention for interaction research is computer-mediated communication (CMC) (Blake, 2000; O'Dowd, 2011). Because of the possibility of CMC to bring together interlocutors from various places, it has the potential to provide learners with access to linguistic input and interaction that was not available a few years ago (Pasfield-Neofitou, 2012). Although in some cases, the input and interaction may be more pedagogical in nature, there is also an unprecedented opportunity for learners to interact with authentic materials and real native speakers.

From an interaction perspective, synchronous CMC is of the most interest (Sauro, 2011). This type of interaction happens in real time as participants communicate with each other either orally or in writing via the computer. In terms of written synchronous CMC, also known as text chat, several advantages have been put forward for this type of interaction. One is that it slows down the communication process, which might help learners focus more on the accuracy of their language production. Slower interaction could also provide more time for learners to draw on their explicit knowledge as they attempt L2 production. Written synchronous CMC also leaves a written record so that learners can go back and look at what was written, which may be particularly useful in helping learners notice the difference between their own errors and the target forms provided in any corrective feedback (Smith, 2009; Smith & Sauro, 2009).

Synchronous CMC can also be voice-based, either with or without accompanying video (Bueno-Alastuey, 2013). At the moment, it appears that synchronous audio CMC shares more characteristics with face-to-face interaction than with written CMC; however, research in this area is in its early stages. No doubt interaction research will continue to adapt as the means by which humans communicate continues to evolve.

EMPIRICAL EVIDENCE

The research that has investigated interaction in the L2 classroom can be divided into two broad categories. First, there is research that has described the effects of specific variables on the frequency or features of interaction. Examples of this type of research can be seen in studies examining the effects of one-way and two-way information gap tasks on the frequency and types of negotiation for meaning. A second type of research has investigated the effects of interaction on L2 development. In some cases, such studies have also investigated moderator variables such as task type and interlocutor characteristics; however, the primary goal has been to determine their effects on acquisition. Both types of research can further understanding of the effects of interaction, and a selection of studies will now be explored.

Factors Affecting Interaction

The previous sections above presented several conclusions from early research on task-based interaction, particularly regarding the effects of task characteristics. Although task characteristics still receive some attention, this review will focus on more recent works that have investigated interlocutor and context characteristics. For example, several recent studies have examined the effects of proficiency and proficiency pairing in learner dyads. In particular, the interaction of learners with similar proficiency levels has been compared to that of learners of unequal proficiency levels. In one such study, Kim and McDonough (2008) investigated the interactional dynamics of 16 intermediate and 8 advanced learners of Korean, placed in either same or different proficiency level dyads. Kim and McDonough found that proficiency played a role in pair dynamics, with learners taking a more passive or novice role when their interlocutor was of a higher proficiency level, while being more collaborative with partners at their own proficiency level. Kim and McDonough conclude that expert and novice roles are not necessarily fixed in L2 interaction and may be open to negotiation.

In another study, Storch and Aldosari (2013) investigated the interaction of 36 EFL students in Saudi Arabia who were paired into one of three proficiency groups: high-high, high-low, and low-low. Storch and Aldosari found a greater focus on language use among high-high proficiency pairs than in the other two pairings. In addition, lower proficiency learners appeared less likely to talk if they were paired with higher proficiency speakers. Based on these results, Storch and Aldosari recommend pairing lower proficiency learners together if fluency is the goal of the task-based interaction. However, if accuracy is the goal, then pairing lower proficiency learners with higher proficiency learners may be more likely to result in a focus on language forms.

One concern regarding learner-learner interaction is that learners will use the L1 while conducting a task, thereby negating the positive effects that tasks can have on L2 interaction and output. Furthermore, lower proficiency learners might be more likely to revert to the L1 because of their lack of L2 proficiency. To that end, Storch and Aldosari (2010) investigated L1 use in two meaning-focused and one forms-focused task conducted by 15 pairs of Saudi students, grouped equally into high-high, high-low, and low-low pairs. Results showed minimal L1 use, with less than 7% of total words and 16% of turns being in the L1. Storch and Aldosari found that task type had the greatest impact on L1 use, although proficiency was a factor as well. Overall, more L1 use occurred in the forms-focused task, which was considered to be the most demanding. Furthermore, lower proficiency pairings relied more on their L1, as they needed all their resources to complete the task. The L1 was used primarily for task management and to discuss the meaning of vocabulary words.

In addition to individual interlocutor differences, there has also been investigation into the impact that the context has on interaction. In this regard, two main settings, namely the classroom and the laboratory, have been studied, with a third context of CMC receiving more attention with the increasing use of technology for communication.

The influence of context on interaction has been investigated to determine if interaction in face-to-face classrooms is similar to interaction in laboratories, thereby allowing researchers to generalize the findings of laboratory-based studies to the classroom. Several studies have found low levels of interaction in the classroom. For example, Foster (1998), in a study of an ESL classroom in Great Britain, observed learners engaged in a variety of tasks during their regular classroom activities. An analysis of their interaction revealed that, although several students engaged in considerable interaction, many students did not speak or engage in negotiation for meaning. In a replication of Foster's study, Eckerth (2009) examined the interaction of lower intermediate British learners of German. Working in pairs, participants completed three tasks: a picture differences task, a consensus task, and a consciousness-raising task focusing on a specific grammatical point. Similar to Foster, Eckerth found low rates of negotiation, suggesting that classroom interaction may not result in much negotiation of meaning. However, at least one study, Gass et al. (2005), found that context did not make a difference in the frequency or features of interaction for university-level L2 learners of Spanish performing tasks in laboratory or classroom contexts; however, differences were found according to task type, with the tasks requiring information exchange containing more interactional features than the task that did not did not. Because of these contradictory findings, more investigation into the comparability of interaction in the classroom and laboratory interaction is needed.

In addition to the classroom and laboratory contexts, there has been growing research into the effects of CMC on interaction, with studies investigating a combination of face-to-face interaction, written synchronous CMC, and oral synchronous CMC. For example, Hamano-Bunce (2010) compared face-to-face task interaction with written synchronous CMC in university English classes in the United Arab Emirates. He found fewer language-related episodes in written CMC than in face-to-face interaction, which he explained, in part, by suggesting that the typed nature of the text chat made language production difficult. When comparing face-to-face interaction with oral CMC on Skype, Yanguas (2010) found that university-level L2 learners of Spanish in California had equal amounts of negotiation in the two contexts when conducting a jigsaw task. Finally, a study by Gurzynski-Weiss and Baralt (2013) examined the interaction patterns of intermediate-level learners of Spanish at an American university performing information-gap tasks conducted either face-to-face or using synchronous written CMC. In addition to investigating learners' perception of feedback, Gurzynski-Weiss and Baralt analyzed the opportunities that learners had to produce modified output in response to feedback. Results indicated that learners in the face-to-face condition had more opportunities to produce modified output and were more likely to take advantage of those opportunities than were learners in a CMC condition. Although these studies suggest that technology can affect interaction, particularly when it occurs in a written modality, there are also similarities with face-to-face interaction in the classroom. As CMC becomes more integrated into instructional contexts, the importance of better understanding its potential strengths and weakness for interaction will continue.

Effects of Interaction

Turning now to the empirical evidence regarding the effects of interaction on L2 development, the first thing to consider is the role of interaction in general before considering various aspects of it. There are multiple individual studies, as well as meta-analyses, that have found interaction in the classroom to be beneficial for L2 development. For example, Keck et al.'s (2006) meta-analysis examined the effects of task-based interaction on the acquisition of L2 grammar and vocabulary. They examined 14 quasi-experimental interaction studies published between 1980 and 2003, and their overall finding was that immediate posttests showed a large effect for L2 learning for learners involved in interaction compared to those who were not. However, Keck et al. did not find any differences in the effectiveness of interaction for the acquisition of grammar or vocabulary. They also compared six different types of tasks, according to whether the tasks required one-way or two-way information exchange, and convergent or divergent outcomes. Keck et al. did not find any differences in the effects of task type on acquisition; however, they suggested caution in interpreting these results due to the small number of studies per task type. On the other hand, they found that tasks in which the use of specific language structures was essential were more beneficial than tasks in which the use of those structures was merely useful; however, this difference was found only on delayed posttests and not on immediate ones, which they say suggests that the effects of interaction may not be immediate. Indeed because interaction does not generally provide explicit attention to linguistic items, the type of learning involved may be more implicit in nature. (See Chapter 2.)

In another meta-analysis exploring the effectiveness of conversational interaction on vocabulary and grammar, Mackey and Goo (2007) examined 28 studies from between 1990 and 2006; they found that learners who engaged in interactive tasks, often accompanied by feedback, improved considerably more than learners who did not. These effects were seen on immediate posttests, but the differences were even greater on delayed posttests, suggesting again that the effects of interaction may take time to be fully realized. Unlike Keck et al.'s study, Mackey and Goo found that, on immediate posttests, interaction was more beneficial for the acquisition of vocabulary than grammar; nevertheless, both areas benefitted, and the differences between the two disappeared on the delayed posttests. Similar to Keck et al., Mackey and Goo cautioned that the small number of studies included in their meta-analysis made robust comparisons of some features difficult.

While these meta-analyses have investigated the effects of interaction as a whole, there are also studies that have investigated the effectiveness of specific aspects of interaction. For example, Bitchener (2004) investigated the longer-term effects of the negotiation for meaning that occurred when 30 ESL learners in New Zealand completed two interactive tasks. The tasks were repeated three times, with the second occurrence happening one week after the initial performance, and the third happening 12 weeks later. Bitchener found that during the first task performance, there was considerable negotiation for meaning, and more than 60% of the negotiation resulted in learners producing modified output. One week later, there was a 69% retention rate for the linguistic items that had been negotiated. Twelve weeks later the retention rate was 62%. Bitchener concludes that negotiation for meaning was beneficial for L2 acquisition and that the benefits were relatively durable.

In addition to negotiation for meaning, other studies have investigated the controversial role of output in interaction. For example, Loewen (2005), in his study of classroom interaction in ESL classes in New Zealand, found that if learners successfully modified their output following communication breakdowns or corrective feedback, they were more likely to get those linguistic items correct on subsequent posttests. Similarly, McDonough (2005) also found that output was beneficial for learning. She examined the development of English question forms in a group of 60 Thai EFL students during information exchange and information gap activities. Learners were placed into one of four groups: (a) feedback plus enhanced opportunity to modify output, (b) feedback plus opportunity to modify output, (c) feedback with no opportunity to modify output, and (d) no feedback. McDonough found that modified output in response to feedback was the only significant predictor of English question development.

As seen in the previous meta-analyses and individual studies, research has largely found benefits for L2 interaction; however, several individual studies have not. For example, Kuiken and Vedder (2005), in their study of 34 Dutch high school students performing dictogloss tasks in pairs (+interaction) or individually (-interaction), did not find any effect for interaction in learners' knowledge of English passives. However, analysis of learners' discourse during the tasks and their reflections after the task revealed numerous examples of interaction resulting in increased noticing, a necessary prerequisite for acquisition. In a similar vein, Garcia Mayo (2005) found that advanced Basque/Spanish bilingual learners of English as a foreign language did not engage in negotiation of meaning to any considerable extent during information gap and decision making tasks. Furthermore, learners often overlooked grammatical inaccuracies in the interaction. Her results echo the findings of Foster (1998) who also found little negotiation of meaning in classroom interaction. Garcia Mayo argues that some type of focus on form should be added to communicative activities in order to help learners notice, and correct, linguistic errors. Finally, Tomita and Spada (2013) examined the classroom interaction of 24 Japanese high school learners of English and found that learners did not always communicate in English during classroom tasks in order to avoid the socially undesirable attribute of showing off their English speaking abilities. However, if students were able to establish identities as learners of English by displaying grammar and vocabulary difficulties, their use of English was viewed as socially acceptable by other students. Tomita and Spada suggest the importance of examining the social contexts of interaction in addition to the cognitive effects, in order to gain a fuller understanding of the complexities of L2 classroom interaction.

In sum, the fact that communicative interaction can have a positive effect on L2 acquisition has been demonstrated by multiple studies; however, it is also clear that not all interaction is successful in all contexts. Thus, consideration of how these findings might relate to classroom pedagogy is important.

PEDAGOGICAL IMPLICATIONS

Interaction in the L2 classroom often occurs as learners engage in tasks, and indeed, task-based approaches to L2 learning and teaching have developed within the communicative language teaching tradition. Such approaches have been described as a more theoretically- and empirically-based pedagogy for communication and interaction in the L2 classroom (Littlewood, 2011; Mackey, 2007; Skehan, Bei, Qian, & Wang, 2012). Furthermore, task-based interaction can facilitate the development of L2 grammar (Carless, 2012), as well as other aspects of linguistic and communicative competence (Shehadeh, 2012). Van den Branden, Bygate, and Norris (2009, p. 11) go so far as to say that 'tasks might be able to offer all the affordances needed for successful instructed language development.' Indeed, the benefits of tasks in the classroom potentially include more student output, autonomy, and involvement; additionally, task-based interaction can help learners develop communicative skills that can transfer outside of the classroom (Griggs, 2005).

Given the benefits of interaction that have been found, the question arises as to what teachers should do in their classrooms. The first suggestion is to bring communicative tasks into the classroom (Mackey, 2007; Naughton, 2006). Teachers are well placed to manipulate instruction, including interaction, in ways that are most beneficial for learning. From the previous theoretical and empirical discussions, there is clear evidence that tasks that require the exchange of information can encourage learner interaction. Littlewood (2011) details specific features of classroom methodology that support communicative interaction. He highlights the importance of involving pairs and groups of learners in communicative tasks that involve the exchange of information.

The use of substantive content can engage learners' interest while they practice using their own linguistic resources.

In addition to negotiation for meaning, communicative tasks should provide opportunities for modified output. One of the constraints of instructed L2 acquisition, particularly in foreign language contexts, is that learners have limited opportunities for communication outside of the classroom. Learners may have difficulty encountering L2 input, finding partners to interact with, and opportunities to produce the language. Indeed, even in second language contexts, it may be difficult for L2 learners to find occasions to interact with native speakers (Ranta & Meckelborg, 2013). One of the advantages of ISLA is that it can provide opportunities to communicate in the L2, something that is important for the development of implicit knowledge, procedural knowledge, and communicative competence.

In addition to providing opportunities for interaction and modified output, teachers can raise learners' awareness of the benefits of peer interaction. For example, Sato and Ballinger (2012) conducted awareness-raising sessions in Canadian elementary L2 classes about the benefits of interaction. The teachers used role plays, games, and discussions to encourage learners to interact with each other; teachers also provided instruction on how to recognize learning opportunities during interaction and how to seek and provide communicative assistance. Although raising learners' awareness took time and planning, Sato and Ballinger argue that persistent instruction paid off in positive attitudes and interaction behaviors. In a similar study, Naughton (2006) provided EFL learners in Spain with an eight-hour training program about the types of interaction that are more successful and contribute to the negotiation of meaning. Because learners do not always engage in the most productive communication strategies, Naughton claims that training learners to interact successfully can be useful. Naughton trained her students in the use of follow-up questions, clarification requests, corrective feedback, and requests for assistance. As a result, learners were largely successful at engaging in these types of interactional behaviors.

One final way of raising learners' awareness about the effects of communicative interaction is by providing them with examples of authentic L1 interaction. For example, Barraja-Rohan (2011) used conversation analysis techniques to teach L2 speakers about features of successful interaction. By using transcripts of actual conversations, Barraja-Rohan wanted to draw learners' attention to how interaction occurred outside of the classroom. By having explicit knowledge of the structure of interaction, learners could potentially incorporate important features into their own interaction.

In addition to raising learners' awareness about the nature of interaction, it can be important to inform leaners (and teachers as well, for that matter) about the importance of interaction for L2 acquisition. Learners often expect overt attention to language in the L2 classroom (Lyster & Mori, 2006). Indeed, Gatbonton and Segalowitz (2005) point out that many teachers, as well as students, prefer explicit instruction to implicit communication activities because when grammar rules are taught, learners are aware of having acquired something tangible. The development of communicative competence is much less visible, but if learners are made aware that developing communicative competence through interaction is important, such knowledge may help learners feel that they are indeed learning.

Finally, because interaction sometimes occurs differently with native speakers than with other learners, it might be important to consider what types of possibilities there are to encourage learners to engage with L2 speakers outside the classroom, particularly through computer-mediated communication (Fernandez Dobao, 2012). This idea will be discussed in more detail in Chapter 9 on different contexts of ISLA.

CONCLUSION

Although considerable research has provided convincing evidence for the benefits of interaction in the L2 classroom, it is also the case that meaning-focused interaction may not make linguistic structures as salient to learners as is needed for acquisition. Some researchers (e.g., R. Sheen, 2005) suggest that interaction alone does not provide the conditions necessary for L2 development, and in many cases, they lament the lack of explicit language instruction in task-based language learning. Indeed, interaction has not been found to be beneficial or superior to other types of instruction in all contexts. As a result, current views of task-based language learning suggest that more explicit attention to language structures may be needed during communicative activities. For many researchers, this attention is provided through a focus on form (Long, 1991, 1996), and although focus on form was originally primarily concerned with negotiation for meaning that occurred as a result of communication breakdown, the term has been extended to refer to any attention to language form within a larger meaning-focused context (Han, 2008). Within focus on form, the amount of overt, explicit attention to form can vary from minimal to extensive (Doughty & Williams, 1998; Loewen, 2011). Indeed, there is an acknowledgment that a variety of such classroom activities, from communicative interaction to explicit instruction, may be necessary for developing L2 learners with well-rounded communicative competence who exhibit high levels of both fluency and accuracy (Nassaji & Fotos, 2011).

The current chapter has considered approaches to interaction that preclude attention to form, as well as those that allow for attention to form but are mostly focused on the characteristics of interaction (e.g., Task-based Language Learning). Approaches that combine meaning-focused communication with more explicit types of attention to form, such as corrective feedback or input enhancement, will be considered in Chapter 4.

ACTIVITIES

The scholarship task is an information gap and opinion gap task that has been used to investigate L2 interaction. What aspects of the task might encourage interaction and negotiation for meaning? Perform the task with a partner, but invent two additional pieces of information about each candidate so that you have unknown information to exchange. As you perform the task, pay attention to your interaction. Does any communication breakdown or negotiation of meaning occur? If so, what triggers the negotiation and what characteristics does it have? What other features do you notice about the interaction? How do you think the interaction from this task would differ if low or intermediate English L2 learners were performing it? How would their level of proficiency affect their interaction? For a larger project, invite two English L2 speakers to perform the task, and observe the interaction that occurs between them.

Scholarship Task

Directions: In this task you will discuss two different candidates for a scholarship. First read the background information about the scholarship, and then read the information about each of the candidates. You and your partner both have the same two candidates, but you each have different information about them. Tell your partner about the information that you have for each candidate. (Do not show them the information sheet.) Decide which candidate should receive the scholarship.

Scholarship Requirements

Your government places great value on education and has decided to send some young people overseas to America to be educated in a leading university. These young people will get a scholarship to pay for all their university fees and living expenses for four years.

The candidates do not need to speak fluent English. But, if a candidate doesn't speak fluent English, he or she will have to take an English course in America before starting their university study. This costs the government more money.

The purpose of the scholarship is to help young people in your country to understand the world better. The government wants young people to have experiences overseas, and then come back home to help build a better society.

Please write down the name of the candidate that you think should get the scholarship.

Scholarship Winner: _____

Information Sheets

Sheet 1	Sheet 2
Candidate 1: Albert • Male • IQ of 110 • Hard-working (studies 8 hours every day) • Hobbies: soccer, captain of the national high school soccer team • Visited America at the age of 15 as a soccer player • ? • ?	**Candidate 1: Albert** • Age: 18 • High grades in every subject • Loves everything about America • Wants to be a professional soccer player, but plans to study business at the university • Current level of spoken English: pre-intermediate • ? • ?
Candidate 2: Gina • Age: 20 • Sometimes lazy at school • Difficult childhood: parents killed in a car crash • Good at music • Possibility of having lessons with a famous teacher in America • Uncle and aunt live in America • Current level of spoken English: upper-intermediate • ? • ?	**Candidate 2: Gina** • Female • IQ of 140 • Usually A grades in school, but failed a class because she was partying before the final exam • Difficult childhood: stole a cell phone. and was arrested at age 14 Was sent to a special school for troubled youth • Has never been to America • Wants to study painting and art history • ? • ?

ADDITIONAL READING

Ellis, R. (2003). *Task-based language learning and teaching.* Oxford: Oxford University Press.

Gass, S.M. (1997). *Input, interaction and output in second language acquisition.* Mahwah, NJ: Lawrence Erlbaum Associates.

Mackey, A. (Ed.). (2007). *Conversational interaction in second language acquisition.* Oxford: Oxford University Press.

McDonough, K., & Mackey, A. (Eds.). (2013). *Second language interaction in diverse educational contexts.* Amsterdam: John Benjamins.

4

Focus on Form

The previous chapter has considered classroom instruction primarily in relation to meaning-focused interaction, accompanied by negotiation for meaning when breakdowns in communication occur. However, as has been shown, there is reason to believe that meaning-focused interaction alone may not result in the desired levels of communicative competence in learn- *meaning* ers because while interaction may result in a better ability to communicate, ✳ + interaction without any attention to linguistic accuracy does not necessar- *linguistic* ily improve linguistic accuracy. One approach to L2 instruction that has been proposed to develop learners who can communicate fluently but also accurately is focus on form (Long, 1991, 1996), which occurs when learn- ers briefly pay attention to linguistic items within a larger meaning-focused context. In this way, learners are still engaged in interaction, which is benefi- cial for communicative fluency, but they are also developing their linguistic competence by attending to the accurate use of language during communi- cation. Interest in focus on form has grown since its original inception, and today is considered 'a leading paradigm for SLA research on the interface between theory and practice' (Han, 2008, p. 45). This chapter will discuss the theoretical and empirical support for focus on form and the more implicit methods of instruction that it advocates.

THEORETICAL CONCERNS

Features of Focus on Form

The primary theoretical concern of focus on form is how attention to both meaning and form can be combined to create an optimal learning environ- ment in which both implicit and explicit learning occur, and in which implicit and explicit knowledge are developed. In an attempt to highlight the unique aspects of focus on form, (Long, 1996; Long & Robinson, 1998) contrasted it with what he termed 'focus on meaning' and 'focus on forms.' Focus on meaning consists of activities in the classroom that are entirely communicative with no attention to specific language items unless there is a breakdown in communication, as discussed in Chapter 3. Focus on forms, on the other hand, encompasses explicit types of L2 instruction in which language and language rules are the overt objects of instruction. In an attempt to illustrate the relationships among these various types of instruction, Loewen (2011) divides L2 instruction into two main categories: meaning-focused instruction and form-focused instruction. As stated, meaning-focused instruction consists principally of communicative tasks that focus on language items only when there is a breakdown in communication. Form-focused instruction, on the other hand, is comprised of any type of instruction that includes some attention to language items, ranging from an implicit focus on form to an explicit focus on forms. However, the dashed line connecting focus on form with meaning-focused instruction represents the fact that focus on form occurs within a larger meaning-focused context. Within form-focused instruction there exist a range of instructional techniques with varying degrees of explicitness (Nassaji & Fotos, 2011). The more implicit ones (i.e., focus on form) will be considered in this chapter, while the more explicit ones (i.e., focus on forms) will be explored in Chapter 5.

A primary feature of focus on form instruction is that attention to form should be relatively implicit. If attention to form becomes too explicit during communicative interaction, there is concern that the interaction will shift from being primarily meaning-focused to mainly focused on linguistic forms, thereby negating the efficacy of a combined focus on form and meaning (Long, 2007b). However, there is also a concern that if focus on form is too implicit, then learners will not notice the linguistic features and no acquisition will take place (Lyster, 1998b). Thus, finding the optimal degree of implicitness/explicitness for instruction is a key interest in focus on form research.

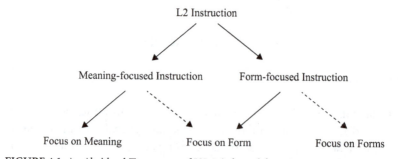

FIGURE 4.1 An Abridged Taxonomy of ISLA (adapted from Loewen, 2011)

Related to the issue of explicitness is the intensity with which focus on form is provided (Han, 2008; Kuiken & Vedder, 2005). Long's (1991) original conception of focus on form implied that even a one-off negotiation on a specific linguistic item could have the ability to positively influence acquisition; however, more research has investigated the effects of intensive focus on form in which the amount of exposure to specific target linguistic structures is increased. In this regard, Ellis (2001) makes a distinction between incidental and planned focus on form. Incidental focus on form consists of unrepeated attention to various linguistic items as they arise spontaneously during classroom interaction, while planned focus on form involves a more concentrated focus during the interaction on one or two structures, with the target structures generally being determined before instruction begins. Although incidental focus on form is closer to Long's original version of focus on form, there may be beneficial effects for both incidental and planned focus on form. Incidental focus on form may better facilitate opportunities for proceduralizing knowledge since it occurs unobtrusively, while planned focus on form may affect explicit knowledge by making the forms more salient. Although this distinction has not yet received much specific research attention, the difference is often indirectly operationalized in terms of the length of treatment that learners receive (Loewen, 2011). In addition, more studies have investigated planned focus on form, in large part because researchers can control the specific linguistic structures being researched. In contrast, the spontaneous nature of incidental focus on form makes it difficult to pretest, and thus to investigate quasi-experimentally.

The timing of focus on form is another important consideration (Doughty, 2003). Long's original version of focus on form stated that it occurred within the context of meaning-focused activities; thus, focus on form was not decontextualized from the communicative context, and the benefits of focus on form were suggested to come from attention to meaning and form at the same time (Long, 1996). The issue of timing is particularly pertinent for one type of focus on form that has received considerable attention, namely oral corrective feedback, because the immediate juxtaposition of the incorrect and correct forms is argued to be crucial for noticing. Although several studies have examined delayed feedback, occurring some time after learners have produced an error, it seems likely that immediate and delayed feedback function differently and result in different types of knowledge. Delayed feedback is more like focus on forms because it does not occur in the immediate context of communication and generally involves explicit attention to language items.

Another issue for focus on form is who initiates it. In general, most focus on form is provided by the teacher either in the guise of corrective feedback or preemptive attention to form; however, some research has investigated student-initiated focus on form, both in terms of corrective feedback by peers

(Adams, 2007), and by the initiation of questions about language forms during interaction. In many cases these queries address lexical items (Williams,
1999). The benefit of student initiation is that the students themselves can
focus on what they feel to be problematic for them, and thus they may be more
likely to benefit from the focus on form. Teachers, in contrast, may or may not
be accurate in judging what is difficult for the students, in which case, time
may be spent on linguistic structures that are already known by the students.

Finally, it should be acknowledged that focus on form can be directed to any
aspect of language, including grammar, vocabulary, pronunciation, and pragmatics (R. Ellis, 2001; Loewen, 2011; Nassaji & Fotos, 2011; Williams, 2005).
In practice, most focus on form research has investigated its effects on the
acquisition of morphosyntactic features, with an increasing interest in lexical
items (Laufer, 2005a). However, the learning of pronunciation (Saito, 2013a,
2013b) and pragmatics (Jeon, 2007) through focus on form has also begun to
garner some attention. Because of the substantial interest that focus on form
research has given to morphosyntax, this chapter will concentrate primarily
on grammar, while the following chapters will discuss focus on form in relation to their respective linguistic areas.

Noticing

One of the most important theoretical supports for focus on form relates
to noticing. Researchers argue that attentional resources are limited; consequently, learners often have difficulty attending to both form and meaning
during communication (VanPatten, 1990). Generally, learners prioritize the
semantic content of an utterance as opposed to its morphosyntactic components because the goal of most interaction is to understand one's interlocutor and to make one's self understood. Because of this tendency to focus on
meaning, learners often do not notice or attend to all of the morphosyntactic
information in the input, particularly if that information is redundant or nonsalient. For example, third person –s in English present tense is both redundant because it is not needed to indicate the subject since an overt subject is
required and nonsalient as it is a single, word-final phoneme. Thus, learners
do not need to process the morpheme in order to understand who the subject
of the sentence is. Furthermore, the inconspicuous nature of third person –s
intensifies the difficulty that learners may have in noticing its presence during
interaction.

The argument for focus on form, then, is that learners need to notice linguistic forms in order to acquire them (Leow, 2007; Schmidt, 1990, 1995,
2001). Probably the most influential proposal in this regard related to focus on
form has been Schmidt's Noticing Hypothesis (1990, 1995, 2000; Schmidt &
Frota, 1986) which states that L2 acquisition does not happen unconsciously;

rather, there must be some awareness of the linguistic forms in order for learning to occur. Schmidt (1995) makes the distinction between awareness at the level of noticing and awareness at the level of understanding. Noticing he defines as 'conscious registration of the occurrence of some event' (p. 29) while understanding is defined as 'recognition of a general principle, rule or pattern' (p. 29). Similarly, Robinson (1995) puts forward a model of attention and memory in which he defines noticing as 'detection plus rehearsal in short-term memory, prior to encoding in long-term memory' (p. 296). In contrast to Schmidt's position regarding the necessity of awareness for L2 acquisition, Tomlin and Villa (1994) argue that attention is necessary for learning but awareness is not. They argue that the central components of attention are alertness, orientation, and detection.

Focus on form argues that noticing of linguistic structures is most likely to occur when meaning is relatively clear and learners have the attentional resources to give to linguistic form. Long (1996) states that it is the combination of input, learner internal processes, particularly noticing, and output that is the most important aspect of focus on form. Given the theoretical importance of noticing, much of ISLA research on focus on form has investigated: (a) the best methods to induce noticing, and (b) if such noticing really does result in L2 development.

Indeed, it is the issue of explicitness that is a central issue in focus on form and focus on forms research (Doughty & Williams, 1998). On the one hand, focus on form proposes that attention to language should be implicit so as not to distract from the communicative nature of the activities. On the other hand, intervention that is too implicit will not be noticed, and noticing is a prerequisite for acquisition. The implicit-explicit distinction is manifest at the pedagogical level, but the theoretical argument is based on the issues of noticing and attention. Long argues that the optimal conditions for L2 acquisition are when learners' attention is drawn to form when meaning is already relatively clear to them. Thus, the attention to form should not be more explicit than it needs to be because it will detract from the communicative nature of the task; however, if it is not explicit enough, then learners will not notice the form and thus not benefit from it.

A variety of factors can influence noticing (Kuiken & Vedder, 2005). As has been discussed already, the salience of forms and their frequency in the input can be important. Additionally, if some forms are not salient in the input, then strategies for enhancing them may be important. In addition, other modifications to input or tasks and activities can increase noticing, and this is what much of the focus on form research has investigated in terms of pedagogy. Finally, there are individual differences, such as working memory or anxiety, which might affect noticing. Such individual differences will be explored more in Chapter 10.

Related to noticing, is Swain's (1995) concept of noticing the gap. When learners receive corrective feedback or are pushed to produce modified output, learners may notice the gap between the target language norms and their own interlanguage production. Learners might notice this gap either in response to feedback on their erroneous utterances, or as they try to produce an utterance and realize that they do not know all of the linguistic forms necessary to express their intended meaning. In this way learners' attention is drawn to specific linguistic forms.

Negative Evidence

The role of positive evidence in terms of input that learners receive has been explored in Chapter 3. The role of negative evidence, however, is most relevant to focus on form and corrective feedback. Some researchers argue that L2 learners do not benefit from negative evidence and should therefore not receive correction in response to their non-target-like utterances (Truscott, 1999). However, there is some ISLA evidence to support the idea that negative evidence might be necessary for learners to acquire higher levels of competence, as well as acquire nonsalient grammatical features.

The theoretical rationale behind negative evidence, particularly corrective feedback, is that it draws learners' attention to problematic language forms during meaning-focused interaction. If learners' incorrect utterances are addressed through feedback that either provides the correct form or attempts to elicit it, then learners may notice the gap between their own production and the target language norms. In the case of recasts, which provide the correct forms to learners, noticing occurs when learners compare their own erroneous utterances with the corrections provided by their interlocutors. In the case of prompts, which attempt to elicit the correct forms, learners are forced to reflect on their own utterances and try to come up with the correct version. In either case, learners are involved in cognitive comparisons of their own interlanguage forms and the target language forms. One difference between uninstructed and instructed L2 learning is that negative evidence in the form of corrective feedback is not generally provided outside of instructional contexts. Thus, if negative evidence is necessary for the acquisition of some features, then learners are more likely to get such feedback in the classroom; however, being in a classroom does not guarantee that negative feedback will occur (Foster, 1998).

Types of Focus on Form

Given that the goal of focus on form is to combine attention to meaning and form, it is important to consider the ways in which this may be done in the classroom. The next sections will explore various options, beginning with the most implicit types of focus on form and moving towards the more explicit types. A definition of implicit instruction states that it involves activities in which there is no specific attention given to language rules (Andringa et al., 2011; Hulstijn, 2002); instead, it involves exposing learners to specific forms without any discussion of the rules that underlie the structure (Ur, 2011). Many studies have investigated various types of implicit focus on form, and several meta-analyses (Norris & Ortega, 2000; Spada & Tomita, 2010) have categorized the following activities as types of implicit instruction: input flood, interaction, and recasts. In addition, input enhancement and language-related episodes have been considered to be relatively implicit (Loewen, 2011; Swain & Lapkin, 1995).

Input flood. One of the most implicit types of focus on form is an input flood, in which the input that is provided to learners is seeded with multiple examples of a target structure (Hernández, 2011). For example, a communicative activity in which learners must choose among several applicants for a scholarship might be seeded with conditional sentences detailing what each applicant would do if they received the award. Input flood is subtle and implicit because the only manipulation that is done is to ensure that multiple exemplars of the targeted structure occur in the input. The goal of input flood is for it to facilitate implicit and incidental learning by causing learners to notice the numerous examples of the target structure (Loewen, Erlam, & Ellis, 2009; Reinders & Ellis, 2009).

Input enhancement. Input enhancement occurs when some aspect of the input is highlighted in some way (Sharwood Smith, 1991, 1993). In many cases, the input enhancement occurs with written language, with the enhanced forms being bolded, underlined, put in a different font size, or highlighted in some other way. It is possible to enhance oral input as well, but little research has addressed this aspect of input enhancement. The theoretical rationale for input enhancement is based on the fact that learners tend to prioritize meaning over language form (VanPatten, 1990), and thus they may not benefit acquisitionally from input that is primarily communicative in nature. Therefore, attention needs to be drawn to linguistic forms in some way. For example, an input flood may not draw learners' attention to the targeted grammatical feature because the learners may be primarily focused on the semantic content of the input. Consequently, learners tend not to notice nonsalient and redundant morphosyntactic forms in the input (Han, Park, & Combs, 2008). To counteract this tendency, teachers and researchers can manipulate the input by targeting and highlighting linguistic features in a way that is intended to draw attention to linguistic forms that may otherwise go unnoticed. Such noticing of language features is a first step towards acquisition. However, the effectiveness of input enhancement in drawing learners' attention is debated due to its subtle nature. Enhancement may be more salient than just numerous exemplars of a linguistic structure, but it still may not make learners aware of the structures that are being highlighted.

Corrective feedback. One of the central components of focus on form research regards the role of corrective feedback (Mackey, 2007; Plonsky & Gass, 2011), and there are numerous primary studies and synthetic reviews on the topic (e.g., Li, 2010; Lyster & Saito, 2010; Lyster, Saito, & Sato, 2012; Russell & Spada, 2006). Corrective feedback is important theoretically because it can provide relatively unobtrusive attention to form during meaning-focused interaction. In addition, corrective feedback, unlike input flood and input enhancement, occurs in reaction to learners' errors, and thus targets forms that are demonstrably difficult for learners, something that the previous two types of focus on form do not necessarily do. Finally, from a practical standpoint, corrective feedback is also easy for teachers (or fellow learners) to provide in an inconspicuous manner during the flow of meaning-focused interaction.

Corrective feedback can occur in a variety of ways. One distinction that has been made is between input-providing and output-prompting feedback, depending on whether the teacher gives the correct form to learners or attempts to elicit it from them. A common type of input-providing feedback is a recast, which maintains the general meaning of an utterance while correcting the linguistic error. In Example 1, Will and the teacher are discussing his army experiences. When Will makes a preposition error, the teacher provides the correct form in a recast. After Will repeats the correct form, the conversation continues about his experiences.

Example 1: Recast (Loewen, 2005, p. 371)

Will:	when I was soldier I used to wear the balaclava
Teacher:	and why did you wear it Will, for protection from the cold or for another reason
Will:	just wind uh protection to wind and cold
Teacher:	**protection from**
Will:	uh from wind and cold
Teacher:	right, okay not for a disguise

One advantage of recasts is that learners get positive evidence about what can be said in the L2. In addition, they may receive negative evidence if they notice the difference between their own erroneous utterance and the correct form, something that Swain (1995) refers to as noticing the gap. Furthermore, recasts are generally very implicit and do not disrupt the flow of conversation (Long, 2007). However, there is acknowledgment that depending on the features of recasts, they may be more or less implicit (Loewen & Philp, 2006; Y. Sheen, 2006). Recasts that isolate the incorrect form from the surrounding discourse and are given with declarative intonation are considered to be more explicit than recasts that are incorporated into the surrounding discourse and provided with interrogative intonation.

Because recasts tend to be implicit, one criticism is that they are sometimes too implicit for learners to notice (Lyster, 2004). Another disadvantage of recasts is that learners may simply parrot back the correct form without actually having to think about it or process it. Finally, the assumption that the learners' meaning is maintained and that only the linguistic form is changed has been questioned (Han, 2008; Hauser, 2005). Consequently, the meaning may not be as clear to the learner as is sometimes thought, and if the meaning is not clear, then learners may have more difficulty attending to the targeted language items.

In contrast to input-providing feedback, output-prompting corrective feedback includes prompts or elicitations in which the teacher attempts to elicit the correct form from the student. In Example 2, from a task in which learners had to solve riddles, the researcher produces a clarification request in response to the learner's incorrect gender marking on *un village*. In this case, in response to the prompt, the learner is able to provide the correct form.

Example 2: Clarification Request (Lyster & Izquierdo, 2009, p. 472)

Researcher: Je suis comme une ville mais plus petite et à la campagne.
              [*I am like a city but smaller and in the country.*]
Participant: Une village. [*A village-F.*]
Researcher: **Pardon?** [*Pardon me?*]
Participant: Un village. [*A village-M.*]
Researcher: Oui, on continue. [*Yes, let's continue.*]

Elicitation may be relatively implicit as seen in Example 2, or if a teacher responds with something such as *What?* or *Can you repeat that?* Alternatively, other elicitations, such as *Can you say that again correctly?* are much more explicit. Elicitations have the advantage of engaging learners in deeper cognitive processing as they are required to come up with the form themselves. Elicitations also usually result in learners producing modified output, which has been argued to also be beneficial for learning (Lyster & Ranta, 1997). However, learners must have some knowledge of the linguistic form being targeted, a requirement that works for linguistic structures that have developmental stages, or for other types of explicit knowledge that may not be proceduralized enough to use in spontaneous communication. However, learners will not be able to come up with forms that are completely new or unknown to them.

One other type of corrective feedback is metalinguistic feedback, which provides information about the nature of the error. Metalinguistic feedback is much more explicit and disruptive of communication. As such, it may detract considerably from the meaning-focused interaction that learners are involved in, as they orient more towards the linguistic structures. However, because metalinguistic feedback overtly identifies the error, the feedback and the targeted structure are more likely to be noticed. The metalinguistic feedback in Example 3, taken from a task in which learners had to describe a character's activities from the previous day, leaves little doubt as to the nature of the error.

Example 3: Metalinguistic Feedback (Ellis, Loewen, & Erlam, 2006, p. 353)

Learner: He kiss her
Researcher: Kiss—**you need past tense**
Learner: He kissed

Language-related episodes. Similar to corrective feedback, language-related episodes (LREs) are portions of meaning-focused discourse in which learners briefly discuss linguistic items, but unlike corrective feedback, LREs do not necessarily focus on errors that learners produce (Swain & Lapkin, 2001). Rather, LREs consist of incidental attention to linguistic items during meaning-focused interaction, regardless of whether or not there is an error in production. In many cases, LREs involve learners asking one another or a teacher about linguistic items during communicative tasks. In other cases, LREs involve learners discussing a problematic linguistic item. LREs often occur in text reconstruction activities because learners are pushed to produce target-like output as they work together to accurately reproduce a text that they have previously heard or read. In terms of focus on form, LREs are considerably explicit, and may blur the boundaries between focus on form and focus on forms. They do arise spontaneously during interaction, but they can be quite explicit in their discussion of language forms.

EMPIRICAL EVIDENCE

Having presented various focus on form possibilities, the chapter now turns to considering the empirical evidence concerning the various options. Early research in this area spent considerable time investigating and describing the occurrence of focus on form, particularly corrective feedback, in naturally occurring classroom interaction. As descriptive studies provided a clearer picture of the occurrence of focus on form, subsequent studies have increasingly used quasi-experimental research designs in order to examine how focus on form can best be manipulated to increase noticing and acquisition.

Occurrence of Focus on Form

One question that has been investigated regards the occurrence of focus on form in the L2 classroom. Numerous descriptive studies have investigated this question (Ellis et al., 2001a, 2001b; Loewen, 2003, 2004; Lyster, 1998a, 1998b;

Lyster & Ranta, 1997; Y. Sheen, 2004), and they have found that focus on form does occur, but it does not occur at the same rate in all classes. For example, Ellis et al. (2001a) investigated 12 hours of communicative activities in two ESL classes in New Zealand. They found that a focus on form episode occurred roughly every minute and a half, and that successful uptake, in which learners produced modified output correcting their errors, accounted for about 50% of responses. Similarly, Iwashita and Li (2012), in their study of corrective feedback in EFL classes in China, found an average of roughly one focus on form episode every two minutes, with a successful uptake rate of 50%. However, Y. Sheen (2004) compared the occurrence of corrective feedback in general, and recasts in particular, in four different contexts. Three contexts had been reported in previously published studies: Canadian Immersion (Lyster & Ranta, 1997), Canadian ESL (Panova & Lyster, 2002), and New Zealand ESL (Ellis et al., 2001a, 2001b), while Sheen added data from a Korean EFL class. She found that corrective feedback occurred most frequently in the Canadian Immersion context, with a corrective feedback episode every minute and a half. The context in which corrective feedback occurred the least frequently was the Korean EFL, with a corrective feedback episode only every three and a half minutes. Additionally, the type of corrective feedback varied, with recasts constituting 83% of the feedback in the Korean EFL context, 68% in the New Zealand ESL classes, and 55% in both the Canadian Immersion and ESL contexts. In sum, these studies suggest that focus on form and corrective feedback do occur naturally in the L2 classroom; however, the amount and type vary.

In general, focus on form is provided by the teacher, and the previously mentioned studies investigated teacher-initiated focus on form. Nonetheless, several studies have examined student-initiated focus on form. For example, Moore (2012) found that learner-generated focus on form was not common during learner-learner interaction in a Japanese university setting. In addition, most studies have found that learner-initiated focus on form, when it does occur, pertains to lexical items rather than other areas of language (Ellis et al., 2001b; Moore, 2012; Williams, 1999).

Occurrence of Language-Related Episodes

In addition to focus on form in general, several studies have looked at the occurrence of LREs during interaction. In their comparison of classroom and laboratory-based learner-learner interaction, Gass et al. (2005) found that, on three different tasks, intermediate-level learners of Spanish engaged in considerable amounts of negotiation for meaning, particularly through the use of confirmation checks and clarification requests; however, learners engaged in LREs relatively infrequently, with an average of only one or two occurring during the 50-minute interaction sessions. Gass et al. did find that task type affected the number of LREs with a task containing no obligatory exchange of information resulting in fewer LREs than tasks with required information exchange.

Other studies have also found variables contributing to the occurrence of LREs in learner-learner interaction. For example, Yilamz (2011) had dyads of university-level learners of English perform jigsaw and dictogloss tasks through synchronous computer-mediated communication (CMC). Yilmaz found an average of almost three LREs in the 20-minute tasks. In addition, the dictogloss task contained statistically more LREs, particularly related to spelling. He attributed these differences to the fact that the dictogloss required learners to negotiate in order to produce written reconstructions of specific texts, while the jigsaw task required only the exchange of information. In another CMC study, Bueno-Alastuey (2013) found that in a synchronous voice CMC task, dyads with L2 speakers from different L1 backgrounds produced more LREs than did dyads with learners and native speakers. In turn, dyads with L2 speakers from the same L1 background had the fewest LREs. Phonology was the most frequent linguistic category for the LREs. Finally, Fernandez Dobao (2012), in a laboratory-based study, looked at differences in lexical LREs in learner-native speaker dyads and learner-learner dyads. She found that lexical LREs were more frequent and more likely to be successful in learner-native speaker interaction. In addition, using Storch's (2001) taxonomy of roles that learners can take during interaction (i.e., dominant, passive, expert, or novice), Fernandez Dobao found different patterns of cooperation, with more collaborative dyads producing more LREs.

In sum, both focus on form and LREs occur in classroom interaction; however, the frequency of occurrence varies in relation to certain characteristics. However, the important question for ISLA is not just if focus on form occurs during interaction; it is if focus on form can bring about increased noticing and acquisition of linguistic forms. In addition, can focus on form be manipulated to increase any beneficial effects?

Effects of Focus on Form on Noticing

Because noticing is such an important construct in focus on form, one strand of research has investigated the effects of focus on form activities on noticing. In particular, several studies have investigated learners' perceptions of corrective feedback. For example, Mackey, Gass, and McDonough (2000) investigated English L2 and Italian foreign language learners' perceptions of corrective feedback. After engaging in interaction in which they received feedback on a variety of linguistic forms, learners were asked to watch a video of their interaction and to report what they had been thinking when various feedback was provided. Mackey et al. found that learners were relatively accurate in identifying feedback pertaining to pronunciation, semantics, and lexis; however, learners were not so good at perceiving feedback on morphosyntactic structures. In a study that extended this line of research to CMC contexts, Gurzynski-Weiss and Baralt (2013) investigated learners' perceptions of feedback in face-to-face and written synchronous CMC contexts. Twenty-four intermediate level learners of Spanish participated in interactive tasks, and subsequently reported on their perceptions during a stimulated recall session. Gurzynski-Weiss and Baralt found that participants generally perceived feedback correctly, identifying feedback on lexis and semantics most of the time, and feedback addressing morphosyntax almost half of the time; however, participants were not as accurate for phonological feedback. Additionally, although it was hypothesized that learners would be better able to notice feedback in the written synchronous CMC condition because of its visual record and slower pace of interaction (Smith, 2009), no statistical differences were found in learners' ability to perceive feedback based on the context in which they interacted.

Effects of Focus on Form on L2 Acquisition

Although noticing is an important result of focus on form, the most important consideration in its effectiveness is if it results in L2 development. This section will consider how the different types of focus on form have resulted (or not) in L2 learning.

Before discussing the effectiveness of focus on form, it is worth briefly reconsidering how acquisition is measured, because as has been discussed in Chapter 2, the types of testing instruments that are used affect the claims that can be made about the treatment being investigated. If the goal of focus on form instruction is for learners to develop communicative competence, then it is important to test communicative competence to determine the effects of the treatment. Consequently, explicit tests of grammatical knowledge do not provide the best measures of implicit and proceduralized L2 knowledge. As an example, Norris and Ortega's (2000) meta-analysis on the effects of L2 instruction found that explicit focus on form was more effective for L2 learning; however, they themselves acknowledged, and others (Doughty, 2003) reiterated, that the majority of the instruments used to measure acquisition were biased towards explicit knowledge.

Another measurement issue is when acquisition is measured. Many studies of focus on form and L2 acquisition have a pretest followed by at least one posttest after the treatment. Often, due to logistical reasons, the posttest occurs within a day or two of the treatment; however, there is theoretical and empirical evidence suggesting that the development of L2 knowledge, particularly implicit knowledge, takes time, and the effects of a treatment may not appear until some time has passed (Ellis, 2009; Mackey, 1999).

Input flood. As has been stated, one of the most implicit types of focus on form is input flood, and while only a few studies have examined input flood by itself, their results are mixed regarding its effectiveness. One early study by Trahey and White (1993) investigated the effects of an input flood of English adverbs for French-speaking children studying English in Quebec. After two weeks of input, the learners showed an increase in the use of adverbs, but there was no decrease in the use of inaccurate L1 strategies that resulted in the incorrect placement of adverbs between the verb and object. Trahey and White suggested that positive evidence alone was not sufficient in this instance to effect change in learners' interlanguage forms, and they proposed that negative evidence, in this case corrective feedback and explicit information about the differences between French and English adverb placement, might be necessary for L2 development. In another input flood study, Loewen, Erlam, and Ellis (2009) observed the effects of an input flood of exemplars of English third-person –s on intermediate level learners of English. In the course of a struc-tured input treatment on generic articles (e.g., *A lion eats meat.*), 20 learners in New Zealand ESL classes were also exposed to numerous instances of third-person present-tense verbs. If input flood had been effective in this instance, there should have been an improvement in learners' scores from pretest to posttest, especially in comparison to learners who did not receive the input flood. Learners completed two tests, targeting implicit and explicit knowledge respectively, but no improvement in learners' use of third-person –s was found on either of the tests, indicating, again, that the input flood was not sufficient to increase learners' accurate use of the target structure.

However, several studies have found benefits for input flood. For example, in a study of English inverted negative adverbs (e.g., *Seldom had he seen such a beautiful woman.*), Reinders and Ellis (2009) compared the effects of enriched and enhanced input. Learners in the enriched input condition were given texts containing multiple exemplars of the target structure, while the enhanced input group received the input flooded text as well explicit instructions to pay attention to the target structure. Upper-intermediate ESL learners in New Zealand showed some improvement in both conditions, but there was no dif-ference between the two groups, indicating that being exposed to input flood was just as effective for L2 development as input flood plus drawing learners' attention to the forms through explicit instructions.

In another study, Hernández (2011) compared the effects of input flood and explicit instruction on the use of Spanish discourse markers by English L1 university students. The input flood group was given three texts, each between 200 and 242 words in length and containing 19 or 20 discourse mark-ers. Learners were asked to notice the use of preterit and imperfect past tense, and were given a comprehension test after reading each text. Subsequently, learners had the opportunity to engage in information gap activities in which the use of discourse markers would be helpful. In comparison, the explicit instruction group received the same texts, but they were also provided with explicit instruction about discourse markers. Additionally, they received corrective feedback on any discourse marker errors that they committed during the communicative tasks. Hernández found that both groups improved significantly in their use of discourse markers during picture-description tasks used as pretests and posttests, and, again, there was no additional improvement for the group that received explicit information about the target structure.

Thus, several studies have found some effect for input flood, and interestingly, this effect was just as strong when input flood was combined with explicit attention to linguistic items; however, it should be kept in mind that the number of studies in this area, particularly in comparison to other aspects of focus on form, is quite small. Consequently, the inclusion of input flood conditions in future research on the effectiveness of focus on form would provide additional insight.

Input enhancement. Input enhancement has traditionally been used with written input, and different types of enhancement have been found to be variably beneficial, including methods that involve multiple types of enhancement (Simard, 2009).However, several meta-analyses (e.g., Han, Park, & Combs, 2008; Lee & Huang, 2008) have found that, although simple enhancement can aid comprehension and induce noticing, it does not seem to have a strong effect on L2 acquisition.

Specifically, Han et al. (2008) inspected 21 research studies on textual input enhancement from 1990 onwards. Most studies were quasi-experimental and compared input enhancement with other types of instruction. The 21 studies failed to find consistent results, with some studies suggesting that enhancement was highly effective, with others finding only moderate effects, and still others finding no effect. Han et al. suggest that these varied findings are due to the variety of methodologies that the studies employed to assess L2 acquisition, leading Han et al. to conclude that more research is needed to confirm or disconfirm the benefits of input enhancement. However, they do suggest that input enhancement can facilitate learners' noticing of target forms, as well as improve overall comprehension. Additionally, they propose that multiple types of enhancement may lead to deeper cognitive processing.

In another meta-analysis of 16 input enhancement studies targeting grammar from between 1981 and 2006, Lee and Huang (2008) found that when compared with input flood, input enhancement had only a small impact on learning as measured by immediate posttests, and no differential effect on delayed posttests. In addition, the meta-analysis found only medium effects when comparing gains made by input enhancement groups from pretest to posttest. Lee and Huang urge caution in interpreting their results due to the low number of studies, but nevertheless, the results about the effectiveness of input enhancement appear inconclusive at best.

Corrective feedback. One of the most prolific research areas in focus on form is that of corrective feedback, and multiple studies and reviews have found corrective feedback to be beneficial. In addition, studies have compared the effects of different types of feedback. One such study, Lyster and Saito (2010), in a meta-analysis of 15 studies of oral corrective feedback in the classroom, examined the effects recasts, explicit correction, and prompts. Overall, they found that corrective feedback had a medium effect on L2 learners' post-test performance in comparison to control groups that did not receive corrective feedback. All three types of corrective feedback were effective; however, prompts had higher effect sizes than did recasts, while the effects of explicit feedback were indistinguishable from those of recasts and prompts. Lyster and Saito conclude that corrective feedback may be more effective when pedagogically oriented in the form of prompts than conversationally oriented in the form of recasts. They argue that these results suggest that the most important aspect of feedback is the negative evidence it provides, coupled with the opportunity for modified output. Lyster and Saito also found that the impact of corrective feedback was durable with no statistical difference between learners' scores on immediate and delayed posttests. Additionally, the effects of long treatments, consisting of seven or more hours of instruction, were more effective than short and medium treatments.

In another meta-analysis, Li (2010) examined the effects of corrective feedback in 33 studies conducted in both classroom and laboratory contexts. He also found that corrective feedback showed a medium effect and that the effect was maintained over time. Furthermore, explicit feedback was more beneficial in the short term, while implicit feedback was more effect in the long term. He suggests that this difference might be because implicit feedback is contributing to implicit knowledge, which takes longer to develop, but is more durable. He also found that laboratory-based studies had larger effects than classroom-based ones, suggesting caution regarding the generalizability of such research to classroom contexts.

PEDAGOGICAL IMPLICATIONS

Because focus on form can be implemented in several different ways, teachers have multiple options when wanting to include focus on form in the classroom. For example, Nassaji and Fotos (2011) state that a focus on form 'can be attained explicitly and implicitly, deductively or inductively, with or without prior panning, and integratively or sequentially' (p. 13). Furthermore, because theory and research indicate that including attention to language items during meaning-focused interaction is generally more beneficial for L2 acquisition than interaction alone, there is ample evidence to support the use of focus on form techniques in the classroom. Often times in meaning-focused interaction inside the classroom, there is little attention to language form unless there is a breakdown in communication. However, by introducing focus on form into interaction within the classroom, the teacher can help draw learners' attention to linguistic items.

One way to set up this focus on form is through focused tasks that create obligatory occasions for the use of specific linguistic features (Philp, Walter, & Basturkmen, 2010). In contrast to the unfocused tasks that were discussed in Chapter 3, focused tasks have a communicative goal as well as a linguistic goal. For example a spot the differences tasks creates numerous occasions for the use of question forms as learners ask one another about the items in the pictures (e.g., Mackey, 1999), or a picture description task might require the use of locative prepositions as learners describe the physical layout of the objects in the picture.

Another way to include a focus on form is by seeding tasks with specific linguistic forms, as is done in input flood. For example, in a consensus task in which learners must choose a scholarship recipient, learners may be provided with information about what the scholarship applicants will do if they receive the scholarship. Such a task could be seeded with conditional sentences, with the expectation that learners will need to process them in the input, as well as produce them as they discuss who should be awarded the scholarship. In this type of task it is also possible to provide input enhancement by highlighting the conditional sentences in some way.

In order to increase the focus on form in such focused tasks, another option is for teachers to provide corrective feedback during these meaning-focused activities. Research fairly conclusively shows that corrective feedback can be beneficial for learners' L2 development. Thus, providing learners with either input-providing or output-prompting feedback during communicative activities can draw learners' attention to specific linguistic items.

In addition to teacher intervention, it is also possible to encourage learners to engage in some of the focus on form activities. For example, Sato and Ballinger (2012) used an intervention to raise Japanese EFL learners' awareness of the benefits of peer interaction and focus on form. Sato and Ballinger had students fill out a learning styles survey, which they then discussed in small groups. Next the teacher explained the benefits of various behaviors during peer interaction. Learners were taught about recasts and prompts, with two teachers modeling the behavior of providing corrective feedback. Learners were then given the opportunity to practice giving feedback to each other during role plays and subsequent interactive tasks. Sato and Ballinger found a significant increase in the amount of corrective feedback that learners provided to each other, and the corrective feedback groups also improved significantly on accuracy scores. In a similar vein, Moore (2012), after finding little learner-initiated focus on form in a Japanese university setting, concludes that 'learners may need to be oriented to, or trained in focus on form for it to be effective in influencing task performance and learning' (p. 182).

CONCLUSION

To summarize, there is ample evidence to support the incorporation of focus on form into the L2 classroom. Learners can benefit acquisitionally from attending to language features within the context of communicative activities. In some cases, learners may notice the forms themselves, but in many cases, it is necessary for the teacher to draw learners' attention to the target forms. There are a range of methods that teachers can use in this endeavor, from very implicit methods such as input flood and input enhancement to slightly more explicit options like corrective feedback. Although focus on form can be effective, there are also instances where more explicit attention to language may be necessary. Thus, the effects of more explicit types of instruction in relation to grammar, vocabulary, pronunciation, and phonology will be considered in the next four chapters, respectively.

ACTIVITIES

1. Revisit the scholarship task in Chapter 3. What types of focus on form could you incorporate in it? What specific grammatical structures or lexical items could you target, and how would you do it?
2. The scholarship task was originally designed to focus on conditional sentences, such as 'If Gina gets the scholarship, she will study painting.' In its current form, how well do you think the task does in providing input and eliciting output on the target structure? What could you do to increase the focus on conditional sentences and still maintain the communication nature of the task? Finally, how effective do you think this task is for the learning of conditional sentences or any other linguistic forms? What would be the best way to measure this task's effectiveness?
3. Here are several corrective feedback episodes from ISLA studies. What types of feedback are provided? What impact do you think the feedback had on acquisition? What are the advantages and disadvantages of these types of feedback?

Example 1: (Gass, Mackey, & Ross-Feldman, 2005, p. 589)

Learner 1:   No tiene flores . . . uh un bosco.
              It doesn't have flowers . . . uh, a forest
              [mispronunciation]

Learner 2:   Bosque.
             Forest. [correct pronunciation]
Learner 1:   Bosque.
             Forest. [correct pronunciation]

Example 2: (Mackey, Gass, & McDonough, 2000, p. 480)

NNS: There is a three bird my picture.
NS: Three birds in your picture?
NNS: Three bird yeah.

Example 3: (Loewen & Philp, 2006, p. 538)

S: to her is good thing (.) to her is good thing
T: yeah for her it's a good thing
S: because she got a lot of money there

Example 4: Lyster (2004, p. 405)

Student: *Parce qu'elle cherche, euh, son, son carte.*
           "Because she's looking for, um, her, her (M) card."
Teacher: *Pas son carte.* "Not her (M) card."
Student: *Euh, sa carte?* "Um, her (F) card?"

4. Below are two quotes that express differing views about the effectiveness of focus on form and task-based interaction. What is your reaction to them? What evidence can you provide to support either claim?

    Klapper and Rees (2003), in their comparison of explicit instruction and focus on form instruction, state, '*in a purely classroom based programme [without extended natural exposure], it is suggested that a FonF [focus on form] is not to be recommended*' (p. 308).
       Van den Branden, Bygate, and Norris (2009, p. 11), in their discussion of task-based teaching and learning, state, '*tasks might be able to offer all the affordances needed for successful instructed language development.*'

ADDITIONAL READING

Doughty, C., & Williams, J. (Eds.). (1998). *Focus on form in classroom second language acquisition.* Cambridge: Cambridge University Press.

Fotos, S., & Nassaji, H. (Eds.). (2011). *Form-focused instruction and teacher education: Studies in honour of Rod Ellis.* Oxford: Oxford University Press.

5

The Acquisition of Grammar

This chapter, and three chapters that follow, will investigate issues related to the acquisition of the specific linguistic areas of grammar, vocabulary, pronunciation, and pragmatics. The previous chapters have referred to these various aspects of language in large part because the topics of L2 knowledge, interaction, and focus on form are not limited to any one linguistic area. Many of the issues in those chapters are relevant to ISLA in general, although it must be acknowledged that grammar has been a primary focus throughout SLA research (Nassaji & Fotos, 2011; Ur, 2011). The following chapters, however, will concentrate on the acquisitional challenges unique to each aspect of language, specifically taking into account more explicit learning and instructional perspectives. The current chapter will consider more explicit approaches to the acquisition of grammar, focusing on theoretical and empirical perspectives that support various methods of grammar instruction.

THEORETICAL CONCERNS

Aspects of Grammar

Before going further, it is important to determine what is meant by grammar because grammar can be conceptualized in several different ways. Grammar is the internal cognitive system of rules about the morphology and syntax (sometimes referred to as morphosyntax) of a language. Knowledge of this system is what allows speakers to produce accurate and grammatical language that conforms to the target language norms. In the case of L1 speakers, their use of language is usually considered to be grammatical in the common sense of the term; however, it should be pointed out that there is sometimes a difference between how so-called experts think people should speak, sometimes called prescriptive grammar, and how people really speak in everyday life, referred to as descriptive grammar. Prescriptive grammar rules in English include 'Don't split infinitives,' 'Don't end a sentence with a preposition,' and 'Use *who* as a subject pronoun and *whom* as an object pronoun.' And yet these supposed grammar rules are often violated by many native speakers of English. What would the introduction to *Star Trek* be without the supposedly ungrammatical phrase 'To boldly go where no one has gone before'? Furthermore, many English L1 speakers find the prescriptively correct phrase 'For whom are you calling?' to be stilted and old-fashioned. Instead, many people might say 'who are you calling for?' ISLA researchers are not concerned with prescriptive grammar; rather, they are concerned with descriptive grammar, that is to say, how L1 speakers actually use the language in everyday life.

Exploring the terms morphology and syntax can further help in describing grammar. Morphology is the study of the grammatical components that go into making a word. For example, English contains prefixes and suffixes that add meaning to a word. These are called morphemes, and they are the smallest meaning bearing units in a language. Some morphemes are free, meaning that the can stand by themselves. For example, *bird* is an English free morpheme that cannot be reduced into smaller meaningful components. Other morphemes are bound and must be attached to another morpheme. For example, the plural marker *–s* is a bound morpheme carrying the meaning of *more than one*. However, *–s* cannot occur by itself, and must be attached to a free morpheme. If we attach *–s* to *bird*, we get *birds*, which is comprised of two morphemes. The use of morphemes is one aspect of grammar. The other aspect is syntax, which has to do with the study of grammatical components at the sentence level. Thus in English, word order is an important syntactic structure. A noun at the beginning of a sentence is generally the subject of the sentence, while a noun at the end of a sentence is usually the object. For example, the different position of *bird* and *cat* in the following sentences changes who is doing the seeing and who is being seen:

a. *The bird sees the cat.*
b. *The cat sees the bird.*

In addition, English has complex syntactic rules about turning declarative sentences into interrogative ones, such as '*What did the bird see?*'

Descriptive grammatical rules can also be referred to as pedagogical grammar, which consists of explicit descriptions of the surface structure of grammatical rules in order to help with learning the language. It should be noted that the linguistic field of syntax is also concerned with deeper and more abstract grammatical rules; however, these rules are less relevant for L2 instructional purposes.

One other characteristic of grammar is that while much of it is considered to be rule-based, there are also some components that are item-based. What this means is that for much of grammar there are rules that can be used to produce target-like language, but sometimes there are no rules and these items need to be memorized. For example, English regular past tense is rule-based; there is a rule that can be applied to all regular verbs. In contrast, English irregular past tense is item based; forms such as *went, taught,* and *saw* are individual items that must be memorized and recalled as individual items. This chapter is primarily concerned with rule-based learning. In other words, it will consider the question of what helps learners develop rule-based, implicit grammatical knowledge.

Issues in Grammar Acquisition

For L2 speakers, their production often deviates from the grammatical norms of native speakers. Nevertheless, L2 learners' language production is also systematic and rule-governed, even if those rules are not the same as for L1 speakers. The term 'interlanguage' (Selinker, 1972) has been used to acknowledge the fact that learners do not immediately gain native-like knowledge of L2 grammar. In fact, many learners never achieve native-like mastery of the L2. Instead, learners have an interlanguage system that is rule-governed and dynamic, allowing learners to produce grammatical forms at their current level of development. Interlanguage theory takes into account the developmental nature of learners' grammatical system, and it proposes that learners' L2 knowledge will not be the same as native speakers' knowledge of that language. Consequently, ISLA research should examine L2 interlanguage on its own terms, as a dynamic, rule-governed system that continues to be restructured as new linguistic input and information is added to the system

Developmental sequences. There is considerable agreement that communicative competence is not acquired one grammar rule at a time. However, there is theory and research to suggest that there is a natural order for grammatical development (Klapper & Rees, 2003; Macaro & Masterman, 2006). There are fairly robust findings that grammar development occurs in stages that are similar for most learners, L1 and L2 alike. One theory that supports this idea is Processability Theory (Pienemann, 1998, 2007). Processability Theory and the teachability hypothesis suggest that some grammatical forms are acquired before others based on the automatic and unconscious processing constraints of the human cognitive system. This order appears to be fairly stable in spite of instruction. Thus the implication is that even if teachers try to teach more advanced structures, learners will not acquire them until they are developmentally ready. For example, English plural –*s* is considered to be an early-acquired feature, while third-person –*s* is late acquired. The teachability hypothesis suggests that even if third-person –*s* is explicitly taught before plural –*s*, this teaching will not affect its acquisitional order. Ortega (2007) argues that Processability Theory has little implication for the classroom. Neverthe-less, the ideas proposed by Pienemann's Processability Theory and the cor-responding teachability hypothesis have implications for what teachers and students should expect as a result of classroom instruction. In other words, just because a grammatical structure is taught in the classroom does not mean that learners will be able to use it productively, unless they are developmen-tally ready. Again this highlights the problem of conflating explicit grammati-cal knowledge with implicit procedural knowledge. Teachers and learners may have false expectations about the results of explicit instruction.

In addition to different grammatical structures being acquired in a develop-mental order, there are some linguistic structures that are themselves devel-opmental in nature with clear stages that learners progress through on their way to achieving target-like accuracy. English question formation, regular past tense and negation are several such structures. Some of the stages that learn-ers go through in acquiring these structures may not match target language norms; however, such stages may nevertheless represent development because learners are progressing through the stages. For example, Table 5.1 illustrates the stages that learners go through in acquiring English negation.

Again it appears that teaching cannot change these stages; learners advance through the stages when they are developmentally ready (Ellis, 1989). Thus, these acquisitional sequences are the same for instructed and uninstructed learners. However, instruction may help learners progress through the stages more quickly. Additionally, instruction may help prevent fossilization and allow learners to achieve higher levels of accuracy than they might have other-wise (Nassaji & Fotos, 2011). Finally there has been some research to determine if the presentation of more advanced stages will help learners 'fill in' the lower stages, thereby avoiding the need for instruction to be finely tuned to learners' precise acquisitional stages (Ellis, 2005).

Instruction and Grammar Acquisition

In traditional methods of grammar teaching, grammar rules were taught in discrete components and it was expected that these components would be

TABLE 5.1

Developmental stages of English negation (based on Ellis, 2008, p. 93)

Stage	Description	Example
1	External negation	No you are playing here.
2	Internal negation	Maria not coming today.
3	Negative attachment to modal verbs	I can't play that one.
4	Negative attachment to auxiliary verbs	She didn't believe me. He didn't said it.

learned and combined, thereby building up the L2 (Nassaji & Fotos, 2011). However, many ISLA researchers no longer believe that accumulating grammar rules will, in and of itself, result in communicative competence. Rather the issue of interest is if, and how, explicit grammar instruction can contribute to the processes that SLA proposes for L2 acquisition. Again, a crucial question to ask is, 'what is the goal for grammar acquisition?' In this regard there has been argument, with some researchers claiming that explicit knowledge of grammar rules is vital and a goal unto itself (e.g., Scheffler & Cincała, 2010; R. Sheen, 2005); other researchers suggest that implicit knowledge and the ability to use the rules is of primary concern for grammatical instruction (e.g., Krashen, 2003; Ur, 2011). In general, ISLA tends to focus on the latter, although the notion of language learning as involving the accumulation of language rules still persists (Swan, 2005).

Although the question about the effectiveness of L2 instruction has been somewhat answered in Chapter 1, there remain several issues to consider in the acquisition of grammar. The role of grammar learning and teaching is contentious in ISLA (Nassaji & Fotos, 2011). On the one hand, there are those who claim that grammar cannot be learned—it can only be acquired. For example Krashen's Input Hypothesis claims that grammar is not learned as a result of any type of instruction, rather grammar is acquired through exposure to input. Thus, if grammar cannot be learned in the traditional sense, then there are no methods needed to teach it. What teachers need to do instead is provide an input-rich classroom environment in which learners are exposed to as much comprehensible input as possible. Krashen concedes that grammar rules may be of some use in helping learners monitor their own production, consequently, spending some class time on explicit grammar instruction is not without some benefit, but on the whole, explicit instruction of grammar rules is not going to develop learners' ability to produce language easily for communication.

In contrast, other researchers claim that the best way for grammar learning to occur is through direct explicit instruction (Scheffler, 2012; Scheffler & Cincała, 2010; R. Sheen, 2005; Swan, 2005). For example, Scheffler (2012) argues in favor of more traditional ways of teaching grammar, such as grammar translation, explicit instruction, and PPP (Present, Practice, Produce). Swan (2005) argues that explicit instruction is much more efficient in the L2 classroom than task-based approaches, and he also argues that task-based learning does not work for new forms.

Drawing on Loewen's (2011) taxonomy of L2 instruction, Chapter 3 has covered meaning-focused instruction, while Chapter 4 has addressed the focus on form segment of form-focused instruction. The remaining type of instruction to consider is also a type of form-focused instruction, and it is what Long (1996) has termed focus on forms. Several theorists have placed focus on form and focus on forms on a continuum according to the level of explicit attention that is paid to language in general and to grammar in particular (e.g., Doughty & Williams, 1998; Shintani, 2013). Chapter 4 examined more implicit types of attention to language, such as input flood, input enhancement, and corrective feedback. This section progresses further down the continuum of explicitness, considering consciousness-raising tasks, processing instruction, PPP, and explicit instruction. Such explicit attention to linguistic forms may be necessary for L2 learners to acquire nonsalient or low frequency grammatical structures from the input (Nassaji & Fotos, 2011; Spada & Tomita, 2010). Focus on forms instruction is one way to draw learners' attention to linguistic forms, particularly those that are less salient.

Consciousness-raising tasks. One of the least explicit types of focus on forms instruction is consciousness raising, which is predicated on the assumption that inductively helping learners discover grammatical rules and patterns for themselves will help facilitate L2 acquisition (Ellis, 2003; Nassaji & Fotos, 2004). In this type of instruction, learners are presented with exemplars of a specific structure, and they are asked to extract the pattern or rule that is operating. For example, learners might be provided with a text in Spanish containing multiple exemplars of verbs in the preterit and imperfect forms. Learners could be asked to identify the ways in which the two verb aspects are used, and to extrapolate a rule or set of rules to explain the grammatical patterns. In this way, consciousness-raising activities are inductive because learners must figure out the rules from the data that are given to them. The goal is for learners to develop explicit, declarative knowledge of the targeted grammatical feature (Nassaji & Fotos, 2011). In addition, consciousness-raising tasks strive to make the grammar structure salient to learners so that they might notice the form in subsequent input. Because consciousness raising is inductive, it could be considered one of the more implicit types of focus on forms, and it is possible for the input that is presented to learners to be meaning-oriented. Nevertheless, the primary emphasis of consciousness-raising tasks is to identify linguistic patterns rather than to focus primarily on the semantic content of the input.

Input-based instruction. Another type of pedagogical method with theoretical underpinnings is input-based instruction, also known as comprehension-based instruction. In input-based instruction, learners are provided with verbal or written input, which is manipulated in order for learners to create form-meaning mappings (Shintani, 2013; Shintani, Li, & Ellis, 2013). In many ways, input-based instruction is similar to input enhancement; however, there is generally more of a focus on specific language items, with perhaps less emphasis solely on meaning. Input-based instruction does not necessarily involve learners in producing language; instead, this type of instruction focuses on comprehension of specific structures, with learners indicating their comprehension through tasks such as choosing from a set of pictures the one that matches the input. However, output is not prohibited, and learners may produce language if they so desire. Shintani (2013) suggests that input-based instruction can be good for lower level learners because it can provide exposure to new structures in the input, and it can help reduce learner anxiety.

Processing instruction. One specific approach to input-based instruction is processing instruction, which is predicated on Input Processing Theory (Van-Patten, 2004, 2007), which states, in simple terms, that the cognitive system processes input in specific ways, and learners often use L1 based processing strategies that do not work or work poorly for processing L2 input. Processing instruction involves three stages. The first is making learners aware of an incorrect processing strategy. A common example is the first noun principle, which English speakers use to assign the subject role to the first noun in a sentence. However, this rule is less helpful in other languages, such as Spanish, with more flexible word order and morphological marking of nouns and verbs. The following sentences illustrate the fixed word order of English, but the flexibility of Spanish that allows the subject and object to occur in different positions in the sentence.

(1) a. Mary hates John.
    b. María detesta a Juan.
    c. A Juan María lo detesta.
(2) a. Mary hates him.
    b. María lo detesta.
    c. Lo detesta María.
(3) a. She hates him.
    b. Lo detesta.

—(from VanPatten, 2007, p. 121)

Providing learners with this explicit information is the first stage in process-ing instruction (Henry, Culman, & VanPatten, 2009). Next, learners engage in referential activities in which they listen to input that forces them to process the input correctly in order complete the activity. For the first noun principle in Spanish, learners could be provided with sentences that alternate between placing the subject before and after the verb. In order to ensure that learners are processing the input correctly they might be asked to choose from a set of pictures the one that corresponds to the input that they just heard. Finally, learners may engage in affective activities in which they are presented with input to which they can respond in more personal and open-ended ways. For example, learners might be presented with sentences that describe certain character traits, and learners can express whether or not these descriptions apply to them personally. Again, the input would entail learners processing the target feature correctly. The goal of processing instruction is to change the way that learners process and comprehend language. As such, processing instruction does not focus on learner production; rather, it facilitates the correct processing of input.

Processing instruction is different from what can be considered traditional grammar instruction because although they both involve presentation of explicit information about the L2, processing instruction is followed by input-oriented activities that prompt learners to process incoming language in a more effective manner. In contrast, in traditional instruction, the explicit presentation of information is often followed by activities that require learners to produce the target structures in mechanical exercises and more meaningful activities (Henry et al., 2009).

[handwritten margin note: difference between traditional vs input]

Processing instruction has been considered both an example of focus on form (VanPatten, 2002) and focus on forms (Loewen, 2011; Shintani, 2013), and in part it combines both implicit and explicit grammar instruction. The more explicit attention to form occurs in the explicit information stage in which learners are made aware of inefficient processing strategies in relation to specific linguistic structures. However, in the referential and affective stages, learners must process and focus on the meaning of the sentences. Nevertheless, because the primary goal of processing instruction is for learners to be aware of specific grammatical features and not for them to use their own linguistic resources to focus primarily on meaning, it is being treated as a type of focus on forms for the purposes of this review.

One of the concerns of input-based instruction in general, and processing instruction in particular, is if this type of instruction leads to improvement in learners' L2 production as well as comprehension. Because learners are given instruction and practice on comprehending input, it is generally expected that learners' ability to understand input will improve. However, critics of input-based instruction and processing instruction argue that L2 production is also an important skill, which is not developed in input-based instruction. In contrast, proponents of input-based instruction, and especially processing instruction, argue that learners' production skills also benefit from input-based instruction.

Present, practice, produce. In addition to input-based instruction, there is also output-based instruction in which learner production of output is a primary concern. One type of instruction that contains elements of explicit instruction with more production-based activities is what is known as Present, Practice, Produce (PPP) instruction (Nassaji & Fotos, 2011; Shintani, 2013). This type of instruction begins with an explanation of a grammar point, followed by very controlled production of that grammar structure. Finally learners engage in freer practice using the grammar structure. For example, learners may be provided with the grammatical rules for constructing relative clauses. Subsequently, learners might engage in sentence combination activities in which they are given two sentences that they must combine using a relative clause. Finally, learners could have the opportunity to engage in activities that involve freer production of relative clauses.

An interesting characteristic about PPP is that it can be more meaning-oriented or less meaning-oriented. Obviously, the presentation stage involves explicit attention to specific grammatical rules; however, the ways in which the practice and production components get operationalized can differ. Previously, from a behaviorist perspective, the practice and production components tended to be formulaic and decontextualized, with the emphasis on learners correctly repeating the L2 sentences in order to form good L2 habits. However, with the greater emphasis on communication and task-based learning that has occurred in ISLA, the practice, and particularly the production activities, may be much more meaning-focused. In fact, it is possible for the production component to consist of focused tasks in which learners engage in communicative activities containing specific predetermined linguistic forms (Foster, 2009). However, while there may be a meaning-focused element to PPP instruction, it is also possible that learners still feel that the primary purpose of the activity is to practice the targeted form rather than engage in meaning-focused interaction (Shintani, 2013).

One of the concerns about PPP is that it may not be closely based on the psychological constraints of L2 development, particularly in terms of the natural order of development (Nassaji & Fotos, 2011). Thus even if late acquired structures are presented early in the learning process, the practice and production activities will not help learners skip steps in the natural order of acquisition. PPP also assumes that what is taught explicitly can be used to develop the ability to use the language for spontaneous production. As we have seen, this claim is contentious, with some researchers arguing that it is difficult or even impossible for explicit knowledge to become implicit. While explicit instruction is fairly successful in developing explicit, metalingual knowledge, there are doubts about the usefulness of such knowledge for spontaneous L2 production (Ellis, 2005). However, a skill acquisition theory perspective would suggest that practice is precisely what is needed to turn declarative knowledge into procedural knowledge. For example, DeKeyser (2007c) expressly states that explicit instruction needs to be integrated with input and output practice in theoretically supported ways, following the stages proposed by skill acquisition theory. The ability to use knowledge automatically is the goal of skill acquisition theory, and DeKeyser argues that automatization requires procedural knowledge, which in turn is dependent upon declarative knowledge. Declarative knowledge becomes proceduralized through slow and deliberate practice, while declarative knowledge is acquired through 'the judicious use of rules and examples' (DeKeyser, 2007, p. 107).

Output-based instruction. Although PPP involves learners in producing language, it is not the only type of output-based instruction. For example, Swain's (1995) Comprehensible Output Hypothesis proposes that learners' L2 production can actually play a facilitative role in the L2 development process. Output-based instruction draws upon this perspective to involve learners in classroom activities in which they produce language. One such activity is a dictogloss task, which involves learners in text reconstruction task (Nassaji & Fotos, 2011). Learners are given a text, usually orally, but it is also possible for the text to be provided in writing. After hearing or reading the text once or twice, learners are asked to reconstruct the passage either on their own or in pairs or groups. During the reconstruction process, learners must pay attention to the forms that were used in the original text, and they may need to discuss and negotiate the correct linguistic forms in order to achieve an accurate reproduction of the text (Kuiken & Vedder, 2005; Swain & Lapkin, 2001). Again, dictogloss tasks are somewhat meaning-focused because learners are asked to reconstruct a passage of text that presumably contains coherent semantic content. Indeed, sometimes dictogloss tasks are considered a type of focus on form rather than focus on forms. However, the primary focus of a dictogloss task is not on the meaning of the text; rather, the focus of the task is producing an accurate linguistic reproduction of the text.

Explicit instruction. In addition to the previous types of instruction that arguably place greater emphasis on linguistic forms while still incorporating a meaning-focused element, it is also important to consider the role that more traditional types of explicit instruction play in L2 learning. Explicit instruction occurs when the primary goal of a lesson or activity involves overtly drawing learners' attention to linguistic features, in this case morphosyntactic rules and patterns. In addition, in many instances the presentation of rules is accompanied by the provision of examples of said rules, often in ways that are decontextualized and devoid of larger semantic content (Andringa et al., 2011; Macaro & Masterman, 2006; Ur, 2011). Furthermore, explicit grammatical instruction often involves the use of metalinguistic terminology (Bouffard & Sarkar, 2008). Specific instructional practices that can be considered examples of explicit instruction include grammar rule explanation, L1/L2 contrasts, translation exercises, and metalinguistic feedback. (Jin & Cortazzi, 2011; Norris & Ortega, 2000; Spada & Tomita, 2010).

One of the assumptions of traditional explicit grammar instruction is that language is comprised of a system of grammatical forms and structures that can be acquired consecutively; therefore, instruction should present grammatical rules in a systematic and orderly manner in order for learners to build up their linguistic knowledge piece by piece (Nassaji & Fotos, 2011). Although language acquisition is thought to follow a natural order, the stages that learners progress through are not generally the same ones employed by classroom syllabi. Furthermore, some stages of development are not target-like, and yet they represent progress on the part of the learner.

While the claim that explicit L2 instruction can bring about explicit knowledge is not too contentious, the claim that it can help in the development of implicit knowledge is disputed (Ur, 2011). Those who support the role of explicit instruction claim that it can be facilitative in the following ways. If learners have explicit knowledge of specific grammatical structures, they may be more likely to notice those structures in the input (Scheffler & Cincała, 2010). In this way, explicit instruction and explicit knowledge are not contributing directly to implicit knowledge, but rather they are helping bring about the conditions necessary for the development of implicit knowledge. If learners notice a linguistic form in subsequent meaning-focused interaction, they may be more likely to acquire implicit knowledge of that form (Long, 1996). In addition to helping learners notice forms in the input, explicit instruction can also provide learners with rules that help them monitor their own production.

Another benefit of explicit instruction is that it has the potential to have a positive affective impact on some learners, that is to say it may make learners feel better. Scheffler and Cincała (2010) suggest that for many L2 learners, particularly adults, being able to understand the grammatical rules of the L2 is important. Because formal education consists largely of explicit instruction, adult learners may feel comfortable with such type of instruction. Furthermore, non-linguists often assume that L2 learning consists primarily of memorizing grammatical rules and vocabulary items (Gatbonton & Segalowitz, 2005). Finally, because adults may have lost much of the facility for implicit language learning that served them during their L1 acquisition process, they may be able to make better use of explicit L2 instruction. Consequently, taking advantage of adult learners' experience with explicit instruction can be expedient (Hulstijn, 2002); however, its effects on the development of implicit and explicit knowledge and their role in L2 production must be kept in mind.

One final potential benefit of explicit instruction is that it can also provide learners with positive L2 evidence (Andringa et al., 2011). If explicit instruction occurs in the L2, then that input can function like any other input. In many cases, communicative interaction is about topics other than language, but linguists spend considerable time discussing language, and this type of explicit discussion of grammatical rules can serve as a topic of meaning-focused interaction.

EMPIRICAL EVIDENCE

Having considered some of the more theoretical claims about focus on forms and more explicit types of grammar learning and instruction, this chapter now moves on to address some of the empirical evidence pertaining to this area. In particular, this section will cover the more prominent types of instruction that have received the majority of research attention, specifically input-based instruction and processing instruction, output-based instruction and PPP, and lastly explicit instruction. Finally, it should be pointed out that unlike focus on form research, the research into more explicit grammar instruction has focused almost exclusively on its effectiveness in bringing about L2 development, rather than its value in promoting noticing of L2 structures.

Input-Based Instruction

The effects of input-based instruction, primarily in the form of processing instruction, have received considerable attention. As mentioned, in addition to an interest in processing instruction's ability to result in improved comprehension, there is also a parallel interest in its ability to bring about improved L2 production. One study from a general input-based instruction approach is Shintani's (2012) examination of the effects of input-based tasks on beginning-level Japanese children's knowledge of English vocabulary and plural –s. Shintani compared a control group with an input-based instruction group that participated in three different game-like activities. First, learners chose cards that matched the zoo animal or supermarket vocabulary that the teacher provided. Second, the teacher provided sentences in which the animals were looking for certain items, and learners had to choose cards based on the plurality of the nouns that they heard. Finally, the learners played picture bingo in which they again identified cards that corresponded to the items called out by the teacher; these items varied between singular and plural forms. For testing learners' comprehension of plural –s, Shintani used tests similar to the treatment activities; learners had to identify pictures that corresponded to the words that they heard. In addition to hearing words that had been used during the treatment, the learners were also tested on new items that they had not encountered before. For the production test, learners had to describe the pictures that had been used in the treatment. Shintani found that the input-based activities were able to foster classroom interaction in which focus on form and negotiation of meaning occurred. In addition, there was significant improvement for the input-based group compared to the control group on the comprehension tests; however, no increase in accurate use of plurals on the production test was found.

In a related meta-analysis, Shintani, Li, and Ellis (2013) examined 35 studies, from 1991 to 2010, investigating the effects of comprehension-based instruction and production-based instruction on the acquisition of grammatical features. They compared comprehension-based and production-based instruction with each other, as well as comparing each type of instruction against control groups. In addition, pretest to posttest gains were analyzed. The meta-analysis also examined two moderator variables: comprehension-based instruction with processing instruction, and production-based instruction with text creation or text manipulation. The results showed that both types of instruction had large effects on both receptive and production tests. There was a short-term advantage on receptive tests for comprehension-based instruction, but the results on delayed posttests indicated no difference between the two types of instruction. In contrast, on productive tests, the two types of instruction showed no difference on the immediate posttests; however, production-based instruction groups outscored comprehension-based groups on delayed posttests. Finally, it appeared that the effectiveness of comprehension-based instruction was enhanced by the presence of processing instruction. Shintani et al. interpret these results as indicating that comprehension-based instruction may be more effective for the initial stages of acquisition, such as converting input to intake. In addition, comprehension-based instruction may be better suited for introducing new grammatical structures. In contrast, production-based instruction may be more effective for helping learners consolidate partially acquired forms. In this way, these two types of instruction may be seen as complementary, achieving different ends, but useful for acquisition in their own ways.

An example of one of the studies included in Shintani et al.'s meta-analysis is Qin's (2008) comparison of the effects of processing instruction activities and dictogloss activities targeting the active and passive voices for young, beginning proficiency Chinese learners of English. In the processing instruction condition learners received explicit instruction about the first noun principle, and then participated in referential and affective activities. The referential activities were based on two well-known Chinese fables. In the dictogloss condition, the learners received explicit information about the formation of active and passive voices. Then they received written copies of the two fables that were used in the referential activities in the processing instruction condition. After engaging in activities to understand the texts, the learners were asked to reconstruct the texts. Qin found that both methods of instruction were effective in improving learners' test scores. The only difference was that the processing instruction group outperformed the dictogloss group on the immediate comprehension test. Otherwise, the groups improved equally on immediate and delayed production tests and the delayed comprehension tests. Qin interprets these results as suggesting there are multiple instructional options for promoting L2 development.

Because of the large amount of research investigating the effects of processing instruction, it is useful to consider some of the individual studies that have been conducting, particularly those that investigate the specific stages of processing instruction—explicit instruction, referential activities, and affective activities. For example, Fernández (2008) investigated the effects of the provision of explicit information. She compared two groups of learners who were exposed to a series of structured input items targeting Spanish word order, object-verb-subject, and Spanish subjunctive. One group received explicit information about the structures and the processing difficulties that they created for English learners of Spanish, after which they engaged in referential activities. The other group participated only in the referential activities. Fernández found that explicit information had a positive effect on Spanish subjunctives, but not for word order. She suggests that the type of structure and the accompanying tasks might account for the differential findings. For the subjunctive form, learners had only to notice and process one form within the sentence, but for word order, learners had to consider the grammatical roles of multiple forms.

In a partial replication of Fernández's study, Henry, Culman, and VanPatten (2009) examined the effects of explicit instruction on the correct processing of German word order and case marking by English speaking learners. Henry et al. divided learners into two groups: one group participated in just the structured input activities in which learners had to choose the picture that matched the input they heard. The other group received explicit instruction in addition to participating in the input activities. The explicit instruction involved a brief description of German case marking and word inversion, as well as information about the first noun principle and a warning to avoid assuming that the first noun in a sentence is the subject. Henry et al. (2009) found that the provision of explicit information resulted in better performance on German word order issues than did structured input activities alone. They suggest that that the difference in their findings and those of Fernández is that word order in Spanish, especially with direct object pronouns, is morphosyntactically more complex than the nominative/accusative case in German. Such differences in complexity might mediate the effects of explicit instruction and structured input activities.

Other studies have examined the activities that follow the explicit instruction stage of processing instruction. For instance, Henshaw (2012) looked at referential and affective processing instruction activities for L2 learners' use of the Spanish subjunctive. Referential activities involved learners hearing part of a sentence and choosing the subordinate clause needed to complete the sentence. The choice of clause was either in the present indicative or the present subjunctive. For the affective activities, learners needed to complete a sentence by choosing the description that best applied to them. Both options were in the subjunctive, so there was no right or wrong answer in terms of grammaticality; rather, in keeping with the nature of affective activities, learners were allowed to respond according to their own preferences. Henshaw divided learners into three groups: referential activities only, affective activities only, and referential activities followed by affective ones. She found that all three groups improved on immediate and delayed posttests, but the two groups that participated in the affective activities were better able to maintain their gains over time in comparison to the group that experienced only the referential activities. Nevertheless she argues that both types of structured input activities can be beneficial for learners.

In summary, these studies suggest that input-based instruction, and particularly processing instruction, can be beneficial for improving learners' comprehension and production, but it does appear that these effects may be moderated by specific variables such as the targeted linguistic structure and the presence or absence of explicit information about the processing issues that the structures create for L2 learners.

Present, Practice, Produce

Although PPP has been a popular method of instruction for decades, there has been relatively little ISLA research into its effectiveness because of its close association with audiolingualism and behaviorism (DeKeyser, 1998; Lyster & Ranta, 2007). Instead of investigating PPP per se, researchers have examined its separate components under different research agendas. For example, the impact of free production, and to a lesser extent practice, on L2 acquisition has been a concern of interaction and task-based approaches. (See Chapter 3.) In contrast, the effects of presentation have been explored under the guise of explicit instruction.

Explicit grammar instruction has been both denounced (e.g., Krashen, 2003) and championed (e.g., R. Sheen, 2005) by ISLA scholars over the years. However, the effects of explicit instruction may be subtler than these positions allow, and current research trends explore what aspects of explicit instruction may be more or less effective for L2 acquisition. In addition, the results of explicit instruction must be examined through the lens of the type of knowledge that it can create and how that knowledge is assessed. Explicit instruction is clearly associated with explicit L2 knowledge (Ellis, 2005; Norris & Ortega, 2000; Scheffler & Cincała, 2010). Its effect on implicit knowledge, which allows learners to use the L2 accurately for spontaneous communication is more at issue (Ellis, 2005).

Multiple studies have found positive effects for explicit instruction, including several meta-analyses which have been described in previous chapters, but will be reviewed briefly here. One of the first, by Norris and Ortega (2000) examined 49 ISLA research studies of the effects of both implicit and explicit L2 instruction. The main finding of the meta-analysis was that explicit instruction was generally more effective than implicit instruction, based on the assessment measures used in the studies that were investigated. Subsequently, Spada and Tomita (2010), who meta-analyzed 41 studies of various types of instruction, also found that the effects of explicit instruction were larger than those of implicit instruction on both simple and complex grammatical structures and on various types of assessment measures.

Another study of interest that compares implicit and explicit instruction is Klapper and Rees's (2003) longitudinal investigation of a German study program at a UK university. The researchers compared two groups of students: one group received instruction that consisted primarily of focus on form, while the other group experienced explicit focus on forms instruction. Klapper and Rees found that in the first two years of study, the explicit instruction group improved significantly compared to the focus on form group. However, the focus on form group reached the same level as the explicit instruction group after a year of study abroad. Klapper and Rees claim that explicit instruction can accelerate the learning process; however, focus on form can help provide a strong foundation for any learning that might occur subsequently due to L2 exposure in more naturalistic contexts. As a result of their study, Klapper and Rees claim that explicit instruction may be best for learners who have very little exposure to the L2 outside of the classroom context.

However, not all research has found in favor of explicit grammatical instruction. For example, Andringa et al. (2011) found mixed results in their comparison of the effects of implicit and explicit instruction for young adult learners of Dutch as a foreign language. Targeting one simple and one complex linguistic structure, Andringa et al. developed computerized lessons to provide learners with explicit instruction, consisting of the presentation and practice of rules targeting the two structures, or implicit instruction, consisting of an input flood of the target features and opportunities to produce them. No explicit attention was given to the forms. A grammaticality judgment test and a free-written response task were used to assess the effects of instruction. Results indicated that the explicit instruction group outperformed the implicit instruction group on the grammaticality judgment test for the simple structure; however, there was no difference between the two types of instruction for the more complex structure. Likewise, on the free-writing task scores, there was no significant difference between the implicit and explicit instruction groups. These results suggest that overall there was no advantage for explicit instruction. Finally, Andringa et al. investigated the relationship between instruction, test scores, and learners' L1s. Results indicated that learners with L1 forms similar in construction to the L2 forms benefited from the explicit instruction; however, learners with different ways of expressing the forms were disadvantaged by explicit instruction. Based on their results, Andringa et al. suggest that implicit instruction should be intensified in the classroom in place of explicit instruction.

In another study, Macaro and Masterman (2006) investigated the effects of an intensive pre-university French grammar course at Oxford University. Before beginning their university studies, 10 students received approximately

30 hours of oral and written instruction designed to develop learners' grammatical knowledge. After this intensive program, they, and an additional 12
students comprising a comparison group, enrolled in a semester-long French
course. Macaro and Masterman wanted to see if the pre-semester intensive
course provided additional learning benefits. Multiple tests that included
measures that favored the use of either implicit or explicit knowledge were
administered as pretests, immediate posttests, and delayed posttests. Results
indicated that the additional intensive explicit instruction helped learners in
correcting sentences that had been identified as ungrammatical; however, it
did not lead to greater grammatical knowledge overall or to improved performance on production tasks. Based on these results, Macaro and Masterman
express doubt about the effectiveness of explicit instruction for leading to successful internalization of grammatical rules.

Finally, in a laboratory-based study of Spanish-English bilinguals, Stafford,
Bowden, and Sanz (2012) investigated the effects of explicit computerized
instruction on the learning of Latin thematic case assignment. Stafford et al.
created four treatment groups using two variables: the presence or absence of
a pre-practice grammar explanation, and the presence of more or less explicit
feedback during practice activities. Results on several different posttests indicated that the explanation of grammatical rules prior to the practice activities
was not beneficial; however, the provision of metalinguistic feedback during
the activities resulted in improved test performance.

Based on this sample of studies, it is clear that the effects of more explicit
types of grammar instruction are mixed. On the one hand, input-based
instruction, accompanied by processing instruction, demonstrates effectiveness across studies. In addition, meta-analyses of implicit and explicit instruction find benefits in favor of explicit instruction. Nevertheless, there are
multiple individual studies that find a limited or lesser effect for explicit
instruction in the development of L2 grammatical ability.

PEDAGOGICAL IMPLICATIONS

There are several pedagogical points that can be taken from this chapter. First
and foremost, it appears that many types of instruction can be effective. While
more implicit types of instruction can bring about language development, as
was seen in Chapter 4, it is clear that more explicit types of instruction can also
be beneficial for learners. For instance, input-based instruction, and in particular processing instruction, has the potential to help learners improve their L2
comprehension and production abilities. However, one drawback to processing instruction is that it is limited in the number of grammatical structures
for which it is relevant, since not all grammatical structures present a processing problem for learners. Furthermore, classroom activities that emphasize

L2 output can also be beneficial for learners, particularly if that production occurs in more meaning-focused communicative contexts. Finally, the provision of explicit information regarding grammatical rules appears to have some benefit as well, although this may not be the case for all structures on all occasions. In summary, then, it seems that the best type of L2 instruction may be that which integrates both implicit and explicit types of instruction (Nassaji & Fotos, 2011; Swan, 2005).

ACTIVITIES

In their research study into the effects of explicit and implicit grammar instruction, Andringa et al. (2011) state that 'the goal of the instruction was to create between-group differences in explicit knowledge while controlling for the amount of exposure to the target structures' (p. 881). Table 5.2 presents examples of the two types of instruction that they employed. How would you characterize the instruction? Do you agree with the explicit and implicit designations? What do you think accounts for the fact that Andringa et al. found little difference in the effectiveness of these two types of instruction?

TABLE 5.2

Explicit instruction	Implicit instruction
Degrees of comparison (DoCs) Which word is a form of the DoCs? When a commercial is funny, people think it is nicer.	This statement is about the text you just read. Is it true or false? When a commercial is funny, people think it is nicer.
Degrees of Comparison These three sentences are taken from advertisements. Which sentence does not contain a form of the degrees of comparison? A- X now washes even cleaner. B- With X, colors stay nicer. C- X is not expensive.	What does this advertisement try to tell you? A- X now washes even cleaner. B- With X, colors stay nicer. C- X is not expensive.
Degrees of comparison Fill in one of the (three) words in the sentence below. Use a form of the DoCs: X is one of Holland's [high/fast/ small] skaters.	Fill in one of the (three) words in the sentence below. Make the sentence agree with the text: X is one of Holland's [high/fast/ small] skaters.

Note: Examples of explicit and implicit instruction are translated from the Dutch and are based on Andringa el al., 2011, p. 883.

ADDITIONAL READING

DeKeyser, R. (2007). *Practice in a second language: Perspectives from applied linguistics and cognitive psychology*. Cambridge: Cambridge University Press.

Nassaji, H., & Fotos, S. (2011). *Teaching grammar in second language classrooms: Integrating form-focused instruction in communicative context*. New York: Routledge.

VanPatten, B. (2004). *Processing instruction: Theory, research and commentary*. Mahwah, NJ: Lawrence Erlbaum Associates.

6

The Acquisition of Vocabulary

Although the acquisition of grammar has received substantial attention in ISLA research, learning vocabulary is also an essential part of L2 acquisition, and learners need large L2 vocabularies to communicate successfully (Schmitt, 2008). Particularly in the last few decades, researchers have turned their attention to lexical acquisition, and there is now substantial research in this area. With vocabulary acquisition, as with other areas of language, it is important consider the scope of the acquisition process; in other words, what is involved in learning vocabulary. Schmitt (2008) states that 'the first step in the vocabulary acquisition process is establishing an initial form-meaning link' (p. 335), and indeed much vocabulary research has focused on this aspect of learning. However, beyond the form-meaning connection, there are other aspects of vocabulary knowledge that have been explored and will be covered in this chapter.

Furthermore, the most effective ways in which to acquire various aspects of vocabulary knowledge is still under investigation (Schmitt, 2008). Because the establishment of form-meaning connections is largely a conscious process, there has been a tradition of intentional vocabulary learning and explicit instruction. Nevertheless, there are strong advocates for incidental vocabulary acquisition occurring through extensive exposure to the L2, particularly through reading (Krashen, 2003). Additionally, proponents of focus on form suggest that vocabulary can also benefit from brief attention during meaning-focused activities (Laufer, 2005a), and research in this area has considered what levels of explicitness might be optimal in such occasions.

Finally, there has been some consideration as to the type of knowledge that occurs as a result of vocabulary learning. Much vocabulary knowledge is explicit, consisting of learners' conscious awareness of the connection between a word's form and its meaning. However, there has been growing interest in aspects of vocabulary knowledge that learners may not be consciously aware of possessing, and which could therefore be considered implicit knowledge. Unlike grammar, vocabulary does not consist primarily of rules that learners may hold consciously or unconsciously; nonetheless, there are aspects of vocabulary knowledge, for example regarding word frequency or collocations, which may be implicit for learners. This chapter will consider these and other acquistional issues that are at the forefront of vocabulary learning in the classroom.

THEORETICAL CONCERNS

Aspects of Vocabulary

Form-meaning mapping. At its most basic, vocabulary learning involves the mapping of meaning onto form (Schmitt, 2008). That is to say, learners need to associate specific semantic concepts with specific phonological or orthographic forms. The primary unit in vocabulary learning is the word, but the precise definition of a word is important to consider. It is clear that words such as *bird* and *fish* have different forms and different meanings. However, words such as *fish* and *fishing* have overlapping forms and meanings; thus, while they are clearly different tokens (i.e., words on a page), there is more of relationship between them than there is between *bird* and *fish*. In ISLA, the general tendency when talking about lexical acquisition is to refer to word families, which include the head word plus the inflected and derivational words that can be formed from the head word (Nation, 2001). The grouping of words in this way is done in large part because the semantic relatedness of the words decreases the learning burden that is associated with learning the forms of one word family compared to those of different word families. Consequently, *fish*, *fished*, and *fishing* all belong to the same word family, and the learning burden for the other forms is greatly reduced if learners know the head word.

The phonological and orthographic shape of a word is an important component of the form-meaning relationship because without the phonological or orthographic form, the word does not exist. Thus, learners need to have knowledge of the pronunciation and spelling of words (Sturm, 2013a). Pronunciation will be considered in more detail in Chapter 7, while spelling has not received much attention in ISLA research, except perhaps for its role in synchronous computer-mediated communication. Consequently, spelling will not be addressed further in this chapter.

Other aspects. In addition to form-meaning connections, there are other aspects of vocabulary knowledge for learners to acquire (Nation, 2001). For example, vocabulary knowledge also encompasses knowing the grammatical properties of words, including their derivational and inflectional morphology. In order to use lexical items accurately, learners need to know if words can function as verbs, nouns, adjectives, or other parts of speech. In some instances, L2 learners may acquire this knowledge incidentally, but in many cases, such information is presented explicitly in the L2 classroom. Words of similar categories, such as nouns related to professions or adjectives describing personalities, might be presented together in a single vocabulary lesson. Furthermore, learners can be taught what morphological features can turn one type of word (e.g., adjectives such as *quick* or *slow*) into another type (e.g., adverbs such as *quickly* or *slowly*).

One aspect of vocabulary knowledge that is often late acquired is the knowledge of which words frequently occur together in multiword units, collocations, and idioms (Boers, Lindstromberg, & Eyckmans, 2013; Nation, 2001). For example, in English one can *go fishing*, but not *do fishing*. In contrast, one can *do karate*, but one *plays tennis* or *football*. In some cases, knowledge of collocations may be implicit, having been acquired incidentally without learners' awareness; however, collocations can also be the target of direct, explicit instruction.

Related to collocations are formulaic chunks, which are groups of words that are stored and retrieved as whole units, meaning that learners have not necessarily analyzed the grammatical constituents of the chunk (Boers & Lindstromberg, 2009; Wray, 2000). For example, *I don't know* and *I want to X* are often learned by beginning learners of English as unanalyzed chunks. The learners do not know the rules that produce these phrases, and they cannot change the subject of the sentence or the form of the verb; nonetheless, they can produce the whole chunk or phrase in the appropriate context. The advantage of chunks is that they reduce learners' cognitive load because they can be retrieved from memory more quickly than they can be generated by the learner's knowledge of grammar rules (Boers & Lindstromberg, 2009).

In addition to knowledge of the linguistic contexts in which lexical items are likely to co-occur, vocabulary knowledge is also comprised of knowledge about the larger contexts in which words are likely to appear. For example, knowledge of a word's domain refers to the content areas in which it is likely to be used; some words are more common in business settings, while others occur more frequently in academic contexts. Indeed, there are courses, such as Chinese for Business, or English for Academic Purposes, that focus exclusively on the vocabulary and other linguistic features that occur in specific domains. The English Academic Word List is an example of roughly 570 words that have been found to occur frequently in academic contexts and thus are particularly important for learners studying at the university level (Coxhead, 2000; Nation, 2001). Another related context that affects vocabulary is the social setting. For instance, the register of a word refers primarily to the formality of a word; some words occur more frequently in informal contexts, while others occur more frequently in more formal contexts. It is possible for domain and register to overlap, and an example of this interplay can be seen in the following words: *excrement, shit, poop, manure, bowel movement, feces,* and *scat*. They all have the same basic meaning, but some are more likely to be encountered in certain domains rather than others (e.g., medicine, agriculture, or biology). The words also differ in register, with some words being considered more acceptable in polite company, while others may be considered offensive.

One final aspect of vocabulary knowledge that learners can acquire pertains to the relative frequency or commonness of words in daily discourse. Some words occur more frequently than others. In fact, ISLA researchers have produced frequency lists in multiple languages that categorize the occurrence rate of words, based on collections of millions of words in corpora taken from newspapers, books, television, radio, and other sources (e.g., Davies, 2006; Nation, 2001). Usually these lists are broken down into bands of one thousand words each, so there is a list of the one thousand most common words in a language, the two thousand most common words, et cetera. Again, knowledge of word frequency may be largely unconscious, but frequency-based word lists are also sometimes used in L2 instruction.

Issues in Vocabulary Acquisition

Depth of knowledge. The many aspects of vocabulary knowledge that have just been covered—grammatical function, collocation, frequency, register, and domain—all contribute to learners' depth of vocabulary knowledge. As a result, learners have the task of not only learning the form-meaning connections of words, but also building up their knowledge of these other components. If learners know only the basic form-meaning connections of lexical items, then their depth of knowledge of is limited.

Breadth of knowledge. Breadth of knowledge refers to the number of words that learners know, with the knowledge in question consisting simply of the basic form-meaning relationships and not the multiple aspects that comprise depth of that knowledge. In considering breadth of vocabulary knowledge, there is some discussion about the optimal size of L2 speakers' vocabulary. Of course, larger is better, but vocabulary learning takes time, and it is important for learners to have realistic learning goals.

The average adult English L1 speaker is conservatively estimated to have a vocabulary size of roughly 20,000 word families (Nation, 2001). For L2 learners, the method often used for calculating a desirable vocabulary size is to calculate what number of words would allow learners to easily comprehend L2 input. It is assumed that readers need to know about 95%–98% of the words in a text in order to read easily for comprehension and to be able to make informed guesses about unknown words. By some calculations, this means that learners need to know roughly the 3,000 most frequent words in the L2 (Nation, 2001; Webb, 2010). However, much of the research on word frequency has focused on English, and Shen (2010) suggests that learners of Chinese need to know about 8,500 Chinese words in order to read nonacademic texts with minimal difficulty.

Frequency of exposure. Related to the frequency of words in the input is the issue of the amount of exposure that learners need to words in order to learn them. Most researchers agree that multiple exposures to a word are necessary before it is learned; however, there is no agreement on the optimal number of encounters. Some studies suggest between 8 to 12 encounters are needed to solidify knowledge of lexical items (e.g., Horst, Cobb, & Meara, 1998), while others argue that only two or three exposures may be sufficient (e.g., Rott, 1999). Laufer and Rozokski-Roitblat (2011) conclude that different frequencies of exposure may provide different degrees of learning, based on the characteristics of the lexical items involved.

Although the number of times a word is encountered is important, the quality of those encounters is also important. Schmitt (2008) refers to this as engagement, and he advocates that the more engagement learners have with a word, the better it will be retained. Similarly, Laufer and Rozokski-Roitblat (2011) suggest that how well words are processed is an essential component of vocabulary acquisition. Finally, Eckerth and Tavakoli (2012) draw on the depth of processing hypothesis (e.g., Lockhart & Craik, 1990) to support the argument that the intensity of exposure to lexical items is just as important, if not more important, than frequency of exposure. Shallow processing of a word, involving perhaps no more than processing the orthographic or phonological features of a word, is less beneficial for vocabulary learning than a deeper analysis, which would include processing the semantic and conceptual characteristics of the word.

Receptive and productive vocabulary knowledge. Another distinction that is made in vocabulary learning is between productive and receptive knowledge, also referred to as active and passive knowledge respectively (Laufer, 1998; Laufer & Paribakht, 1998; Webb, 2008). Productive knowledge is comprised of words that learners can use when they are creating either written or spoken L2 output. In contrast, receptive knowledge consists of words learners can recognize in the input, but are unable to come up with on their own. Research shows that in general, learners' receptive vocabulary knowledge is larger than their productive knowledge.

Implicit and explicit vocabulary knowledge. The distinction between implicit and explicit knowledge has received considerable attention in relation to the acquisition of grammar; however, there has been less research in this area pertaining to vocabulary. In part, this lack may be due to the fact that most vocabulary knowledge is considered to be explicit. Learners are usually consciously aware of the word meanings that they know, and there is often conscious, intentional, explicit learning that is done in order to acquire those form-meaning connections.

However, not all vocabulary knowledge is necessarily explicit; some aspects may be implicit (Sonbul & Schmitt, 2012). For example, knowledge of the collocations, frequency, domain, and register of a lexical item might be implicit. Learners may not be taught this information explicitly, but it is possible that they might acquire this knowledge implicitly without being aware of doing so (e.g., Rebuschat, 2013).

Instruction and Vocabulary Acquisition

Incidental and intentional learning. Two divisions are often made in vocabulary acquisition research, namely that of intentional and incidental learning (Hulstijn, 2001). In terms of the overall ISLA taxonomy (Loewen, 2011), incidental learning is more likely to transpire in meaning-focused instruction in which the goal is for learners to engage in communicative tasks, with learners acquiring grammar and vocabulary incidentally along the way. Incidental learning occurs when the main goal of L2 instruction is something other than vocabulary learning, such as reading for content, meaning-focused interaction or grammar-focused activities; however, incidental learning does not necessarily imply that learning happened without awareness. For example, learners may pause from their reading and look up an unknown word, in which case any learning would be incidental because vocabulary acquisition was not the primary goal of the activity. Nevertheless, the learning process would be explicit because the learner would be aware of looking up the meaning of the word. Thus, learners may learn words intentionally even if they encounter the word incidentally. In contrast, definitions of implicit learning (e.g., Rebuschat, 2013) state that implicit learning happens without awareness.

In contrast, intentional vocabulary learning fits well with form-focused instruction, which involves varying degrees of attention to language items. In focus on form, the attention to language items, in this case vocabulary, is brief, and it may occur through pedagogical techniques such as input enhancement or corrective feedback. In contrast, focus on forms involves primary attention to language items along with intentional types of learning. These pedagogical options will be explored, beginning with the most implicit and progressing to the most explicit.

Exposure and incidental learning. One of the more controversial issues in the ISLA vocabulary debate is the role of implicit vocabulary learning, particularly through extensive reading for pleasure. Some people argue that the incidental learning of vocabulary while reading is the most crucial and efficient way to learn vocabulary (Krashen, 2003). Extensive reading involves learners reading numerous self-selected texts, primarily for personal enjoyment rather than for language learning purposes (Al-Homoud & Schmitt, 2009). The argument in favor of extensive reading for vocabulary learning is that the task of learning large numbers of vocabulary items through direct instruction is beyond what is possible in the L2 classroom; however, it is possible for learners to encounter large amounts of vocabulary as they read for enjoyment.

In part, the argument for incidental vocabulary acquisition is based on L1 lexical acquisition. Laufer (2005b) contends that the default hypothesis for L1 vocabulary learning claims that most L1 vocabulary is acquired through extensive exposure to input, both written and oral, rather than through instruction. However, when it comes to L2 learning, Laufer (2005b) argues that there are several factors that make extensive reading a poor option for vocabulary learning. First, there is an assumption that learners will be able to recognize words that they do not know, and then it is assumed that learners will be able to infer the meanings of these words from the surrounding context. However, Laufer questions whether such assumptions are warranted. Furthermore, learners need multiple encounters with words to achieve long-term retention; however, learners may not experience such recurrent exposure through extensive reading, especially for low frequency words. A word may be encountered only once in a text. Finally, Laufer states that it cannot be assumed that the acquisition gains that learners make from reading short texts can be extrapolated to longer texts. Just because learners acquire five words from reading a 200-word text does not mean that they will be able to learn 50 words from a 2,000-word text.

Involvement Load Hypothesis. One theoretical position pertaining to incidental L2 vocabulary acquisition is the Involvement Load Hypothesis (Laufer & Hulstijn, 2001), which states there are three important task factors for incidental vocabulary acquisition; these factors are *need*, *search*, and *evaluation*. *Need* refers to whether or not knowledge of a word is necessary for completion of the task. Need is moderate when it is imposed by the task, and strong when it is imposed by the learner. *Search* is the cognitive aspect of trying to find or figure out the meaning of the new word. Keating (2008) implies that search requires effort on the part of learners, so it is present if they have to look up words in the dictionary, but it is not present when, for example, glosses are provided in the margins. *Evaluation* refers to comparing a new word to other words and deciding on its suitability in a given context. Evaluation is moderate when learners have to recognize differences between words, and strong when a task requires making decisions about the suitability of new words and then using them. In a 2008 study, Keating used the above criteria to calculate an involvement load index, which gave a rating of 0 (absent), 1 (moderate), or 2 (strong) to a task, based on the strength of each component. Tasks with higher involvement loads are hypothesized to result in higher lexical retention, and focus on form is seen as one way of increasing involvement load (Keating, 2008). One of the criticisms of the Involvement Load Hypothesis is that if learners are left to their own devises to search for and evaluate appropriate lexical items in specific contexts, they may or may not be successful in coming up with the correct meaning, and if they are unsuccessful, they may 'learn' the wrong thing (Eckerth & Tavakoli, 2012)

One area of research that still needs to be done in relation to the Involvement Load Hypothesis is its effect on lower proficiency learners (Keating, 2008). Furthermore, research needs to address learning in terms of both receptive and productive L2 knowledge.

Lexical focus on form. With incidental vocabulary acquisition through exposure to extensive input, the attempt to directly manipulate the input or learning process is minimal. In contrast, focus on form attempts to incorporate brief attention to linguistic items during more meaning-focused interaction, and while focus on form has concentrated extensively on grammar, it is also possible for focus on form to target vocabulary (Ellis et al., 2001a; Laufer, 2005a; Loewen, 2005; Tian & Macaro, 2012). As has been discussed in Chapter 4, focus on form attempts to situate brief attention to form within a larger meaning-focused context. Again, the rationale for focus on form is that learners will be able to pay attention to language items when the meaning is largely clear to them, and this attention will facilitate learning. Learners' attention may be drawn to lexical items through an input flood of the targeted vocabulary, input enhancement in which specific lexical items are highlighted, or corrective feedback that targets learners' incorrect use of vocabulary items.

Explicit instruction. In addition to calls for vocabulary learning through incidental exposure and focus on form, there are also proponents of vocabulary instruction that is explicit and isolated from other communicative contexts (Laufer, 2005b; Nation, 2001). There have been several different approaches to the explicit instruction of vocabulary.

Contrastive analysis and translation. One type of explicit instruction relies on the use of the L1 through contrastive analysis and translation. Although translation activities have fallen out of favor with more emphasis on the development of communicative competence, there are those who argue that translation does have some theoretical and empirical support (Hummel, 2010). Drawing on the depth of processing model (Lockhart & Craik, 1990), Hummel (2010) argues that translation activities can help with vocabulary learning because they provide elaboration, consisting of more extensive processing of lexical items. Thus, the processing effort required by translation activities, particularly when learners translate from their L1 to the L2, can be beneficial for learning. Similarly, Laufer and Girsai (2008) propose the contrastive analysis and translation (CAT) method of vocabulary teaching, in which learners are involved in comparing L1 and L2 structures and lexical items. They argue that translation can be an effective method of learning vocabulary.

One final argument in favor of translation activities for vocabulary acquisition relates to the efficiency of providing translations or L1 glosses of L2 words, particularly for ensuring comprehension. Providing circumlocutory explanations of lexical items in the L2 can be cumbersome and time consuming, although such explanations can provide input for learners. It should be noted, however, that while translation activities may be convenient in foreign language contexts where learners often share the same L1, they are logistically problematic in classes in which the teacher and students do not share the same L1.

Engagement. Finally, Schmitt (2008) discusses 'engagement' as being the construct that encapsulates what is needed for vocabulary acquisition. From his perspective, engagement is a combination of multiple components that create the optimal vocabulary learning conditions. In this sense, his concept of engagement encompasses aspects of incidental learning, focus on form, and explicit instruction. From the incidental learning position, Schmitt argues that increased frequency of exposure is important. Therefore, extensive reading and tasks that recycle vocabulary can be helpful for learning. From a focus on form perspective, increased interaction with, attention to, and noticing of lexical items are important. The multiple methods for achieving a focus on form can provide opportunities for such conditions to arise. Finally, from an explicit learning perspective, increased intentionality by the learner to focus on lexical items, and increased requirement from the teacher or task to use lexical items are important. In addition, having more opportunities to manipulate and engage with the lexical item is better for learner acquisition.

EMPIRICAL EVIDENCE

Now that various theoretical positions regarding the acquisition of vocabulary have been presented, the chapter turns to discussing some representative studies related to those positions. The first perspective to be explored is that of implicit learning through incidental exposure. In particular, some of the research investigating the effects of extensive reading will be examined. The next several options to be considered relate to focus on form and its combination of attention to form and meaning during classroom activities. Finally, this section ends with a look at more explicit options for vocabulary instruction.

It should be noted that vocabulary, unlike other areas of language, has not been the attention of larger scale meta-analyses into the effects of instruction. However, there have been several smaller scale meta-analyses specifically in the area of vocabulary and computer-assisted language learning. These reviews will be presented in their appropriate contexts; however, the need for broader meta-analyses to inform vocabulary instruction is evident.

Incidental Exposure

The research into the effects of incidental exposure to input on the acquisition of vocabulary has been largely positive. For example, Al-Homoud and Schmitt (2009) examined the effects of extensive reading in EFL classes in Saudi Arabia.

They compared two classes, one that received intensive vocabulary instruction, while the other was involved in extensive reading. Learners in the intensive instruction class were taught new words, quizzed, and drilled on reading strategies. In addition, they had to read new passages and do comprehension activities for homework. Learners in the extensive reading group performed some of the intensive exercises, but they had far fewer and less frequent exercises, with more class time being spent reading. Results showed that both the intensive instruction and extensive reading groups improved equally and statistically on the 2,000 and 3,000 most frequent English words, as well as the academic word lists. However, the extensive reading group had a more positive reaction overall to the learning conditions to which they were exposed.

In an earlier study, Horst (2005) also found that extensive reading had a positive effect on vocabulary acquisition. She conducted a longitudinal study with 21 immigrant learners in Canada, who participated in two hours of reading a week outside of regular class time. Horst identified low frequency words in a set of graded readers, and tested learners on them at the beginning and end of a six-week reading program. Although encountering relatively few unknown words due to the simplified nature of the reading materials, learners were nonetheless able to acquire roughly half of the new words, a result that Horst found quite encouraging.

Focus on Form

In addition to examining the effects of incidental exposure on vocabulary acquisition, researches have investigated the ways in which brief and relatively implicit attention to form can be incorporated into more meaning-focused vocabulary activities. One of the more implicit types of focus on form comes from Boers et al.'s (2013) study in which the authors proposed that learners' attention would be drawn to the phonological patterns of multiword units, particularly the alliteration of the first sound in each word. In this experiment, learners were provided with alliterative and nonalliterative word pairs, and then given a surprise recall test. Learners also were not told that some word pairs were alliterated and some were not. The alliterated phrases were better recalled than the nonalliterated phrases on an immediate posttest; however, there was no advantage for alliteration on the delayed posttest one week later. Boers et al. conclude that in order for the mnemonic advantages of alliteration to be realized, learners' awareness needs to be raised about the usefulness of such strategies.

Another one of the more implicit methods of vocabulary instruction is the provision of glosses of potentially unknown vocabulary items in larger reading texts, an option investigated by two recent meta-analyses. The first, Abraham (2008), investigated the effects of computer-mediated glosses on L2 vocabulary learning, as reported in 11 research studies. Abraham found that learners who read texts and had access to computerized lexical support had large learning effects on both immediate and delayed vocabulary tests, when compared with learners who did not have access to extra vocabulary support. Abraham found no significant effects for proficiency level, indicating that beginning, intermediate, and advanced students in these studies benefitted equally from the treatment.

In a similar study, Yun (2011) examined the effects of hypertext glosses on vocabulary L2 acquisition during computerized reading. He found 10 studies, conducted between 1996 and 2007, that compared groups of learners who read texts with and without hypertext glosses, and his analysis revealed a moderate effect size for acquisition in studies that included glosses compared to those that did not. Unlike Abraham's (2008) study, Yun's analysis of moderator variables indicated that learner proficiency affected the impact of glossing, with beginning learners receiving larger benefits. Although both meta-analyses urge caution in the interpretation of their results due to the small sample sizes, there is some reason to believe that the effects of extensive reading can be augmented by the relatively unobtrusive inclusion of additional lexical information.

Another focus on form related option can be seen in the Involvement Load Hypothesis, which argues that the elements of need, search and evaluation are necessary to induce incidental vocabulary acquisition during meaning-focused tasks. In one study, Keating (2008) investigated the involvement load hypothesis with 79 beginning-level Spanish students, divided into three treatment groups that received instruction with differing involvement loads. The group with the lowest involvement load participated in reading comprehension activities in which marginal glosses were provided for target vocabulary items. The level of need for this group was moderate; however the search and evaluation conditions were absent. The next treatment group participated in the same reading and comprehension activities as the lower involvement load group; however, instead of being provided with glosses, the learners were provided with a vocabulary list which they had to use to place each vocabulary item in its appropriate location in the text. The level of need for this group was also moderate, and the search condition was absent; however, the level of evaluation was moderate because learners had to choose the appropriate vocabulary item. The third group, having the highest involvement load, was provided with a list of the target vocabulary items, and, after studying them for 10 minutes, had to create original sentences with the words. Although the levels of need and search were the same as the two other groups, the level of evaluation was strong. Keating found that the group with the lowest involvement load scored significantly lower than the other two groups on both immediate and delayed passive recall tests. On an active recall test, the highest involvement load group scored higher than the other two groups on the immediate test but not on the delayed test, suggesting that a high level of evaluation was effective only in the short term. Keating concluded that the evaluation stage was a crucial component of word learning; however, recycling of vocabulary items is important in order to maintain gains in knowledge.

In a similar study, Eckerth and Tavakoli (2012) manipulated frequency of lexical exposure and task-induced involvement load for 30 ESL students in the UK who were asked to read a series of three texts. In one text, learners were provided with marginal glosses for 10 target lexical items. In a second text, learners filled in gaps in the text with words from a vocabulary list, while in the third text, learners were provided with marginal glosses and they engaged in a writing task after reading the text. The differences in these three tasks reflected weak, moderate, and strong involvement loads. To manipulate frequency of exposure, Eckerth and Tavakoli included five of the target words only one time each in the text, and the other five words five times each. On the immediate posttests, learners displayed an influence for involvement load, with test scores increasing with the level of involvement load. Word frequency was also found to be a factor on the immediate test; however, its influence declined on the posttest. In contrast, the effects of involvement load appeared to be stable over time. Eckerth and Tavakoli also found that scores on tests in which learners had to produce the vocabulary items were lower than on recognition tests. The authors conclude that incidental word learning can occur through extensive reading, but vocabulary learning is contingent on both frequency of exposure and amount of elaboration. They also conclude that output provides better conditions for word retention than does input, and that task induced involvement load is better for long term vocabulary retention than is mere frequent exposure.

Another way in which the impact of focus on form has been investigated for vocabulary acquisition is with corrective feedback. Although the effects of corrective feedback have been investigated rather intensely in terms of grammar acquisition, there have been a smaller, but growing number of studies that have investigated corrective feedback on lexical items. For example, Dilans (2010) investigated the effects of prompts and recasts on the vocabulary acquisition of intermediate ESL learners in the US. Learners were placed into three groups, and in addition to engaging in a number of vocabulary learning activities, two groups received corrective feedback on their errors in the usage of target vocabulary items. Both feedback groups showed significantly improvement compared to the control group on immediate posttests of vocabulary knowledge, while there appeared to be a slight advantage for the prompt group on the delayed posttest. Specifically, the prompt group performed better on a test of depth of vocabulary knowledge, which Dilans attributes to the role that prompts play in pushing learners to produce the correct form, and thereby involving them in more elaborate processing.

Recent studies have also investigated more explicit types of focus on form. For example, Tian and Macaro (2012) investigated the effectiveness of providing L1 vocabulary glosses during communicative activities for Chinese-speaking learners of English. The researchers provided definitions or descriptions of target vocabulary words in either the learners' L1 or L2. They found that lexical focus on form led to statistical increases in vocabulary scores over time and in comparison to a control group. However, the benefit of L1 glosses was seen only on the immediate posttest; there was no long-term advantage. Furthermore, although Tian and Macaro expected to find L1 glosses to be more helpful for lower proficiency learners, no such effect was found. Lower proficiency learners did as well as higher proficiency ones. Tian and Macaro conclude that drawing learners' attention to form-meaning connections is a necessary component for vocabulary acquisition. If learners are left to focus on the general ideas of the text, vocabulary learning is less likely to occur.

Another study by Laufer and Rozokski-Roitblat (2011) examined the effects of word frequency and task type on the vocabulary knowledge of 20 EFL learners in Israel. Learners were exposed to target vocabulary words either 2 to 3, 4 to 5, or 6 to 7 times during the treatment activities. In addition, learners engaged in activities in which the target vocabulary items were inserted either into the text, a type of focus on form treatment, or into exercises, a type of focus on forms treatment. The results indicated that after being exposed to four occurrences of a lexical item, the focus on forms group improved in comparison to the focus on form group. Laufer and Rozokski-Roitblat conclude that since the more explicit focus on forms treatment was effective for improvement on recall tests, 'the non-communicative, partly decontextualized activities characteristic of focus on forms are crucial for learners' future performance of authentic language tasks' (p. 407).

Explicit Instruction

Multiple studies have investigated the effects of explicit instruction on L2 vocabulary acquisition, including several that have examined the effects of translation. In one such study, Laufer and Girsai (2008) investigated the effects of explicit contrastive analysis and translation activities on the incidental acquisition of single words and collocations. High school learners of English were provided with either: (a) meaning-focused instruction in which there was no focus on the target words; (b) form-focused instruction, with contextualized focus on the target words; or (c) contrastive analysis and translation, in which learners translated sentences from the L2 into the L1, and vice versa. Learners were given both active and passive recall tests, and the contrastive analysis and translation group significantly outperformed the other two groups on all tests. Laufer and Girsai claim that the cross-linguistic instruction increased the salience of the target forms, resulting in improved acquisition.

In another study, Hummel (2010) investigated the effects of translation on three groups of French native speaking university students studying English. One group translated sentences from the L1 to the L2, another group translated from the L2 to the L1, and the third group simply copied down the L2 sentences.

Hummel found that although the two translation groups did improve on an immediate posttest, it was the rote copying group that improved the most. She argues that the active translation condition might have overloaded the learners' cognitive system such that they were not able to retain the lexical items to the expected degree. However, the act of copying sentences freed up learners' attentional resources and allowed them to focus on the linguistic forms.

Another method that has been used to make vocabulary instruction more explicit is dual coding, in which vocabulary information is presented in more than one mode. For example, Boers et al. (2009) look at the effects of dual coding of idioms by English learners in Belgium. Learners were presented with 100 idioms, half of which were accompanied by pictures to illustrate the meaning of the idiom. Learners engaged in two hours of activities with the idioms; however, the results indicated that pictorial elucidation did little to aid learners' retention of the idioms, and in fact, the pictures may have even distracted some of the learners, particularly those who were had visual learning styles.

However, Farley, Ramonda, and Liu (2012) explored the suggestion proposed by the dual coding theory that concrete words would be retained better than abstract ones because of the imagery associated with them. Eighty-seven first-year learners of Spanish at an American university were presented with 12 abstract words and 12 concrete ones. Learners were divided into two groups, one of which received computerized instruction containing L2 vocabulary items and L1 translations, while the other group received the same input accompanied by a picture illustrating the target word. After being presented with the L2 words and translations, learners engaged in a series of tasks in which they had to choice the correct meaning of each word. The results, based on immediate and delayed recall tests in which learners supplied the L1 forms of the L2 words, indicated that for the abstract words, the group with pictures outperformed the group without on both posttests, although there was a loss of retention for both groups. In contrast, for the concrete words there was no effect for the presence of pictures.

Finally, Shen (2010) investigated the effects of single coding (verbal only) and dual coding (verbal plus imagery) on beginning learners of Chinese. Learners were presented with both abstract and concrete words, which were presented orally and in writing for both groups. In addition, one group was provided with visual imagery for the words. Shen found that single and dual coding were equally beneficial for learning concrete words, but dual coding was better for abstract words. It enhanced retention of the shape and meaning of the abstract words but not the sounds of the words.

PEDAGOGICAL IMPLICATIONS

In many cases, the pedagogical implications for vocabulary learning are similar to those for grammar: multiple approaches to instruction are needed for the acquisition of vocabulary in the L2 classroom. Schmitt (2008) argues that having a large vocabulary is an important component of L2 communicative competence, and one of the best ways to rapidly expand learners' vocabulary knowledge is through intentional, explicit learning. Indeed, intentional learning can be an efficient method of learning (Eckerth & Tavakoli, 2012), particularly for beginning L2 learners who might benefit most from large amounts of explicit vocabulary instruction in order to rapidly develop their lexical knowledge.

However, because the amount of class time that can be spent on explicit vocabulary instruction is limited, it is important to provide opportunities for incidental learning through extensive exposure to aural and textual input. There is evidence to suggest that incidental vocabulary learning from extensive reading and exposure to L2 input can be beneficial, particularly for advanced learners. Therefore, learners should be provided with numerous ways of engaging with the L2 for enjoyment. Because of technological advances, learners are no longer limited to reading, and can access audiovisual material (Webb, 2010) as well as authentic input on the Internet. However one caveat about the effects of extensive exposure is that it takes time, and time is often in short supply for instructed learners. Doing extensive reading takes up valuable class time, so there are suggestions to try to engage learners in extensive exposure outside of the classroom as much as possible. Thus, linking in-class activities with out-of-class activities helps maximize benefits for vocabulary acquisition (Webb, 2010).

Another important consideration is having a principled rationale for choosing the lexical items that are selected for vocabulary instruction. Research shows that teachers can target specific frequency levels, domains, and collocations. For example, it seems that the 3,000 most frequent words in a language are especially important, and learners should focus on these. In addition, Boers and Lindstromberg (2009) suggest that the learning of multiword units should be purposive with priority given to those multiword units that learners are likely to encounter most frequently, as well as those that are most helpful for communicative purposes in a variety of contexts that are most relevant for learners. For example, learners in second language contexts might need more social routines than learners in foreign language contexts.

It is also clear that the quality and quantity of learners' encounters with lexical items is important. The more times learners encounter a word, and the deeper they engage with it, the more likely they are to retain it. Also, having learners encounter words in a variety of contexts helps them develop the depth of their vocabulary knowledge. Thus, it would seem that a multi-pronged approach to vocabulary instruction may be called for. Incidental learning through extensive exposure to L2 input can be useful for vocabulary acquisition, but such learning takes a lot of time, something that many classroom L2 learners may not have if they are only studying the L2 a few hours a week. Thus, class time might be better spent engaging in more intentional types of learning, through focus on form and explicit instruction (Laufer, 2005b; Laufer & Rozokski-Roitblat, 2011), while encouraging learners to engage with the L2 through homework and other activities outside the classroom.

ACTIVITIES

Two tests that have been used to assess vocabulary knowledge cofme from Nation (2001) and Qian and Schedl (2004). What aspects of knowledge are being measured here? How effective do you think these tests are for measuring vocabulary? Administer these tests to several English L1 and L2 speakers. Do you think the test is a good measure of proficiency? Why or why not?

Depth of vocabulary knowledge test (Adapted from Qian & Schedl, 2004, pp. 50–51)

Directions: In this test, there are 40 items. Each item looks like this: *sound*

---

logical   healthy   bold   solid   snow   temperature   sleep   dance

Please note:

Some of the words here on the left are similar to the meaning of *sound*.

Some of the words on the right are nouns that can be used after *sound* in phrase of a sentence.

There are eight words above, but only **four** of them are correct. You have to choose which are the four correct words.

On the left, **"logical," "healthy,"** and **"solid"** all share the meaning of "sound."

We do not normally say "sound snow," "sound temperature," or "sound dance," but we often say "sound sleep," so **"sleep"** is the correct answer on this side.

Note: In this example there are three correct answers on the left and one on the right, but in some other items there will be *either* one on the left and three on the right, *or* two on the left and two on the right. Please circle four words for each item.

1. Peak

initial   top   crooked   punctual   time   performance   beginning   speed

2. Accurate

exact   helpful   responsible   reliable   error   event   memory   estimate

3. Dense

transparent   acceptable   compact   thick   hair   view   wood   material

4. Troublesome

annoying irritating dangerous bothersome favor relief weeds opportunity

5. Devoted

dedicated relevant loyal elected follower instance requirement patriot

6. Wild

sound uncultivated uncivilized disappointed calm mob refinement berries

7. Insufficient

ungrateful inexpressible discontented inadequate lack resources amount need

8. Considerable

significant   outright   great   large   change   condition   release   nature

9. Obscure

---

unclear   unknown   vague   old   product   appraisal   origin   demand

---

10. Minute

---

tiny timely incorrect hard adjustment preconception imperfection particle

---

Vocabulary levels test (Adapted from Nation, 2001)

Directions: This is a vocabulary test. You must choose the right word to go with each meaning. Write the number of that word next to its meaning. Some words are in the test to make it more difficult. You do not have to find a meaning for these words.

The 2,000 Word Level

---

1. copy
2. event
3. motor   _____ end or highest point
4. pity   _____ this moves a car
5. profit   _____ thing made to be like another
6. tip

The 3,000 Word Level

---

1. bull
2. champion   _____ formal and serious manner
3. dignity   _____ winner of a sporting event
4. hell   _____ building where valuable
5. museum   objects are shown
6. solution

The 5,000 Word Level

---

1. analysis
2. curb   _____ eagerness
3. gravel   _____ loan to buy a house
4. mortgage   _____ small stones mixed with
5. scar   sand
6. zeal

Academic Vocabulary

1. area	
2. contract	_____ written agreement
3. definition	_____ way of doing something
4. evidence	_____ reason for believing some-
5. method	thing is or is not true
6. role	

The 10,000 Word Level

1. alabaster	
2. chandelier	_____ small barrel
3. dogma	_____ soft white stone
4. keg	_____ tool for shaping wood
5. rasp	
6. tentacle	

Productive Levels Test

Directions: Complete the underlined words. The first one has been done for you.

He was riding a bicycle.

The 2,000 Word Level

1. I'm glad we had this opp_____ to talk.
2. There are a doz_____ eggs in the basket.

The 3,000 Word Level

1. He has a successful car_____ as a lawyer.
2. The thieves threw ac_____ in his face and made him blind.

The 5,000 Word Level

1. Soldiers usually swear an oa_____ of loyalty to their country.
2. The voter placed the ball_____ in the box.

The University Word List Level

1. There has been a recent tr_____ among prosperous families towards a smaller number of children.
2. The ar_____ of his office is 25 square meters.

The 10,000 Word Level

1. The baby is wet. Her dia_____ needs changing.
2. The prisoner was released on par_____.

ADDITIONAL READING

Nation, I. S. P. (2008). *Teaching vocabulary: Strategies and techniques*. Boston: Heinle.
Schmitt, N. (2010). *Researching vocabulary: A vocabulary research manual*. New York: Palgrave Macmillan.

7

The Acquisition of Pronunciation

The acquisition of pronunciation has received less attention from ISLA researchers and theorists than other linguistic areas such as grammar and vocabulary (Derwing & Munro, 2005). Nonetheless, pronunciation is an important component of linguistic communicative competence, and there is a body of research that has addressed this area of L2 acquisition (Lee, Jang, & Plonsky, 2014). In the 1970s and 1980s, pronunciation instruction was influenced by behaviorist theories of learning, which were manifested in ISLA by: (a) contrastive analysis, focusing on similarities and differences between the L1 and L2; and (b) audiolingual drills, entailing extensive amounts of correct repetition of phrases and sentences without much consideration of meaning. Pronunciation was an important aspect of both of these activities, exemplified by the identification of L1/L2 pronunciation sound contrasts (Jenkins, 2004) and the repetition of correct pronunciation through drills. Consequently, the current lack of emphasis on pronunciation in the classroom may have come in part as a reaction to the considerable amount of attention it previously received, at the expense of more meaning-focused classroom activities (Nation, 2011). Finally, the critical period hypothesis, which argues that there are biological and maturational constraints on adult L2 learning, has considerable adverse implications for L2 pronunciation, suggesting that native-like pronunciation may not be attainable for L2 learners unless they have started learning the L2 by the age of 6 or 7 (Long, 2007a). Indeed, some feel that the age of onset of learning is the most important constraint for pronunciation acquisition, and thus there may be little that can be done to facilitate adult L2 learning in this area (Moyer, 2011). Although these factors may partially explain the lack of large-scale pronunciation research, there are a number of researchers who have maintained an interest in the effects of instruction on the acquisition of pronunciation in the L2 classroom, arguing that age of onset of learning is not the only determining factor in learners' pronunciation abilities.

THEORETICAL CONCERNS

Aspects of Pronunciation

Put simply, pronunciation concerns itself with the sounds of a language. There are several aspects of these sounds that need to be considered. In phonology, the phoneme is considered to be the minimal unit of sound, and different languages possess different phonemic inventories. One way to identify a phoneme is to consider minimal pairs of words that differ in only one sound. For instance, the differences between English *sheep* and *ship* or Spanish *pero* and *perro* exemplify different phonemes. In pedagogical terms, these individual sounds are often called segmentals, and individual sounds have been a primary focus of pronunciation instruction. In particular, in contrastive analysis, the identification of the different segmentals between the L1 and L2 was important because the differences indicated areas where L1 transfer might make learning difficult (Jenkins, 2004). For example, the fact that English /r/ is different from the flapped /r/ and trilled /r/ found in Spanish may suggest learning problems for English learners of Spanish. Contrastive analysis suggests that if teachers are aware of these difficulties, they can address them in the classroom.

In addition to segmentals, pronunciation research is also concerned with suprasegmentals, that is the pitch, prosody, and stress given to syllables, words, or phrases (Derwing & Munro, 2005; Jenkins, 2004). Again, different languages use these suprasegmental features in different ways, and proficiency in suprasegmentals may be just as important as segmental proficiency. An example of a suprasegmental prosodic contrast in English is the difference between declarative intonation and interrogative intonation which can change the statement *Austin likes to race* into a question such as *Austin likes to race?* In terms of word stress, the difference can be seen in the two uses of *record* in the following sentence: *Patrick is going to record a record.*

Issues in Pronunciation Acquisition

Perception versus production. An important distinction pertaining to pronunciation in ISLA is that of perception and production, and the relationship between the two. Perception involves learners' ability to identify L2 phonemes and suprasegmental components in the input and to discern contrasts between various L2 phonemes, as well as differences between L2 and L1 phonemes. Production involves the ability to articulate the sounds of the L2.

In terms of L2 learning, it is important to consider the relationship between perception and production (Hanulíková, Dediu, Fang, Banaková, & Huettig, 2012). It is possible that perception and production are independent of each other, and therefore develop independently. Alternatively, it may be the case that perception and production are more closely related, with changes in one affecting changes in the other. One theoretical perspective is that perception precedes production (Jenkins, 2004; Saito, 2013a). Learners first need to recognize sounds in the L2 before they can produce them. Thus, the initial stage of L2 pronunciation acquisition is for learners to begin to be able to perceive the difference between a new L2 phoneme and a similar L1 phoneme, or between two similar L2 phonemes.

Another consideration related to the link between perception and production is if instruction in perception of L2 phonological characteristics can also influence production of those sounds or if production needs its own set of instructional activities. There are those who propose that L2 production problems may stem from issues in perception and that instruction that addresses perception can automatically lead to improvement in production (Derwing & Munro, 2005).

Goals of pronunciation learning. The purported goal of much L2 learning in general is native or near-native proficiency in the L2. However, this goal is particularly controversial with regard to pronunciation. Levis (2005) suggests that two principles have driven research in L2 pronunciation: the nativeness principle, and the intelligibility principle. The nativeness principle holds that native-like pronunciation is the goal for L2 learners, and teachers and learners should strive to achieve this goal. However, many researchers suggest that native-like pronunciation is an unattainable goal for L2 learners (e.g., Jenkins, 2002; Levis, 2005). The effects of age on language development do not allow most learners to achieve native-like proficiency if they started studying the L2 after puberty. Late learners have entrenched motor skills that are accustomed to producing L1 sounds and altering these L1 articulatory patterns may be extremely difficult. A similar issue may arise with perception. Learners' established mental representations of phonemic categories may make it challenging to establish new perceptions of L2 phonemic categories (Moyer, 1999; Saito, 2013b).

Instead of native-like pronunciation, many researchers and theorists suggest that intelligibility should be the guiding principle for L2 pronunciation instruction. Thus, rather than sounding like native speakers, learners should strive for a level of pronunciation proficiency that is comprehensible to others (Levis, 2005). In addition, it is not necessarily the case that accentedness and intelligibility go hand in hand (e.g., Saito, 2011). Reduction in the degree of accentedness can be difficult, particularly for adult L2 learners; however, it is possible for learners to make themselves understand even with a relatively strong foreign accent. The intelligibility principle also maintains that different aspects of pronunciation may play greater or lesser roles in facilitating or hindering intelligibility, and one strand of research has sought to identify those components that are the most important for intelligibility (Levis, 2005). Furthermore, there is more of an expectation that L2 instruction, particularly explicit instruction, can help learners in the production of more comprehensible and intelligible speech (Derwing & Munro, 2005; Saito, 2011).

The issue of pronunciation goals is particularly controversial for L2 English. English has become a de facto international lingua franca, with the result that there are more L2 speakers of English than there are native speakers. Because of this fact, some researchers (e.g., Jenkins, 2002) argue that there should be a set of pronunciation norms based on English as a lingua franca, and not based on standardized British or American accents. The main guideline for pronunciation in English as a lingua franca is comprehensibility, and this, proponents argue, should be the goal of pronunciation instruction. One way to address comprehensibility is to look at the phonological issues that create problems in non-native—non-native interaction, rather than those pertaining to non-native speaker interaction with native speakers (Jenkins, 2002). This norm has been referred to as English as an International Language (Jenkins, 2002).

Age and aptitude. As has been mentioned, an important variable in the acquisition of pronunciation is age. While some may consider age to be the final arbiter of pronunciation success in L2 learning, there are others who feel that age does not account for the entire picture (Levis, 2005; Moyer, 2011) and other factors may also influence the ultimate success of L2 pronunciation learning (Díaz-Campos, 2004; Moyer, 1999). For example, it should be pointed out that it is not just age of onset of learning that is important. If learners begin learning a foreign language early, but do not receive sufficient input over time, they may not be able to take full advantage of the benefits that a younger age of onset provides (Moyer, 1999).

In addition, there are several studies that suggest that high language aptitude may be able to compensate for a late start in L2 learning, even for pronunciation. In fact, phonemic coding ability, the capacity to distinguish between sounds, is one of the components of language aptitude that will be considered in more detail in Chapter 10. However, because there is little that teachers and researchers can do to manipulate age or aptitude for L2 instruction, this chapter will not seek to further explore these issues in relation to instructed SLA.

Identity. Another issue that appears to be related more specifically to pronunciation than to other areas of language is the role that pronunciation plays in establishing and maintaining learners' social identities (Levis, 2005; Nation, 2011). As has been commented on, there is very much a reaction against the nativeness principle in pronunciation that suggests that learners need to conform to native speaker phonological norms; in contrast, there does not seem to be a corresponding negativity towards native speaker norms in the acquisition of L2 grammar or vocabulary. It is not entirely clear why there is such a strong emphasis on the link between identity and pronunciation, and not to grammar and vocabulary. Clearly, L2 learners can rely on non-standard grammatical forms or specific lexical items to mark their identity and solidarity with specific groups, and indeed, interlanguage grammar is an important construct in morphosyntactic development. However, the pervasiveness of pronunciation and identity may have to do with the fact that accent is present in almost everything that an individual says. On the other hand, it is possible, especially for advanced learners, to say a fair number of things without using marked vocabulary or non-standard grammar, which would identify them as an L2 speaker.

Multiple researchers and theorists claim that maintaining a non-native accent can help support an identity separate from the L2 culture, and that this identity may be important and beneficial for learners (e.g., Gatbonton, Trofimovich, & Magid, 2005). Learners may feel that they are rejecting their L1 ethnic affiliation if they identify too strongly with the L2, its culture, and its speakers. Maintaining non-native-like accents that contain L1 influences can signal that learners are not abandoning their origins. The use of accent to express identity may be not be done consciously by learners.

disagree

Not only do individual learners have feelings about their own identities in relation to their L1 and L2 cultures, so do the people around them. Their fellow L1 speakers may accuse individuals with native-like L2 accents of being disloyal to the L1 speaking group. Furthermore, individuals of the L2 speaking culture may exert pressure on learners to uphold a certain identity. Thus, although many learners may outwardly express a desire to sound native-like, the difficulty in doing so, coupled with the limited rewards—or even negative consequences—of achieving such high levels, means that many learners are content, either consciously or unconsciously, to have a level of pronunciation proficiency that enables them to communicate effectively but that still retains L1 phonological influences.

Explicit and implicit pronunciation knowledge. As has been discussed, in research on grammar (e.g., Ellis et al., 2009) and to a lesser extent vocabulary (e.g., Sonbul & Schmitt, 2013) there is a focus on the nature of L2 knowledge, which is often described as implicit and explicit knowledge or declarative and procedural knowledge (e.g., DeKeyser, 2007c). However, with pronunciation there has been less discussion and consideration of these issues. Nonetheless it is worth exploring the status of pronunciation in this regard in order to attempt to provide a theoretical perspective that potentially applies across all linguistic aspects of L2 knowledge.

In the case of L1 speakers, much of their pronunciation knowledge is implicit, especially for those who have had very little interaction with speakers of other dialects or languages. But of course, it is also possible for L1 speakers to have explicit knowledge about pronunciation. For example, many L1 speakers can identify and describe phonological differences among various

L1 accents. For L2 speakers, it is clear that they can possess explicit knowledge about L2 phonology. For instance, many English speaking learners of Spanish know that the flapped and trilled /r/ in Spanish are different from the English /r/ and that these sounds are hard for some learners.

At some point, however, there must be implicit or procedural knowledge that underlies L2 speaking because relying on explicit knowledge to produce coherent, real-time oral production is difficult. Thus, it would seem that L2 learners either: (a) develop implicit knowledge of L2 pronunciation that allows them to produce L2 sounds, or (b) transfer their L1 pronunciation knowledge and skills to their L2 production.

One of the arguments for the transfer of L1 knowledge into L2 production is that learners' articulatory muscles are trained in the L1 patterns, and it can be difficult, particularly for adult L2 learners, to retrain their muscles. In considering the development of implicit/procedural knowledge from explicit/ declarative knowledge, one issue is whether explicitly knowing the phonological rules of a language allows learners to use them in spontaneous production. It would seem here that biology is a mitigating factor in making it difficult for learners to turn declarative knowledge into procedural knowledge.

In terms of L2 pronunciation knowledge, Saito (2013b) suggests that it is first gained in word-sized units. That is to say, learners acquire the phonotactic and prosodic features of individual words initially without analyzing or being aware of the characteristics of each constituent phoneme. Saito goes on to argue that as learners' vocabulary size increases, they begin to pay attention to the individual phonetic characteristics of the L2 input. By paying attention at the individual phoneme level, learners are able to distinguish between minimal pairs and other words that are phonologically similar.

As has been stated in reference to other aspects of language, instruction can help in the development of explicit knowledge. In this case, explicit instruction can produce learners with explicit knowledge about the phonology of the L1. In addition, this knowledge may be able to assist learners' performance during closely monitored tasks, such as careful reading of individual words or sentences; however, explicit knowledge may be less useful for spontaneous use of the L2 in more communicative settings (Kissling, 2013). Indeed, it is not clear to what extent explicit instruction allows students to transfer what they have learned in the classroom to their spontaneous speech outside the classroom (Saito, 2013a). Again, the role of explicit instruction in terms of developing communicative competence is controversial. Teaching learners about Mandarin tones or French nasals could alert them to be on the lookout for those sounds in the input they receive and the output they produce. Indeed, such noticing potential is one argument for explicit instruction. It may also be the case that such declarative knowledge is necessary to develop procedural knowledge.

Instruction and Pronunciation Acquisition

Unlike with grammar and vocabulary, there has not been a large emphasis in ISLA on implicit or incidental acquisition of pronunciation. Thus there will be no section in this chapter on it. Instead, this chapter will begin with focus on form as the most implicit type of instruction, followed by more explicit types.

Focus on form. In addition to addressing morphosyntactic and lexical aspects of language, focus on form can also draw attention to L2 phonology (e.g., Ellis et al., 2001a). Indeed, negotiation for meaning may occur as a result of a communication breakdown caused by phonological errors. In addition to being addressed in negotiation for meaning, pronunciation can be the topic of brief attention during the context of meaning-focused interaction. For example, learners might receive corrective feedback on their phonological errors (Ellis et al., 2001a; Saito, 2013b), or they might ask a question about the pronunciation of a certain word. Focus on form enables learners to notice phonological forms as they are using them.

Explicit instruction. Of course, explicit instruction is another option for learning pronunciation. In fact, Saito (2013a) argues that over the past 20 years, pronunciation teaching has been largely explicit and decontextualized from meaning-focused contexts, consisting of phonetic transcriptions, minimal pair drills, and imitation of appropriate models. One of the central aspects of pronunciation instruction has typically been the explicit teaching of the phonetic properties of the L2, particularly in terms of the segmental components of the language and their manner of articulation (Kissling, 2013). In addition, explicit pronunciation instruction has often emphasized the differences between the learners' L1 and L2.

Another component of explicit instruction can be repetition (Trofimovich & Gatbonton, 2006). Perhaps more so than in other areas of language, repetition drills have been a common practice in pronunciation instruction. The drill and repeat methodology is a pedagogical method of audiolingualism. However, in the past, this type of repetition was often decontextualized and lacking any focus on meaning. Currently, skill acquisition theory makes an argument for repetition and practice as a means of developing procedural knowledge, but it places this practice in a larger context that has more concern with semantic content than has often been the norm with this type of instruction (DeKeyser, 2007b).

Technology. Although applicable to all areas of instruction, technology is seen as particularly conducive for the acquisition of pronunciation (Blake, 2011; Derwing & Munro, 2005; Jenkins, 2004). Technology has been used in a number of ways in pronunciation learning. One early use was to enable learners to practice hearing the phonological properties, either segmental or suprasegmental, of the L2. Learners would listen to recordings of speakers, and often repeat what they heard. In this way, learners had access to different models of pronunciation, something that is particularly important in a foreign language context where there is little opportunity to hear the language. More recently, technology has been used in other types of pedagogic activities. For example, computer programs can present learners with visual representations of sounds, such as waveforms and pitch contours, in an effort to help learners visualize pitch and sound duration. There are also computer programs that provide 3D animations that show the actions of the lips and tongue during pronunciation. These types of activities are based in the explicit instruction tradition that is common to pronunciation.

One other use of technology that relies more on a focus on form perspective is the use of speech recording and speech recognition software. Learners can record their own utterances, and the software can provide learners with feedback regarding the accuracy of their production. Some programs also allow learners to compare their own production with that of native speakers. These types of activities assume that learners will be able to notice the differences between their own production and that of the speakers on the recordings. In addition, the corrective feedback that can be provided by some programs constitutes negative evidence, which is argued to draw learners' attention to linguistic form thereby facilitating acquisition.

EMPIRICAL EVIDENCE

The evidence concerning pronunciation instruction is generally positive about its effects on improving L2 learners' perception and production abilities; however, as with other types of instruction, there are some variables that seem to increase the effectiveness of instruction (Kissling, 2013). Relevant studies that have investigated the effects of various types of focus on form and explicit instruction will now be explored.

Focus on Form

Focus on form research has not been primarily concerned with pronunciation. Moreover, much pronunciation instruction research has investigated the effects of explicit instruction; nevertheless, there have been a few studies that have employed more implicit types of instruction when exploring the effects of instruction on pronunciation ability. Generally, these studies have investigated the effects of corrective feedback in comparison to other types of instruction.

For example, Dlaska and Krekeler (2013) compared the effects that incidental corrective feedback and listening activities had on improving the comprehensibility of L2 learners' speech. They divided 169 adult learners of

German into two groups. One group recorded themselves while reading a text, after which they listened to their recording. Subsequently, they listened to a recording of the teacher reading the same text, and they were asked to compare their own recording with that of the teacher. The feedback group also recording themselves and listened to their recordings, but before they listened to the teacher's recording, learners were provided with a two- to four-minute interactive feedback session in which the teacher provided information about pronunciation errors that learners had made. Dlaska and Krekeler found that corrective feedback was more effective than listening activities alone in improving the comprehensibility of learners' production, and they suggest that in many instances, learners may need to have negative evidence in order to notice that their own phonological production is not target-like.

In a study by Saito and Lyster (2012), form-focused instruction with and without corrective feedback was explored. One group of Japanese learners of English was provided with meaning-oriented activities that incorporated the targeted form, English /r/, in the input. A second group participated in the same activities, but also received corrective feedback on their pronunciation errors. A control group was also included. Using a series of word reading, sentence reading, and picture description tasks, Saito and Lyster found that form-focused tasks alone were not sufficient for L2 development, but providing learners' pronunciation errors with corrective feedback resulted in improved performance. They suggest, again, that the negative evidence is helpful because it draws learners' attention away from the whole word and focuses it on individual sounds.

Explicit Instruction

In many cases studies have indicated that explicit instruction can have a positive impact on learners' pronunciation abilities. The most comprehensive evidence comes from Lee et al.'s (2014) meta-analysis of 86 studies investigating the effects of pronunciation instruction. Overall, they found that instruction had a large effect on learners' pronunciation abilities; additionally, they found some noticeable, although not statistically significant, differences in moderator variables influencing the effects of instruction. Variation related to the type of instruction included: (a) greater effects for instruction involving corrective feedback, (b) greater effects for instruction that was more than four hours in duration, and (c) lesser effects for computer-based instruction than for teacher-led instruction. The context of instruction also played a factor in the effectiveness of instruction, with larger effects found in second language and laboratory contexts than in foreign language or classroom contexts, respectively. Furthermore, pronunciation instruction was more effective in high schools than university or language institute settings, and intermediate learners appeared to benefit less than did beginner or advanced learners. All aspects of pronunciation benefitted roughly equally from instruction, although instruction targeting word stress had the highest effect size. Finally, scores on tests of controlled production were generally higher than those on free response measures.

While Lee et al.'s study provides a useful overview of trends in pronunciation instruction, it is also informative to examine some of the individual studies in this area, particularly in relation to the types of explicit instruction that have been provided. Several studies have investigated the impact of explicit knowledge of the phonological structures of the L2. For example, Al-Jasser (2008) provided explicit information about the phonetic properties of the L2 in an attempt to help Arabic-speaking learners of English with word segmentation, which involves hearing the division between words in the incoming speech stream. Al-Jasser instructed learners regarding the consonants clusters that were permissible at the beginning and end of English words and those that were not permissible. In the treatment, learners were told about these phonotactic constraints and then were given a list of 12 sound clusters that cannot appear in the onset or coda of English words. Al-Jasser claims that providing this explicit information allowed learners to notice the features in the input, something that they might not do otherwise. Indeed, his treatment group improved significantly in their ability to segment English words.

In another study, Venkatagiri and Levis (2007) investigated the relationship between learners' general phonological awareness and the comprehensibility of their speech. Phonological awareness was defined as 'the conscious knowledge of the sounds, syllable structure, phonotactics and prosody of the target language' (p. 265). The researchers found a strong positive correlation between phonological awareness and learners' comprehensibility scores, which they suggest points to the benefits of providing explicit information about the phonological features of the L1 and L2.

A number of recent studies by Kazuya Saito have investigated the effects of explicit instruction together with focus on form on several different phonological features for Japanese learners of English. Saito (2011) investigated the effects of instruction on a number of English-specific segmentals. A treatment group received four hours of explicit training regarding the pronunciation of eight English segmentals. Saito used native English speaking raters to assess the comprehensibility and accentedness of learners' production during two tasks: a sentence-reading task to measure learners' pronunciation in a controlled context, and a picture-description task for more spontaneous production. He found that explicit phonetics instruction had a significant effect on learners' comprehensibility, especially in a sentence-reading task; however, learners were not judged as having a reduction in foreign accent, indicating that intelligibility and accentedness were not identical.

In another study, Saito (2013b) looked at the effects of form-focused instruction and recasts in the acquisition of English /r/ by Japanese learners. Of his two treatment groups, one received four hours of form-focused instruction consisting of explicit instruction, structured input, typographically enhanced input, and focused tasks, all targeting English /r/. The second group received the same form-focused instruction, but in addition, they were given recasts in response to errors in production of the target structure. There was also a control group that did not receive any pronunciation instruction. Overall, the form-focused instruction led to improvements in both perception and production tests. However, the effects were seen primarily on words that had been used during the treatments. In contrast, the form-focused instruction plus recasts group improved their performance on familiar words as well as words that had not been encountered during the treatment. Based on his results, Saito concludes that form-focused instruction can have a positive effect on phonological perception and production, both in controlled and spontaneous contexts. In addition, he argues that recasts can draw learners' attention to phonetic aspects of their L2 production, and in fact, recasts may be more successful for phonological errors than for other types of errors, with previous studies (e.g., Mackey, Gass, & McDonough, 2000) finding that learners are more likely to accurately perceive corrective feedback provided to phonological errors than corrective feedback provided to morphosyntactic errors.

In yet another study targeting English /r/ for Japanese learners, Saito (2013a) investigated the effects of the provision of explicit pronunciation information before form-focused instruction. The explicit instruction consisted of exaggerated models of the phonological forms, as well as information about the manner of articulation. The form-focused instruction entailed opinion gap activities with the target forms enhanced. An acoustic analysis was performed on pretest and posttest data collected from both a controlled and spontaneous production task. Form-focused instruction appeared to impact development on items used during instruction, but the form-focused instruction group that also received explicit information not only improved on familiar items but was also able to generalize to new contexts.

However, not all studies have found an effect for instruction. For example, Kissling (2013) investigated the effects of explicit phonetics instruction for English-speaking learners of Spanish. Instruction targeted eight sounds that such learners find problematic, and included four computer-delivered modules. The first one focused on articulatory phonetics in general, while the other three provided explicit information about the phonemes targeted in the study. A comparison group also completed computerized tasks that provided input, practice, and feedback, but no explicit phonetics instruction. A production test involved learners reading a list of words and phrases, with an acoustic analysis conducted on the resulting data. Results indicated that both groups improved equally on the immediate posttest, leading Kissling to speculate that input, practice, and feedback may be the most important components of instruction, rather than the provision of explicit information.

PEDAGOGICAL IMPLICATIONS

Previous researchers have argued that L2 teachers receive little training in pronunciation instruction, and that much of what they do is based on ideology and intuitions (Levis, 2005). Nevertheless, research can support several recommendations regarding pronunciation instruction. First, the conclusion is that, in general, pronunciation instruction can be beneficial, if not for erasing L1 phonological influences, then at least for improving learners' comprehensibility (Derwing & Munro, 2005; Díaz-Campos, 2004; Lee, Jang, & Plonsky, 2014). Therefore, teachers may wish to incorporate more pronunciation instruction into their teaching. For example, Saito (2103b) suggests that learners' awareness and perception of new L2 sounds needs to be increased, and learners also need to be given the opportunity to practice producing those sounds. Additionally, some researchers argue that explicit instruction is necessary for learners to achieve high levels of pronunciation accuracy (Moyer, 1999).

As has been stressed in many chapters already, it is important to be clear on the goal for pronunciation learning. In this regard, teachers may wish to stress to learners that native-like proficiency is not a realistic goal for most learners, and that comprehensibility is a better goal to strive for (Saito, 2011). In addition, if teachers recognize that native-like proficiency might not be desirable for the establishment of learners' identities, this may help them understand any potential resistance to native-like pronunciation. Also if learners are made aware of the role of pronunciation and accent in the maintenance of their identities, they may be able to decide more consciously what their own personal goals should be, as well as to understand the social pressures that may be exerted upon them (Gatbonton et al., 2005).

Next, teachers may wish to decide if they wish to incorporate explicit pronunciation instruction, as well as more implicit types of pronunciation focus, such as corrective feedback. Both appear to be helpful for learners, but if teachers already employ numerous meaning-focused tasks, it may be a more efficient use of class time to plan to incorporate brief attention to specific phonological features, as well as to address those that occur incidentally during the tasks.

ACTIVITIES

Here is some of the explicit phonetics information that Kissling (2013) provided in her study on Spanish pronunciation of native speakers of English. Kissling did not find any additional effect on learner pronunciation for the provision of this type of explicit instruction. Why might this be the case? What impact might we expect such information to have? How could this information be modified so that it would have an impact on learners' L2 pronunciation abilities?

> *The Spanish sounds /b, d, g/ are occlusive consonants. We explained in Module II that an occlusive consonant is articulated by creating an obstacle in the articulatory tract and letting air build up behind this obstacle: this air is then released suddenly.*
>
> *Another group of consonants are fricative consonants. These sounds are created by forming only a partial obstruction in the articulatory tract, rather than a complete closure. In articulating fricative consonants, the air never stops completely but rather passes through this partial obstruction with friction. The English and Spanish sounds /s/ and /f/, for example, are fricative sounds. You will notice that you slightly modify the airflow with your tongue or lips and teeth, but you never stop it completely as with the occlusive consonants. (In fact, some people call occlusive consonants "stops" because the air stops, while they call fricatives consonants "continuants," because the air continues without stopping.)*
>
> *This module presents the /b, d, g/ sounds along with their fricative variants /ß, ð, ɣ/, which occur in certain required contexts, as will be explained further in the next sections.*
>
> —(Kissling, 2013, p. 741)

ADDITIONAL READING

Hansen Edwards, J., & Zampini, M. (2008). *Phonology and second language acquisition*. Amsterdam: John Benjamins.

8

The Acquisition of Pragmatics

The acquisition of pragmatics probably figures only minimally in many learners' minds when they contemplate L2 learning. And yet pragmatics, the use of language in social contexts, is an important component of communicative competence that has begun to receive a considerable amount of attention in ISLA (Bardovi-Harlig, 2013). The acquisition of L2 pragmatics is considered to be one of the most difficult and latest acquired aspects of L2 learning (Bardovi-Harlig & Vellenga, 2012). As a result, it could be argued that it is important to help learners acquire L2 pragmatics in instructed contexts; however, attention to pragmatics often does not occur in the classroom. In addition, while it is possible for learners to receive considerable amounts of grammatical, lexical, and phonological input, especially in communicative classes, input regarding pragmatics is much more constrained in the classroom because the contextualized nature of pragmatics depends on the social situation, and yet L2 learners, especially foreign language learners, often find themselves in only one social context in which the L2 is used, i.e., the L2 classroom. Thus, there is little opportunity for learners to observe or to use language in different social contexts. As a result it can be even more crucial for teachers to intentionally highlight L2 pragmatic usage.

A common difficulty in acquiring L2 pragmatics is that learners often transfer their L1 pragmatic norms into the L2. Thus, they may be using language that is socially appropriate for the context in their L1, but not in their L2. Such a lack of L2 pragmatic skill is often viewed not as a linguistic deficit when the pragmatic rules are broken, but as a character trait—the speaker is rude, arrogant, pushy, et cetera (Nguyen, 2013). Thus, learners' L2 pragmatics errors outside of the classroom may have larger social consequences than errors in other linguistic areas.

THEORETICAL CONCERNS

Aspects of Pragmatics

Pragmatics has been defined as the way that individuals use language in social contexts; in other words, the study of 'how-to-say-what-to-whom-when' (Bardovi-Harlig, 2013, p. 68). Other definitions include 'the ability to communicate and interpret meaning in social interactions' (Taguchi, 2011, p. 289) and 'the study of how people accomplish their goals and attend to interpersonal relationships while using language' (Rose & Kasper, 2001, p. 2). As such, pragmatic competence is viewed as an essential component of L2 proficiency, although it is seen as distinct from grammatical, discourse, and strategic competencies (Taguchi, 2011).

Pragmatics can be broken down into two general categories: pragmalinguistics and sociopragmatics. Pragmalinguistics refers to the linguistic resources that are available to learners when they want to convey pragmatic intent, such as respect or politeness, or when they want to use language to accomplish things, such as making requests or giving compliments (Bardovi-Harlig, 2013; Félix-Brasdefer & Cohen, 2012). In other words, pragmalinguistics is comprised of the lexical, morphosyntactic, and to a lesser extent phonological, resources that learners possess and use to convey and interpret meaning in specific social settings. For example, Korean has a system of honorific morphemes which speakers use when addressing or speaking about someone to indicate the social relationship vis-à-vis one another (Ahn, 2013). Knowledge of these morphemes constitutes pragmalinguistic knowledge. Another example pertains to English modal verbs, which imply varying degrees of obligation. Thus, *Winona must study* conveys a stronger degree of obligation than *Winona should study*. Pragmalinguistic knowledge is comprised of the knowledge of what pragmatic meanings these linguistic forms convey.

The other component of pragmatics is sociopragmatics, which consists of an individual's knowledge about the contexts in which specific pragmalinguistic features should be used (Taguchi, 2011). Individuals have a sense of formality, politeness, and/or respect that a specific situation requires. Thus, in the case of Korean honorifics, sociopragmatic knowledge would enable L2 learners of Korean to assess the social context they are in and chose the appropriate honorific morphemes to use when speaking about someone older as opposed to a close family member. For English modals, sociopragmatic knowledge entails knowing the degree of obligation that is appropriate in a given social context when making a request of a friend (*Can I borrow a pencil?*) or of a professor (*May I have an extension for turning in this essay?*).

Having one type of pragmatic knowledge does not necessarily imply knowledge of the other. For example, a learner may have pragmalinguistic knowledge without sociopragmatic knowledge, in which case learners know the pragmatic force that linguistic forms convey, but they may be unclear on when those specific occasions occur. In the case of Korean honorific morphemes, learners may know which forms denote higher and more formal status, but they may be uncertain as to how to determine relative social status in a given situation. On the other hand, it is possible to have sociopragmatic but not pragmalinguistic knowledge. In this case, learners are aware of the social demands of a situation, but they do not know which linguistic forms would express the appropriate level of politeness. For example, learners may realize that they need to use more polite forms when making a request of a professor, but they may not know which modal reflects the stance they wish to take.

Speech acts. Related to both pragmalinguistics and sociopragmatics are speech acts, which are the actions that speakers can perform with language (Loewen & Reinders, 2011). For example, language is used to make requests, give compliments, make complaints, and accept invitations, among other things. Pragmatics research has investigated how both L1 and L2 speakers accomplish these activities, examining closely the ways in which language is used and modified in various social contexts. For example, Taguchi (2006) investigated the perceived appropriacy of various means of students requesting to reschedule an exam. Although often accompanied by additional discourse moves, the basic request ranged from *Is there any chance, like, maybe I can take [the exam] earlier or later or some other time?* (p. 525) to *I want to take the test another day* (p. 527).

Issues in Pragmatics Acquisition

Explicit and implicit pragmatics knowledge. Just as with other linguistic areas, the nature of pragmatics knowledge is an issue that has been considered, although to a lesser extent than for other linguistic areas, in ISLA. Clearly, some pragmatics knowledge is explicit and declarative. SLA researchers and L2 teachers can provide specific information about the pragmatic requirements for specific social contexts (Bardovi-Harlig, 2013).

Presumably, however, some pragmatics knowledge is also learned implicitly and stored as implicit knowledge (Hulstijn, 2002). That is to say, speakers do not always have to think consciously about what pragmatic forms to use in a given social contexts. From another theoretical perspective, one could argue that declarative knowledge of pragmatics can become proceduralized. Taguchi (2011) discusses the declarative knowledge that learners might have in relation to both pragmalinguistic and sociopragmatic aspects of pragmatics. She goes on question whether or not instruction helps promote the development of procedural knowledge as well as declarative knowledge, indicated in fluency and accuracy respectively.

Again, much less consideration has been given to this topic in comparison to grammar or vocabulary, but Bardovi-Harlig (2013) argues that ISLA researchers are interested in the development of implicit pragmatics knowledge, even if they might not state it so clearly. She maintains that the use of conversations and simulated conversations to teach and assess L2 pragmatics knowledge demonstrates the field's interest in implicit pragmatic knowledge. Language production in such types of activities typically draws on implicit and procedural knowledge as learners produce language relatively spontaneously. However, it is possible for learners in these situations to monitor their production and pause when there is uncertainty about the pragmatic requirements of the situation or the linguistic forms necessary to adequately fulfill those requirements. Furthermore, Bardovi-Harlig (2013) claims that explicit pragmatic knowledge has been largely overlooked in the development of tasks designed to elicit language samples for empirical studies. This may be due in part to two reasons: native speakers are not aware of much of their own pragmatic behavior, and there is no tradition of explicit pragmatic teaching the way there is in grammar or vocabulary teaching.

Similar to the other areas of language, the ability to measure the types of L2 learners' pragmatic knowledge depends on the instruments that are used. Many commonly used pragmatics tasks might involve explicit knowledge (Bardovi-Harlig, 2013). For example, discourse completion tasks, in which learners are given various scenarios and asked to judge or provide the most appropriate discourse, are generally not time-pressured, allowing learners time to reflect on and access their explicit knowledge. In contrast, free production tasks often occur in real time, and require learners to rely more on their implicit L2 knowledge (Bardovi-Harlig, 2013).

Developmental stages. One issue of concern to pragmatics researchers relates to the possible developmental nature of pragmatics knowledge. Most research studies investigating pragmatic knowledge employ cross-sectional designs in which data are taken from learners at only one point in time, and any claims made regarding gains across proficiency levels are made based on comparing different levels of learners. In order to better assess the existence of developmental stages for pragmatics, it is important to employ longitudinal studies that follow learners over a longer period of time and chronicle their development sequences (Bardovi-Harlig, 2013). However, this has not been a common practice in pragmatics research (Belz, 2007).

When considering the development of pragmatics knowledge, Kasper and Rose (2002) proposed a five-stage process for the development for L2 requests. The first stage is the prebasic stage in which learners are dependent upon the situational context and perhaps a few lexical items to make their request. At this stage, learners do not have productive use of syntax, and they are not able to use language to address the social context and relationships. The second stage is the formulaic stage in which learners have specific phrases that they rely on to make their requests or to perform other speech acts. Learners have not analyzed the individual components of the formulaic chunks; instead they use them as a whole unit. An example might be *Can I have an X?* Learners can use the phrase as is, but they cannot alter it except for the object being requested. The third stage involves unpacking the formulas and beginning to analyze these formulaic chunks so that learners can manipulate the phrases as the context might dictate. Furthermore, there is a shift toward more indirectness at this stage. Stage four is pragmatic expansion in which learners add new pragmalinguistic forms to their repertoire. Learners are also able moderate the force of their utterances with the use of downgraders or upgraders, and they can also use more complex syntax. The final stage is fine-tuning in which leaners have considerable control in regulating the pragmalinguistic features of their requests or other speech acts to best reflect their understanding of the demands of the situation.

In addition, to the above proposed stages, Bardovi-Harlig (2013) suggests that it is important to consider how development in areas of grammar and vocabulary leads to greater pragmatic expression, particularly since pragmalinguistics is closely tied to learners' proficiency in grammar and vocabulary. Similarly, Félix-Brasdefer and Cohen (2012) stress that teachers should make clear the links between grammatical structures and the functions that they perform in meaning-focused communication. One example that they provide regards the use of English progressive aspect and the conditional to express politeness, deference, and respect when making appropriate requests in formal settings (e.g., *I was wondering if you would write a letter of recommendation for me* versus *Write me a recommendation letter*).

L1 transfer. One issue related to pragmatics is negative L1 transfer, which occurs when learners try to use their L1 pragmatic features in the L2 (Félix-Brasdefer, 2004; Huth, 2006). Learners have been found to rely on their L1 pragmatics knowledge in a variety of areas, including the frequency, order, content, and perception of pragmatic strategies. As an example, research has investigated the ways in which speakers react to compliments. In some cultures it is polite to disagree with compliments, and thereby minimize self-praise; however, in other cultures it is acceptable for individuals to agree with a compliment (Huth, 2006). The way in which learners transfer these L1 strategies into their L2 may have negative social consequences, for instance if the person giving the compliment perceives the learner as proud rather than humble based upon a dispreferred response to the compliment.

Perception versus production. Another issue that is considered in pragmatics acquisition is the difference between perception and production. Rose (2005) argues that most research on pragmatics instruction has investigated the teaching of the production of specific features, with much less attention given to pragmatic comprehension. Félix-Brasdefer (2004) also stresses that pragmatics research and instruction need to consider both perception and production. The majority of studies have examined learners' abilities to produce politeness strategies in target-like ways, but little research has investigated perception.

Social values. One of the issues related to pragmatics is that it involves learning behaviors that reflect and instantiate the values of the societies in which the L2 is spoken (Taguchi, 2011). Thus, similar to pronunciation, which is closely linked to learners' identities and ethnic group affiliations (Levis, 2005; Gatbonton, Trofimovich, & Magid, 2005), the use of pragmatics can show affiliation or detachment from L2 values. For example, some speakers from societies with less social hierarchy may not always feel comfortable when having to mark social relationships grammatically. There are two issues here. One is whether or not learners are aware of these social values, and the other is whether or not they wish to follow the L2 cultural norms (Huth, 2006). Learners may feel that they do not want to embrace the native-like use of pragmatic features, but instead they may use their L2 resources to express other cultural orientations that are important to them.

Instruction and Pragmatics Acquisition

One of the issues that seems to be raised more frequently with pragmatics than with other areas of language is whether instruction is necessary at all (Jeon & Kaya, 2006; Rose, 2005). Kasper and Rose (2002) argue that instruction is necessary because 'pragmatic functions and relevant contextual factors are often not salient to learners and so not likely to be noticed despite prolonged exposure' (p. 237). Furthermore, pragmatics is hard enough to pick up in second language environments where learners presumably have opportunities to interact with native speakers outside of the classroom. However, in foreign language environments, the classroom may be the only context in which learners are exposed to the language, and thus their experience with pragmatics during social interaction is virtually nonexistent (Félix-Brasdefer & Cohen, 2012; Jeon & Kaya, 2006). The variety of social settings that learners can experience in the classroom is quite limited, and although teachers may employ role plays or other such activities to try to simulate various social settings, there is concern that the lack of real-world consequences renders such activities less than ideal (Félix-Brasdefer & Cohen, 2012).

Furthermore, the pragmatics input that learners may receive tends to be constrained in frequency, variety, and authenticity. In fact, pragmatics materials can be modified or structured in ways that do not reflect native-like pragmatic norms. Nevertheless, pragmatics instruction in the classroom can be more efficient for learning than mere exposure alone (Jeon & Kaya, 2006). On the other hand, some researchers (e.g., Belz, 2007; Belz & Kinginger, 2003) suggest that some aspects of pragmatics (e.g., the use of formal and informal second-person pronouns in languages such as German and Spanish) cannot be taught only by rules in the classroom, because the social roles within the classroom are limited and learners do not get exposure to the ways in which these forms are used in real life. In addition, classroom learners do not get frequent opportunities to practice and use various pragmatics features in meaningful interactions.

As with other areas of language, the options for pragmatics instruction range from implicit to explicit, and questions have been raised about the effects of different types of instruction (Belz, 2007; Jeon & Kaya, 2006; Rose, 2005). Implicit instruction does not provide learners with explicit information about pragmatics; rather, it provides learners with input and practice opportunities (Taguchi, 2011). Several researchers have noted that focus on form and the noticing hypothesis provide theoretical support for more implicit types of pragmatics instruction because the context is so important for pragmatics. Thus, noticing the relationship between form and meaning within a specific context can provide learners with information about not only grammar and vocabulary (and to a lesser extent pronunciation), but also about the contexts in which such forms are socially appropriate (Jeon & Kaya, 2006; Taguchi, 2011).

Although focus on form can be an option for pragmatics instruction, explicit instruction is also a possibility. Explicit instruction often takes a PPP form, with information about a pragmatic feature being provided to the learners, who then have a chance to engage in more or less controlled production of the forms. Taguchi (2011) also contends that Input Processing and Skill Acquisition Theory have supported pragmatic research, with the latter proposing that learners start with declarative knowledge of pragmatics, which becomes proceduralized through practice with the target forms.

In addition to instruction inside the classroom, one area of research that has received considerable attention in pragmatics development is the role of study abroad opportunities because of the possibility to provide what many researchers argue is not available inside the traditional L2 classroom, namely exposure to language in a variety of social contexts. Thus the effects of exposure to input, particularly in study abroad will also be considered here. However, Bardovi-Harlig (2013) suggests that, in addition to the length of time spent abroad, there are other factors that need to be considering regarding L2 pragmatics learning on study abroad. For instance, lower proficiency learners might not be able to take advantage of the opportunities to interact in the L2 environment; thus, longer duration might not always be better if there is limited interaction with L2 speakers.

Explicit instruction. Unlike other areas of language, where it seems that L1 children receive little overt instruction or corrective feedback, pragmatics is an area of language in which children are often taught rules and are instructed in the politeness system of the L1 culture (Pearson, 2006). This fact, coupled with a lack of naturalistically occurring pragmatics input in the classroom, makes a good argument for including explicit pragmatics instruction in the L2 classroom. Indeed, explicit pragmatics instruction seems to be the norm, if pragmatics is taught at all (Jeon & Kaya, 2006).

Explicit instruction can involve activities such as output practice, explicit correction, as well as the provision of metapragmatic information (Nguyen, 2013). If pragmatics instruction occurs at all, it tends to be explicit, involving: (1) teacher-fronted instruction on pragmalinguistics or sociopragmatics, (2) complete disclosure of the goals of instruction to the learner, (3) frequent use of metalanguage and metapragmatic information, (4) unidirectional flow of information from teacher to students, and (5) structural exercises (Jeon & Kaya, 2006).

One argument for teaching pragmatics explicitly is that the greater cognitive involvement resulting from explicit instruction makes it more successful than implicit instruction for L2 pragmatic learning (Takahashi, 2010). Additionally, teaching metapragmatic awareness is argued to be helpful in developing learners' ability to notice and analyze pragmatic phenomena, particularly as they relate to the linguistic forms that are used to express specific cultural norms in various situations. Metapragmatic information can also help learners notice the difference between their own pragmatic norms and those of the L2 (McConachy, 2013). In fact, House (1996) concludes that metapragmatic information is essential in order for learners to avoid negative pragmatic transfer, and to promote the increase of learners' pragmatic fluency by promoting the use of more and more varied pragmatics features.

As with other areas of language, the way in which proficiency and development are measured is important for the conclusions that can be drawn about the learning of pragmatics. The types of data collection methods that are commonly used include written and oral discourse completion task, elicitation through role plays, and audio recordings of authentic conversation (Bardovi-Harlig, 2013; Jeon & Kaya, 2006). One benefit of more constrained measures such as discourse completion tasks is that they provide data that are comparable across learners; in comparison, free conversation is high in construct validity and authenticity, but it may not provide data that can be compared across learners. Unsurprisingly, open-ended methods of data collection tend to result in longer, more complex and richer data than discourse completion tasks. Furthermore, the use of control groups and delayed testing is rare in instructed pragmatics research (Jeon & Kaya, 2006).

EMPIRICAL EVIDENCE

A few studies have looked at the developmental process of pragmatics acquisition. For example, Félix-Brasdefer (2007) conducted a cross-sectional study of the development of requests of three proficiency levels of learners of Spanish in a foreign language context. Learners engaged in a series of role plays in which the social distance and power relationship between the characters was manipulated. Félix-Brasdefer found that the beginning learners employed mostly direct requests regardless of the social distance or power relationships in the scenarios, suggesting that these lower-level learners had limited pragmalinguistic resources. In contrast, the intermediate and advanced learners demonstrated a strong preference for conventionally indirect requests across the situations. Furthermore, there was a decrease in direct strategies as proficiency increased. Félix-Brasdefer argues that these learners' sociopragmatic norms were already developed from their L1, but their pragmalinguistic abilities showed differences according to proficiency levels. However, in spite of greater pragmalinguistic skill by the higher proficiency learners, Félix-Brasdefer argues that the requests were still not target-like and that pragmatics instruction in the classroom is needed.

Exposure. Rather than investigating explicit instruction, some studies have investigated the effects of exposure alone. Belz and Kinginger (2003) investigated learners' use of German formal and informal second-person pronoun forms. They used emails and synchronous written chat to set up language partners in the US and Germany as part of a class assignment. There was no explicit intervention. Students simply interacted with their peers. Belz and Kinginger conclude that learners' participation in these communicative activities leads to an increase in appropriate pronoun use over time. This study demonstrates that mere exposure helped with an aspect of pragmatics use. In addition, it showed how technology could be used to facilitate extra input and output practice outside of the classroom, in authentic situations with native speakers of the L2.

Regarding the effects of time spent in an L2 environment, Taguchi (2013) investigated the effects of study abroad and proficiency on learners' pragmatic production. She examined three groups of Japanese university students studying at an English university in Japan. One group had lower proficiency and no study abroad experience, while the other two groups had higher proficiency, but one had study abroad experience while the other did not. Students completed oral discourse completion tasks in which they were asked to respond to situations in which native speakers often provided routine phrases. For example, when asking for the time, native English speakers often ask *Do you know the time?* or *Can you tell me what time it is?* In turning down offers of help from a salesclerk, common responses are *I'm fine* or *That's alright.* Taguchi found that both proficiency and study abroad experience impacted the appropriacy of learners' production, as well as their speech rate and amount of planning time. She argues that higher proficiency in itself may not lead to pragmatic improvement; rather, the exposure brought about by study abroad

contributed to learners' pragmatic skills by being in an L2 speaking environment in which it is possible to have considerable exposure to a variety of social
situations and contexts. Learners can gain awareness of these routines and
practice them as well. Taguchi argues that higher proficiency may give learners
better pragmalinguistic ability, but study abroad exposure helps them put it to
use because they can observe and practice in real-world contexts. However,
it should be noted that none of the learners achieved native level proficiency.

Explicit Instruction

In general, explicit instruction is considered to more beneficial for the acquisition of pragmatics than mere exposure to input (Kasper & Rose, 1999; Rose,
2005; Taguchi, 2011). In addition, explicit instruction is considered to be
better than implicit instruction (Rose, 2005). In a meta-analysis of 13 quasi-
experimental studies of pragmatics instruction conducted between 1984 and
2003, Jeon and Kaya (2006) conclude that instruction was beneficial for learners
in comparison to no instruction. They also suggest that explicit instruction
was better than implicit instruction, although the differences between these
two types of instruction were not substantial.

Additional studies have also found positive effects for explicit instruction. For
example, Takimoto (2006) focused on teaching lexical/phrasal downgraders and
syntactic downgraders in English request forms to ESL students in Japan. One
group of learners performed structured input activities, while another group, in
addition to conducting the structured input activities, received explicit feedback
on their judgments of the politeness of the requests. Both groups participated
in four 40-minute treatment sessions over a two-week period. There was also a
control group. In both the treatment and testing stages of the study, Takimoto
varied the power relationship, degree of imposition of the request, and social
distance to achieve sociolinguistic variables that could not otherwise be achieved
in the classroom. He used a discourse completion task, a role play, and an accept-
ability judgment test to measure learners' development. The results indicated
that both treatment groups improved significantly in comparison to the control
group; however, they did not differ from each other, suggesting that the addition
of feedback did not provide additional learning benefits. The gains were also
evident on the delayed test four weeks after the treatment.

Another study, by Huth (2006), examined the use of compliment sequences
between German native speakers and English speaking learners of German.
He provided learners with explicit instruction by involving them in a variety
of activities: (1) a general in-class discussion about conversational practices,
(2) a comparison of German and American English compliments, (3) practice listening to and reading transcripts of authentic complement sequences,
(4) practice using compliments in role plays, and (5) a class discussion about

the cultural implications of the compliment sequences. Huth found some evidence of improvement in simulated role plays, but he also found considerable evidence of L1 transfer. Learners reported that they felt uncomfortable with the German routines, because they would be considered rude in American English. Huth takes his findings to suggest that the use of authentic materials to provide learners with explicit information about L2 pragmatics can help learners improve their pragmatics performance in spite of the limited pragmatics exposure in the classroom.

In a relatively early pragmatics study, House (1996) examined the effects of input and output opportunities, as well as explicit instruction on learners' use of discourse strategies, including opening gambits and opening and closing speech acts. She used two advanced level English classes for German students. One class received explicit metapragmatic information during a 14-week course, while the other class did not. Tape-recorded conversations were used for assessment purposes. Both the implicit and explicit groups improved over the 14 weeks in their initiating behavior, although the explicit group employed a wider variety of discourse strategies. However, both groups remained poor in their uptaking and responding abilities. House concludes that metapragmatic information does not necessarily result in pragmatic fluency for all aspects.

In another study, Nguyen (2013) investigated the ability of learners of English to provide their peers with constructive criticism in classroom contexts. Specifically she examined their ability to soften criticism rather than intensify it. She used two groups of Vietnamese high-intermediate-level students of English as a foreign language. The treatment group received 10 weeks of instruction involving explicit instruction regarding eight types of criticism modifiers, while the control group did not receive any instruction on providing criticism. The instruction involved three different stages. The first stage consisted of consciousness-raising activities and metapragmatic instruction. Following this stage, learners engaged in controlled practice of the forms, and this was followed up with communicative practice in which learners received corrective feedback on their production. Nguyen found that instruction had a positive effect, with learners being better able to modify their criticism.

In an investigation of speech acts, Pearson (2006) looked at explicit instruction on directives and requests for second semester, English speaking learners of Spanish. Two groups of learners received instruction concerning speech acts, while a third group continued with their normal classroom instruction. The two treatment groups viewed videos containing the speech acts, and in addition, one group received metapragmatic information about the speech acts. Pearson found no significant effects for the speech act instruction on learners' oral production on posttests, a result that she attributes in part to the limited amount of instruction, the limited range of speech act strategies that were presented, and the low proficiency of the learners.

In summary, although explicit pragmatics instruction seems to be generally positive, there appear to be some factors that enhance its effects. In fact, Taguchi (2011) comments that the types of instruction that had lasting effects 'were often characterized as having cognitively demanding tasks, such as comparison of interlanguage and target language forms or awareness raising activities targeting pragmatic conventions' (p. 292).

PEDAGOGICAL IMPLICATIONS

Because of their limited exposure to a wide range of L2 social contexts, learners often have few opportunities to develop pragmatic competence outside the classroom. Furthermore, because of the restricted social roles in the classroom, learners' pragmatics input is further limited. Thus, if learners are to improve in this area of language, they will need instruction that includes pragmatics, especially if they are to achieve high levels of pragmatic proficiency. Teachers should strive to incorporate authentic materials as much as possible, because the classroom represents a constrained and limited environment in terms of social roles and routines. In addition, instructional materials are not always authentic or accurate in their portrayal of pragmatic norms (Belz, 2007; Huth, 2006). Also the use of technology can be important to foster opportunities for authentic input, interaction, and output. Providing learners with oral or written examples of naturally occurring interaction can be a good way to heighten their metapragmatic awareness (McConachy, 2013). Finally, it is possible for study abroad to provide opportunities for learners to improve their pragmatic ability; however, that improvement is not guaranteed if learners do not interact with L2 speakers while in the host country.

ACTIVITIES

1. Below are instructions for two role plays regarding requests. What would you say in these situations? Ask several other people to respond to these scenarios. How closely do their responses match? How well do you think these role plays measure pragmatic ability? What other methods might you use to elicit information about L2 learners' ability to make pragmatically appropriate requests?

Role play from Félix-Brasdefer (2007)

Student-professor: Asking for a letter of recommendation

Imagine that you are in a Spanish-speaking country of your preference. You are in the final year of your undergraduate studies and you have decided to ask your Spanish professor, Professor 'X,' to write you a letter of recommendation.

You have been a good student in the class and although your professor has always treated everyone equally, you're sure that he wouldn't have any reason not to write a letter for you. You prefer that the letter be written by this professor because this class has been an important one for your major and the material is representative of classes you have taken toward your major. The relationship between you and your professor is strictly academic and you have only interacted with one another at the university either in class or during office hours. You need the letter of recommendation and you go to his office to ask him to write you one. What do you say?

Classmates: A student asking a classmate for notes

Imagine that you are in a Spanish-speaking country of your preference. It is the last day your Spanish professor is going to lecture before reviewing for the final next week. You did not attend class for the past two weeks. Unfortunately, you really need the notes to study for the exam because your professor takes the questions straight from his lectures. However, there is really only one person whose notes you would trust to copy, your classmate Vanessa's. Everybody else in class usually nods off, doodles on their paper, or works on an assignment for another class. You know your classmate is a diligent student and takes excellent notes. You decide to ask her for her notes even though you've only talked to her during group work in class and you are not friends. On the review day, you are able to catch her as she is walking out the door and you decide to ask to borrow them. What do you say?

2. Below is a sample of the explicit instruction from Nguyen (2013, pp. 93–94). What is your opinion of the effectiveness of this type of instruction? Have you ever encountered such explicit information regarding pragmatics in an L2 classroom? How might one provide more implicit types of instruction regarding this topic?

Explicit instruction in corrective criticism.

I. *Recognizing softeners and directness levels*

Each situation below is followed by three possible constructive comments (a–c). For each situation:

1. Identify all the softeners in the responses to each situation.
2. Calculate a relative directness level between 1 and 5, with 1 being most direct and 5 being most softened. Note that perceptions of level of directness may vary.

3. Decide which one of the three responses (a–c) you feel would be most help-ful and most supportive. Would you feel comfortable giving that response? This is a personal decision, so there is no right answer.

Example situation:

In a writing session, Student A had to give critical feedback to Student B's English essay. Student A thought that Student B's essay presented only one-sided arguments, which could make it hard for her to convince her readers. In her feedback, she said:

> *I think* everything *must* be seen from two sides but in this essay you pre-sented only one-sided arguments. So you *have to* address the opposing point of view as well.

Answer:

(1) a. Statement of problem: *You presented only one-sided arguments.*
    b. Statement of advice: *You have to address the opposing point of view as well.*
(2) Softeners: I *think*
(3) Level of relative directness: *Level 1* (due to use of strong modals "must" and "have to" in direct statements). Note that simply using "I think" does not soften this response.

II. Practicing softening criticism

How might you modify the following ways of giving critical feedback to include softeners? Look at the underlined forms and write them in a more softened form (some already incorporate some softeners). Two possible sam-ple answers are provided to the first feedback example.

(1) You know, in this paragraph you changed from passive to active voice and then back to passive, <u>so it was inconsistent</u>. <u>I think you should keep one or the other</u>.

    Sample answer: Below are two possible answers. The first is less softened; the second is more so. Both are appropriate.

a. You know in this paragraph you changed from passive to active voice and then back to passive, so it was *sort of* inconsistent. You *might just* keep one or the other.
b. You know in this paragraph you changed from passive to active voice and then back to passive, so it *may seem sort of* inconsistent. *Do you think it would be a good idea* to *just* keep one or the other?

ADDITIONAL READING

Félix-Brasdefer, J. C. (2008). *Politeness in Mexico and the US: A contrastive study of the realization and perception of refusals.* Amsterdam: John Benjamins.

Kasper, G., & Rose, K. (2002). *Pragmatic development in a second language.* Malden, MA: Wiley Blackwell.

9

Contexts of Instructed Second Language Acquisition

In addition to the various aspects of language that must be learned in ISLA, it is also important to consider the contexts in which ISLA can take place because different contexts provide different challenges and advantages for L2 learning. The first chapter made a distinction between instructed and uninstructed L2 acquisition, with the primary difference between the two contexts being that in the former there is some systematic attempt to manipulate the L2 learning process. Thus, even if L2 learning does not occur inside the four walls of a classroom, it is still of interest to ISLA if there is some manipulation of the learning process. The degree of manipulation can vary from very little to considerable.

For the most part, this book has focused on what could be considered traditional or formal instructional contexts. Now we turn to a variety of issues related to other instructional contexts. Collentine and Freed (2004), in an introductory article on contexts of SLA in a special issue of the journal *Studies in Second Language Acquisition*, suggest that there are three general contexts of instruction for high school and university level L2 students: at-home, immersion, and study abroad. The at-home context is the traditional classroom in which instruction is often heavily biased towards explicit attention to language, rather than using language to communicate. In general, this is the context that has been assumed so far in this book. One important distinction in the at-home context that has not yet been discussed is that of second language and foreign language contexts, depending on whether or not the language that learners are studying is a primary language of the wider society that learners are in.

Turning to the immersion context, Collentine and Freed define that context fairly narrowly as summer programs that create an L2 environment within the larger L1 society. However, immersion has also been used to refer to other types of programs that focus on providing large amounts of L2 input while remaining in the L1 context (Lyster, 2007). Within immersion programs there can be a range in the intensity of focus on L2 learning. In some cases, language learning is the primary goal of instruction, as in Collentine and Freed's usage, while in other immersion contexts, such as content-based instruction (CBI) and content and language integrated learning (CLIL), there is a dual purpose of learning academic content as well as the L2.

Next, there is the study abroad context in which learners are studying the L2 in an environment in which the language of study is also the language of the larger society. The study abroad context may come closest to uninstructed learning because manipulation of the learning conditions on a daily level may be minimal; however, in many cases, the overall goal of a study abroad program is L2 acquisition.

In addition to the previously mentioned contexts, this chapter will address the use of technology in L2 learning, an ever-increasing context with its own advantages and disadvantages.

One assumption made in this chapter is that the context of learning does not alter the cognitive mechanisms that drive learning (Bardovi-Harlig, 2000; Gass, 1989; Howard, 2005). Thus, L2 learning in study abroad or traditional classrooms or in computer-assisted language learning contexts is not a qualitatively different cognitive process. However, social context obviously plays a large role in the amount and type of input that learners receive, as well as the opportunities they have to produce the L2. Furthermore, context may affect how the L2 is perceived. Is it simply another academic subject with information that needs to be memorized? If so, then there might be a considerable amount of explicit learning resulting in explicit knowledge. However, if the L2 is viewed as a communicative tool that is important for everyday interaction, then there may be more emphasis on implicit learning and knowledge.

THEORETICAL CONCERNS

Foreign Language Versus Second Language Contexts

The first context that needs to be considered briefly is the traditional at-home or formal instructional context (Collentine & Freed, 2004; Mora & Valls-Ferrer, 2012) because it can provide a baseline for comparison with other contexts. In the 'traditional' L2 learning context, which may be the most common context in which L2 learning occurs (at least it is the most common focus of ISLA research), learners are generally involved in several hours of classroom instruction a week. Classes may occur for an hour every few days, or learners may be involved in more intensive programs in which they engage in classroom study for multiple hours each day.

One distinction that has been made regarding traditional L2 learning contexts is that of second language learning contexts versus foreign language learning contexts (Shehadeh & Coombe, 2012). Because the cognitive processes in both contexts are thought to be the same (Lyster & Saito, 2010), not all researchers make this distinction; however, it does retain a certain appeal. Conventionally a foreign language context is one in which the target language is not spoken in the wider society, and learners are often fairly homogenous in terms of first language. For example, learning English in Japan would constitute a foreign language context. English is not widely spoken in the larger society, and most students in English classes share Japanese as their first language. In contrast, second language contexts are those in which the L2 being studied is also the language (or at least one of the languages) spoken in the broader society. In addition, in many cases learners in second language contexts come from a variety of L1 backgrounds. Studying English in the United States or Great Britain would be an example of a second language context because English is the language of the wider society, and in many cases, students are heterogeneous and diverse in their backgrounds. The importance of this distinction rests primarily on the assumption that learners in a second language context enjoy considerably more exposure to the L2 and its speakers. Whether this assumption is justified is an empirical question, and some studies have found that not as much interaction with native speakers happens in second language contexts as might be expected or hoped for (e.g., Ranta & Meckelborg, 2013).

Another important question is whether research findings conducted in one context can be generalized to another context. Shehadeh (2012), specifically referring to task-based language teaching, contends that research conducted in second language contexts cannot be applied indiscriminately to foreign language ones. There are differences in institutional factors, such as the prevailing philosophies of education and assessment, as well as in teachers' and students' views of what constitutes good practice in the classroom. Although these may be broad generalizations, such variation may be important when considering the effectiveness of different types of instruction. For example, learners from educational backgrounds that prioritize memorization as an important method of learning may benefit more from explicit types of instruction, and may be more resistant to communicative approaches to L2 instruction.

One difficulty with the distinction between second and foreign language contexts is that learners may not remain exclusively into one context. Howard (2005) calls into question the distinction between the two contexts, since, among other things, it ignores that fact that learners may move back and forth between these environments. In spite of these difficulties, the distinction between second and foreign language learning contexts is commonly used and has some broad descriptive adequacy, even if it may not be appropriate in every individual instance.

Study Abroad

One distinctive context for L2 learning is study abroad, in which learners spend time in an L2-speaking society generally as a result of an instructional program. Often some traditional classroom study is associated with study abroad, either before, during, and/or after the study abroad component. Nevertheless, a chief purpose of study abroad for language learning is to expose L2 learners to a wider range of more authentic L2 input and interaction than they would receive in a traditional foreign language context. In some ways, study abroad may not fit within a strict definition of ISLA because some programs have minimal systematic manipulation of the L2 learning process. However, other programs contain considerable manipulation. Furthermore, the act of going on study abroad itself can be seen as an attempt to manipulate the learning process by changing the environment in which learning occurs to one that is presumed to be more conducive to learning by providing more exposure to the L2. Finally, it should be acknowledged that there are also study abroad programs that do not have L2 learning as a goal, but instead may focus on building cultural or academic awareness, and indeed research suggests that study abroad can be a powerful method of developing intercultural understanding (Kinginger, 2011).

There is a belief in many quarters that study abroad is the optimal context for L2 acquisition, and indeed study abroad may provide a powerful opportunity for L2 acquisition, especially if learners receive appropriate institutional and pedagogical support (Kinginger, 2011). However, sometimes there is the assumption that learners who go abroad will automatically pick up the L2 and gain greater fluency simply because they are surrounded by the L2 (Howard, 2005; Kinginger, 2011). This belief is based on the supposition that the implicit learning mechanisms that are at work during L1 acquisition will enable L2 acquisition to occur in the same way. However, there are several issues to consider concerning the effectiveness of study abroad for L2 acquisition, and indeed study abroad may not always be as beneficial as hoped. For example, Wilkinson (2002) speculates 'Perhaps immersion in a target-language community during study abroad does not always take students as far beyond the classroom as one might intuitively believe' (p. 169). Kinginger (2011) adds that 'a sojourn in-country does not guarantee language learning' (p. 63). She argues that learners may vary greatly in the degree to which their L2 proficiency benefits, with many not achieving an advanced level in spite of the learning opportunities.

Nevertheless, one of the primary benefits of study abroad is that it moves learners outside of the classroom and its limited scope of language and social contexts. Indeed study abroad has the potential to expose learners to a multitude of social settings, with the language use that accompanies them. In addition, learners' use of language inside the traditional classroom may have little personal impact apart from a course grade; however, interaction with individuals outside of the classroom in the host society has real social consequences, and learners' use of language may or may not enable them to achieve and maintain the social relationships they desire (Kinginger, 2011). In the end, the experiences of study abroad learners may be highly varied, and not all learners experience its full benefit in terms of language proficiency gains; however, the more that is done to prepare learners ahead of time to take advantage of the opportunities, the better off learners will be (Kinginger, 2011).

As has been mentioned, one of the primary putative goals of study abroad is to get learners outside of the classroom so that they can experience increased L2 input, output, interaction, and feedback (DeKeyser, 2007d). Learners in at-home classes, particularly in foreign language contexts, are often exposed to a limited range of language and social contexts. Moreover, the input that learners receive is constrained and many times it is created for L2 leaners and thus does not reflect authentic language as used by native speakers. Interaction and output opportunities can also be limited in at-home contexts, although the implementation of focus on form and task-based language learning attempts to address this shortcoming. Even so, the language that learners are exposed to in the traditional classroom is generally restricted. Thus, learners do not gain an understanding, for example, of how L2 use can vary according to different social factors.

However, it is becoming clear that study abroad does not automatically create the ideal conditions for learning. Opportunities for L2 practice may not happen as frequently in study abroad contexts as might be expected (DeKeyser, 2007d; Ranta & Meckelborg, 2013). Additionally the interaction that does happen may not be of a very high quality (Wilkinson, 2002). Thus, it is the quality and quantity of interaction with and in the L2 that may be most critical for study abroad learners (DeKeyser, 2007d; Kinginger, 2011). What studies suggest is that time on task, quality of interaction, amount of interaction, input, and output are more important than simply being on study abroad (Du, 2013) or even the length of study abroad (Bardovi-Harlig, 2013). It may be better to have a short stay abroad with high quality interaction, than a longer one with little or no interaction.

Different researchers and theorists suggest that study abroad might be better for some aspects of language in comparison to others. Probably the most important target for improvement on study abroad is oral fluency (e.g., Du, 2013; Llanes & Muñoz, 2013; Mora & Valls-Ferrer, 2012). For example, Mora and Valls-Ferrer (2012) draw on skill acquisition theory to suggest that increased exposure to L2 input and opportunities for interaction in study abroad contexts may help turn declarative knowledge into procedural and automatized knowledge. However, Kinginger (2011) says that study abroad can be beneficial for all aspects of language learning, although study abroad might not always produce the impressive results that students and teachers are hoping for.

Another issue to consider in study abroad is the amount and type of preparation that learners experience (Kinginger, 2011). In order for learners to maximize their time in the L2 environment, it is important for them to be prepared. One type of preparation is to make learners aware of how L2 acquisition works. For example, learners might not be able to take full advantage of all the opportunities afforded by study abroad if they do not understand how language acquisition occurs, and the role played by use of the L2 in communicative interaction. For example, if learners think of L2 learning as merely the accumulation of multiple grammar rules and lexical items, then they may miss the chance to develop their communicative and pragmatic competence by interacting with native speakers (DeKeyser, 2007d; Kinginger, 2011).

Not only are students' perceptions and preparations important, but the host society and its individuals also play a role in the success or failure of learners' study abroad experiences (Kinginger, 2011). Interaction is not one-sided, and even if students try to engage with the larger community, they may find it challenging, In other words the hosts' attitudes might not be conducive to the types of interaction that are necessary for L2 development. Learners may not be viewed as legitimate interaction partners. One issue related to this is the role that identity, and particularly gender, can play. In particular, female learners may be placed in different gender roles than they are used to in their home context. These roles may be viewed negatively by the learners, and thus these roles may negatively impact L2 learning, especially if it keeps learners from interacting with native speakers.

Another factor to consider is learners' proficiency level when they embark on their study abroad (Bardovi-Harlig, 2013). Lower-level learners may be less able to take advantage of study abroad opportunities, especially when it comes to interaction with native speakers. Related to the issue of proficiency is the factor of age. Although study abroad is often associated with university students, at least one study has looked at children on study abroad. Llanes and Muñoz (2013) argue that age interacts with context. Children who study abroad benefit more from the experience than adults because younger learners have a better ability to learner naturalistically and implicitly. However, not all of the benefits go to the young. Implicit learning takes time, and study abroad programs may be only a couple of weeks in length. Thus, for children there seems to be a threshold of two or three months for the advantages of study abroad to be seen. Adults may do better in at-home contexts, underscoring the fact that adults have an advantage for explicit learning, which is common in typical classrooms.

Interestingly, one of the trends that has been seen as a benefit for L2 learning, namely the access to the L2 and its speakers through the Internet, can also be a drawback on study abroad. Learners may be so caught up in their existing social contacts through social media and computer-mediated communication that they may not take advantage of the opportunity to interact with people in the host county (Kinginger, 2011).

In sum, study abroad can be a powerful opportunity for L2 development; however, numerous factors may determine the extent of its effectiveness.

Immersion

Another context that is different from the traditional L2 classroom is the immersion classroom. This type of instruction has also been called content-based instruction (CBI) or content and language integrated learning (CLIL), and while there are some differences among these two, they are all similar in their approach to classroom instruction. In these classes, there is a focus on both nonlinguistic subject material as well as the L2 itself, with the goal being for learners to acquire knowledge of both (Lyster, 2007). The content focus of the course can range from academic subject material, to vocational or professional knowledge (Lyster & Ballinger, 2011; Valeo, 2013), and the primary medium of instruction is the L2. In addition, these content-based programs can be found in a variety of institutional settings, from primary schools to universities, and workplace and adult education programs. However, as shown in Figure 9.1, the degree of emphasis on content or language can vary greatly depending on the details of a specific program (Brinton, Snow, & Wesche, 2003; Valeo, 2013). In some cases, there is an almost exclusive focus on content-learning, while in other cases, there is more equal attention to both language and content. However, at some point, if the emphasis of instruction leans more towards language, then it ceases to be a type of immersion or content-based context, and instead could be considered to represent a more focus on form or task-based approach.

In addition to the scale in Figure 9.1, there are other criteria that have been proposed as being necessary for a program to be considered an immersion program (Cammarata & Tedick, 2012; Fortune & Tedick, 2008). Arguably, it is important that the L2 be used at least 50% of the time by teachers who are fully proficient in the L2. In addition, some contend that the program should provide at least two years of instruction, with the goal of L1/L2 bilingualism.

Content-driven					Language-driven
←					→
Total Immersion	Partial Immersion	Content Courses	Content + Language Courses	Language Classes with Thematic Units	Language Classes with Content Used for Language Practice

FIGURE 9.1 Options in Content-based Instruction (adapted from Lyster & Ballinger, 2011)

The theoretical support for content-based instruction is similar to that of focus on form (Long, 1996), namely that brief attention to language structures during larger, meaning-focused interaction is beneficial for L2 acquisition. In addition, content-based instruction is supported by models of incidental and implicit learning (e.g., Rebuschat & Williams, 2012), in which it is assumed that the L2 will be acquired incidentally as learners focus on content (Dalton-Puffer, 2007). One of the issues related to content-based instruction is attention to and awareness of language (Valeo, 2013). The tension is that there should be enough awareness of language that it enables L2 learning, but not so much that it detracts from learning content.

In describing immersion programs, Cammarata and Tedick (2012) state that the main goal is an integration of content and language, with language being used as 'the vehicle for teaching the subject matter content' (p. 251). Immersion programs can be organized in many different ways. One-way classes involve students with the same L1 studying the L2 – that is, language majority students take subject classes in a foreign language. For example, English L1 speaking learners in the US may be involved in one-way immersion programs in which they study subjects like math, science, and history in Chinese or other foreign language. Another type of immersion is for language minority students in which they study in the dominant language of society, but also receive help maintaining or improving their L1 skills. The goal of these types of programs is additive bilingualism, in which learners become proficient in both languages. However, there are also immersion programs for minority students in which no support is provided for L1 maintenance, and the (perhaps implicit) goal is subtractive bilingualism in which use of the L1 is not encouraged (Cammarata & Tedick, 2012).

In another type of immersion program labeled two-way immersion, there are two groups of learners who are each studying the L1 of the other group as their L2. For example, a group of English L1 speakers could be taking classes in Spanish, while Spanish L1 students are taking classes in English. The goal is the same as other immersion programs, development of both content knowledge and language proficiency, but learners in two-way programs have the additional advantage of having peers who can help support learning as they interact in their respective L2s (Ballinger & Lyster, 2011; Cammarata & Tedick, 2012). Some of the difficulties with two-way immersion programs are that it is sometimes difficult to keep teachers and students using the L2 rather than reverting to the L1, particularly if the L1 is the dominant language of the larger society (Ballinger & Lyster, 2011).

There are many proposed benefits, both linguistic and nonlinguistic, of immersion programs. Ideally, students develop functional proficiency in the L2, while maintaining or even improving their L1 proficiency. In addition, immersion education can foster 'academic achievement, greater cognitive flexibility, better nonverbal problem solving abilities' (Cammarata & Tedick, 2012, p. 253). However, in spite of these benefits, from an ISLA perspective there is acknowledgment that learners' L2 proficiency often does not reach target-like levels of grammatical accuracy, lexical diversity, and pragmatic appropriateness (Cammarata & Tedick, 2012).

Although content-based instruction is a common term in North America, there is also the term content and language integrated learning (CLIL), which is more commonly used in the European context. Both types of instruction aim to integrate content and language instruction, but in Europe, immersion programs are offered in a variety of languages, many of which have official status as a second or regional language of said country. In contrast, CLIL classes focus on a foreign language, which in most cases is English (Lyster & Ballinger, 2011).

There are several issues that affect the implementation of immersion and content-based instruction, with one being whether teachers see themselves as primarily content teachers, language teachers, or both. Ideally, from an ISLA perspective, teachers would see themselves as both, and they would take advantage of the opportunities that content instruction offers for focusing on language, especially vocabulary, but also grammar (Cammarata & Tedick, 2012; Tan, 2011); however, such perceptions are not always the case.

Other issues that arise in implementing immersion programs relate to teachers' lack of experience and training in teaching both content and language. Teachers need to be trained to focus on form during content teaching (Tan, 2011), and lessons should have clear content and language goals in order to emphasize the relationships between the content material and the language used to express it (Kong & Hoare, 2011). In addition, there are external factors such as lack of resources and support for immersion programs (Cammarata & Tedick, 2012; Tan, 2011). Another issue that arises is that language learning will not necessarily take care of itself during content instruction (Cammarata & Tedick, 2012; Kong & Hoare, 2011). Rather there must be some additional attention to language, either during content instruction, through focus on form, or in the shape of additional classes focusing on language.

Computer-Assisted Language Learning

The context of computer-assisted language learning (CALL) is rapidly increasing and creates new opportunities for L2 learners (Blake, 2011; Chapelle, 2009). Learners can now take L2 courses that are entirely computer-based, or learners may be involved in hybrid courses, which include face-to-face as well as online components. Although learners' interaction with technology generally occurs outside of the classroom, in many cases it is the teacher or researcher who facilitates its use. Thus, it fits into the definition of ISLA because there is an intention by the teacher to manipulate learning by having learners engage with computer-based materials or interact through computer-mediated communication. In addition, there is often an effort by the designers of the technology to manipulate the materials that learners engage with to enhance L2 learning.

One of the primary goals of computer-assisted learning is to create materials that will interest learners so that they will engage more with the L2, either intrinsically because they find it interesting, or extrinsically because they are required by their teacher (Blake, 2011). This increased engagement is hoped to lead to increased L2 learning.

Technology, particularly the Internet, has the capability to breakdown the foreign language/second language distinction because one of the main differences between the two contexts is the lack of L2 use in the learners' wider environment. If that wider environment includes the Internet, it is possible for learners to have much more exposure to the L2. Today, learners in foreign language contexts can have considerable access to authentic L2 materials and L2 native speakers with just a few clicks of a mouse.

One of the primary issues in computer-assisted language learning is how different technological arrangements can affect learning. Again, it is not assumed that technology can actually alter the cognitive processes that are involved in L2 learning; however, technology-assisted language learning does have the potential to speed up or enhance the process. In this regard, a possible benefit is that technology may be able to deliver individualized instructional materials that meet learners at their specific levels of proficiency. For example, depending on how learners respond to certain questions or activities, a computer program can lower the level of linguistic difficulty to help learners review and solidify their knowledge. Alternatively, a program can move learners to a higher level if they have mastered the previous material. Blake (2011) refers to intelligent CALL or iCALL as a way of providing individualized instruction that is based on the records of learners' previous interactions with such iCALL systems. iCALL systems should be able to anticipate learners' mistakes and difficulties based on their previous performance, thereby providing individualized feedback and advice on how to proceed in the learning process based on the ways in which learners have engaged with the program in the past. In addition, iCALL systems can assess individual learners' performance in relation to a database of other learners' performances, providing learners with a good way of assessing their own progress in relation to that of their peers.

One of the things that CALL can be used for is explicit instruction in specific areas of language (Levy, 2009). For example, grammar activities can potentially be helpful, especially if they are well-designed. Additionally such 'mechanical' activities could be done outside of class, freeing up class time for other, more interactive, activities. This approach also has the advantage of increasing learners' time on task by having them engage with the L2 outside of class (Blake, 2011). Vocabulary is another area where CALL can provide learners with detailed information about their proficiency level and provide them with input that is tailored to their level. Additionally, computer programs can be designed to ensure that learners encounter new words multiple times and in multiple ways and contexts, thereby increasing learners' engagement with the lexical items (Cobb, 2007; Schmitt, 2008). In addition to providing sections of textual input, computer programs can also highlight specific lexical items that have proven difficult for leaners and provide them with more opportunities to practice these difficult items. Finally, as discussed in Chapter 7, pronunciation instruction has already been making use of the potential of technology to enhance instruction.

In addition to individualizing instruction, CALL can also be used to create additional social and interactive contexts for L2 learning (Blake, 2011). The potential of synchronous CMC, and its support from interactionist approaches to ISLA, has already been discussed in Chapter 3, but other ways in which technology can foster communication is through asynchronous CMC such as discussion boards, wikis, blogs and other social networking options. One area of computer-mediated social interaction that has begun to receive considerable attention is the potential of online gaming environments for L2 learning (Blake, 2011; Thorne, Black, & Sykes, 2009). Gaming can include social interaction in the L2 since many games are played in groups, and it can provide a positive affective element that is missing from many other L2 learning activities (Thorne, Black, & Sykes, 2009). Furthermore, many of these games are task-based, involving learners in quests and missions, which involve the use of language for accomplishing nonlinguistic goals.

In sum, online learning can be an important context for L2 learning. In particular it can help keep learners interested in the learning process, and it can provide additional, engaging exposure to the L2, which can increase learners' time on task, which helps in the time-consuming task of L2 learning (Blake, 2011).

EMPIRICAL EVIDENCE

Second Language Versus Foreign Language Contexts

There have been conflicting findings about the importance of the second language/foreign language distinction for L2 learning. For example, Lyster and Saito (2010), in a meta-analysis of 15 studies on the effects of oral corrective feedback in the classroom, found that corrective feedback had a medium effect on L2 learning; however, there was no difference in the effects of corrective feedback in second language versus foreign language contexts, and they suggest that the distinctions between the two contexts are not such that they affect the L2 learning process inside the classroom.

In contrast, however, Li's (2010) meta-analysis of 33 studies of corrective feedback in both classroom and laboratory studies found that overall the effect for feedback was greater in foreign language contexts than in second language contexts. Li suggested that teachers and learners in foreign language contexts might be more positively oriented towards corrective feedback, which may increase its effectiveness. Similarly, Mackey and Goo (2007), in their meta-analysis of interaction studies, found that the immediate effects of interaction were greater in foreign language contexts as compared to second language contexts. However, on delayed posttests learners in both contexts benefitted equally. One suggestion for the beneficial effects of corrective feedback and interaction in foreign language contexts is that there might have been a novelty effect. In other words learners benefitted from it because it was not like their normal types of study so it was more noticeable and they paid more attention to it.

In summary, it seems that the distinction between foreign and second language classes is not always meaningful, although there does seem to be some empirical support for the distinction. Further investigation into the factors that contribute to potential distinctions could be conducted.

Study Abroad

The effects of study abroad have received considerable investigation, and as one might expect, numerous, and often contradictory results have been found. This section reviews several studies that have found a variety of outcomes regarding the effects of study abroad on L2 acquisition.

Positive effects. There have been many studies that have found benefits for study abroad. Llanes and Muñoz (2013) conducted a study that compared the effects of study abroad and at-home programs for adults and children. Spanish-speaking learners of English spent between two and three months in the United Kingdom or Ireland. The researchers measured multiple aspects of L2 proficiency: oral and written fluency, lexical and syntactic complexity, and accuracy. Results showed that 'the study abroad context was superior to the at-home context, and more advantageous for children than for adults in comparative gains, although adults outscored children in absolute gains' (p. 63). Llanes and Muñoz suggest that the study abroad context was particularly beneficial for children because they had more opportunities for oral interaction and because they were better able to take advantage of the implicit learning opportunities that such interaction afforded. The one linguistic area that the at-home students did better on was the writing task. This finding could be explained by the at-home group receiving more explicit instruction, the effects of which would show up on a writing task; in contrast, the implicit and procedural knowledge gained by the study abroad learners would not necessarily facilitate L2 writing.

At least one study has looked at the effects of study abroad coupled with other types of instruction. Klapper and Rees (2003) looked at learners studying German in a four year university program in the UK. Learners had two years of classroom instruction, a year abroad, and then another year at university. One group of learners experienced more explicit, focus on forms type of instruction; while another group engaged in more implicit, focus on form learning. The researchers found that focus on forms, namely explicit instruction, was more effective for learners in the at-home language context; however, after spending a year abroad, the focus on form group attained a similar level of proficiency to the focus on forms group. Klapper and Rees suggest that focus on form can be useful in laying a foundation if there is an immersion type context following the classroom instruction; however, they maintain that more explicit instruction is better in foreign language contexts.

Mora and Valls-Ferrer (2012) compared the effects of a three-month study abroad with that of formal instruction at home. They looked at advanced-level Catalan-Spanish undergraduate learners of English, who provided speech samples at three points in time over a two-year period. Thus, it was a longitudinal study that investigated the long-term effects of these two types of instruction. The results revealed a variety of different effects. On fluency measures, learners showed robust gains during study abroad; however, there was only a moderate improvement on grammatical accuracy, and no gain in the complexity of the language that the learners produced. The group that received formal instruction did not make any gains in these areas. Mora and Valls-Ferrer conclude that study abroad was effective for the development of fluency; however, they did find that the most significant predictor of fluency gains was a learner's initial fluency scores.

Finally, Du (2013) provides an interesting longitudinal study of 29 American college students studying Mandarin in China in a study abroad program. The data consisted of informal interview sessions that the researcher conducted with the students. From an analysis of the learners' L2 use during the interviews, Du found that overall students' fluency did improve. In her qualitative analysis, Du examined students who kept the language pledge to speak only Chinese and those who did not. She found that personality, being socially outgoing, and creating opportunities for L2 interaction were more important than simply speaking only Chinese. For example, one learner spoke only Chinese, but spoke very little and had little interaction with Chinese speakers. In contrast, one student did not keep the language pledge and spoke both English and Chinese during her stay. However, she had lots of social interaction in both languages. Du found that 'students who interacted with native speakers in a variety of contexts, who created social networks for themselves with Chinese speakers, and who went out into the culture and spoke Chinese improved their language whether or not they followed the pledge to the letter' (p. 141). Du concludes that study abroad was very influential in improving learners' L2 fluency, especially at the beginning of the program. In addition, the amount of time that learners spent using Chinese was the most important factor affecting the development of L2 fluency.

Mixed effects. Not all research into the effects of study abroad has found positive results. For example, Collentine (2004) compared the linguistic gains of American learners in a semester-long study abroad program in Spain, with those of another group who spent the semester in an at-home classroom context. Learners were tested before and after the semester using an Oral Proficiency Interview. Collentine found that learners in the at-home context demonstrated greater increases in their grammatical and lexical abilities. However, he did find that the study abroad group improved in discourse-level features such as their ability to convey information in narratives and in more semantically complex ways.

In another study, Freed, Segalowitz, and Dewey (2004) investigated the effects of three different contexts: at-home, immersion, and study abroad, on the fluency of English-speaking learners of French. The at-home context comprised a typical university L2 learning situation. Classes met for two to four hours a week for 12 weeks, and the curriculum emphasized a communicative approach to language learning. The immersion context consisted of a seven-week summer program, with classes meeting between three and four hours per day. In addition, students were expected to participate in frequent extra-curricular activities that the program organized for them. Students were also expected to sign a language pledge stating that they would use only French during the program. The study abroad students spent 12 weeks studying in Paris, where they attended French classes for two to five hours per day. In addition, they had numerous opportunities to use French outside the classroom. Students were tested at the beginning and end of each program, using an oral interview. The results of the data analysis indicated that the study abroad group was significantly more fluent than the at-home group, but, surprisingly, the immersion group scored significantly higher than both the at-home and study abroad groups. Additional investigation into learners' use of the L2 outside of the classroom found that the immersion group reported spending significantly more time speaking and writing in French than did the at-home group or even the study abroad group.

No effects. Finally, some studies have found no such positive results for study abroad. For example, Wilkinson (2002) investigated the discourse patterns of a cohort of study abroad students during their summer-long program. She found that learners used patterns of interaction typical of the classroom with their host families, thereby missing out on one of the most important benefits of study abroad, the opportunity to have interactions that are different from what is encountered in the classroom, thus exposing the learner to a broader range of language and language use. Again, the quality of the interaction was not as high as might be expected for study abroad.

Díaz-Campos (2004) examined the impact that study abroad might have on learner pronunciation in comparison to an at-home program. Forty-six English-speaking American students studying either abroad in Spain or at-home in an American university participated in the study. Testing at the beginning and end of the program consisted of leaners reading a paragraph containing segmental phonemes difficult for English-speaking learners of Spanish. Overall, Díaz-Campos found no difference in the phonological performance of study abroad and at-home students. Both groups improved on some phonemes, but not on others. He also investigated the influence of various factors on the test scores, and he found a number of variables that contributed to improved pronunciation, including the number of years of formal language instruction and the reported use of Spanish both before the semester and outside the classroom during the semester.

Based on these and other studies, it is clear that study abroad can provide a great opportunity for L2 learners to improve their linguistic abilities, particularly their oral fluency. In addition, learners have the opportunity to engage in interaction that may help them use the language in more native-like ways. However, it is clear that study abroad is not a panacea for L2 acquisition, and that some aspects of language benefit more from certain contexts than others (Collentine & Freed, 2004).

Immersion/Content-Based Instruction

As might be expected with the numerous ways in which immersion and content-based instruction are implemented, there are a variety of results regarding the benefits of these contexts for L2 acquisition.

One of the contexts where there is perhaps the greatest focus on content is in university foreign literature classes. Zyzik and Polio (2008) look at incidental focus on form in university Spanish literature classes. They 'found that recasts were the instructors' preferred form of feedback, with negotiation and explicit correction being extremely rare. Furthermore preemptive focus on form was common, but almost exclusively limited to vocabulary' (p. 53). The authors suggest that content teachers could be encouraged to bring more focus on language into the classroom; however, not all instructors felt that it was their responsibility to provide additional language support for their students.

In a study of a different type of content-based instruction, Valeo (2013) examined a program in Canada in which the goal was to prepare adults to work as professional childcare providers. She compared two classes. One class received content-based instruction with focus on form, which included metalinguistic explanations, tasks that drew learners' awareness to form, and corrective feedback. The other group received entirely meaning-focused instruction. Each met for five hours a week for 10 weeks. Learners participated in recall protocols investigating their noticing of content and linguistic forms. Learners were able to report awareness of both content and language forms, but as might be expected the class receiving focus on form reported more attention to linguistic items. However, in spite of their reported noticing, there was no correlation between awareness and language learning, as measured by gains from pretest to posttest scores. Valeo suggests that these results might be due to a ceiling effect in her study in which higher proficiency learners did not demonstrate learning gains due to high pretest performance; in contrast, lower proficiency learners, who reported lower levels of noticing, focused primarily on the non-linguistic content, and thus did not notice the targeted linguistic items.

In another study, Ballinger and Lyster (2011) looked at patterns of teacher and student language use within a two-way Spanish/English immersion program for Grades 1, 3, and 8 in a U.S. school. They found that students in general preferred to use English; however, they also found that students from Spanish-speaking households were more likely to use Spanish with their teachers and peers. Since more of the communication among peers occurred in English, it was the Spanish L1 students who had the opportunity to practice their L2 the most, while English L1 speakers did not. Ballinger and Lyster conclude that there needs to be considerable effort exerted in an immersion program if the non-dominant language is going to be prioritized. If teachers and administrators are ambivalent about this goal, then these attitudes will most likely be amplified among students, and students' perceptions of the usefulness and importance of the minority language can diminish.

Computer-Assisted Language Learning

A number of studies have investigated the effects of technology in L2 learning, with many of them concentrating on the effects of computer-mediated communication. In one study of learners' communication, Peterson (2006) examined the interaction that occurred when learners used avatars to complete tasks in a virtual world. University-level learners of English in Japan were placed in dyads and engaged in three different communicative tasks: a jigsaw task, a decision-making task, and an information exchange task. Peterson examined the interaction that occurred in the virtual world as the learners completed their tasks. He found that the use of avatars helped facilitate learners' interaction and it increased learners' sense of presence in the virtual world. Peterson also found a high number of politeness strategies occurring in the interaction, and he suggests that the presence of the avatars may have inclined learners to transfer L1 politeness strategies to the L2 context. Peterson suggests that L2 interaction in virtual worlds is a learning context that warrants further investigation.

In another study of CMC interaction, Loewen and Erlam (2006) replicated a study (Ellis et al., 2006), originally conducted face to face, in which lower-proficiency learners of English in New Zealand received corrective feedback on their incorrect use of past tense during task-based communication. Learners performed the tasks in a chat room in groups of four with a researcher who provided either recasts or metalinguistic feedback on past-tense errors. Unlike the face-to-face context, which demonstrated effects for both recasts and metalinguistic feedback, Loewen and Erlam's study found no improvement for either condition, leading them to speculate that the learners may not have been developmentally ready for the structure. In addition, Loewen and Erlam suggested that the interrupted nature of the feedback in chat room discourse, due intervening turns between the error and the feedback, might have lessened the impact of the feedback. Furthermore, learners did not frequently incorporate the correct forms into their own production. Loewen and Erlam suggest that the differences between face-to-face and online learning contexts need to be further explored.

PEDAGOGICAL IMPLICATIONS

The pedagogical implications for these contexts, particularly in study abroad and immersion programs are similar, and pertain to the overall program, as much, if not more, as the individual classroom. In large part, a key suggestion raised by these studies is to ensure that proper training is provided for implementation of the programs. In terms of study abroad, managing expectations about the possible effects of study abroad is important. For example, study abroad is not an unproblematic solution for all aspects of learners' L2 proficiency. Some aspects of language, such as grammar and vocabulary, may benefit more in at-home contexts than in study abroad. However, aspects of language such as oral fluency and pragmatic proficiency seem to be well-supported. Furthermore, studies (e.g., Kinginger, 2011) suggest that training prior to departure is an integral component to ensure success. Learners need to be made aware of the opportunities to improve various aspects of their language, and to realize that language learning is more than just studying grammar and vocabulary in the classroom. Additionally, study abroad programs would do well to develop multiple opportunities and have requirements for learners to use the L2 and interact with its speakers outside of the classroom. These opportunities may happen on their own if learners are left to their own devices, but they are more likely to occur if they are structured into the program.

In terms of immersion programs, there appears to be a strong need for administrators to support the programs to their fullest. Teachers also need to be well-trained and supported, and they should be made aware that they can be both content and language teachers. In fact, such a combination will benefit learners the most. By creating these opportunities, immersion programs can achieve the dual goals of improving content knowledge as well as L2 proficiency.

ACTIVITIES

Zyzik and Polio (2008) investigated the occurrence of focus on form in Spanish literature classes in an American university. In addition to observing classroom interaction, the researchers interviewed several of the teachers, asking them about their thoughts on the role of attention to language in content-focused classes. Teachers provided a variety of response, several of which are provided below. In their discussion of their results, Zyzik and Polio (p. 64) raise the following issues.

How can content-based literature courses . . . provide L2 learners with the linguistic support they need? The question itself makes two critical assumptions that merit explanation. First, we assume that these L2 learners continue to need linguistic support, in other words, opportunities to develop and refine certain grammatical and lexical features of the target language. The second assumption implicit in the question . . . is that literature courses are the right setting for providing such linguistic support.

1. What is your assessment of the two assumptions made in the previous quote? Do you agree?
2. Based on the teachers' quotes below, how do you think the teachers feel about Zyzik and Polio's assumptions?
3. What arguments would you make to convince reluctant content teachers that it is possible to combine attention to language and content in the same course?
4. What types of activities would you recommend to help teachers achieve an integration of content and language within the same course?

Teachers' statements (Zyzik & Polio, 2008, p. 62)

Statement 1

I think that they're [opportunities to focus on language] important, but at the same time, as I just stated, it's a literature course, this is something that should be addressed in a linguistics course. But I mean, I don't want, at the same time with vocabulary, you know, since I deal with very old, very old literature, of course I need to explain that vocabulary, or give them.

Statement 2

Well, we've been through this so many times. The difference between *preguntar* and *pedir*. I mean, I have brought it to their attention. Every day when we start class . . . usually I come in and the common mistakes, we talk about them immediately. And the running joke is "whatever happened to the subjunctive in Spanish?" And the other ones are *pedir* and *preguntar*.

Statement 3

Well, I just want them to open their mouths, so I try not to correct them so much, you know, if they're making mistakes.

Statement 4

I was thinking that they wouldn't understand the word *desafiantes*. That's why I translated it twice and I am writing it down in Spanish. I don't write down in English, I write down in Spanish.

Statement 5

Because a lot of times, at this level, or at any level, the students say that they understand something and know what it means when they really don't. So that's what I try . . . I try to make sure that they understand, or people are embarrassed to say they don't understand something. Because I'm certain that everyone in that room did not know that a *panza* was a belly. So, it's just to make sure that they see the connection.

ADDITIONAL READING

Jackson, J. (2008). *Language, identity and study abroad: Sociocultural perspectives*. London: Equinox.

Lyster, R. (2007). *Learning and teaching languages through content: A counterbalanced approach*. Amsterdam: John Benjamins.

Pellegrino Aveni, V. (2005). *Study abroad and second language use: Constructing the self*. Cambridge: Cambridge University Press.

Shehadah, A., & Coombe, C. (2012). *Task-based Language Teaching in Foreign Language Contexts: Research and Implementation*. Amsterdam: John Benjamins.

10

Individual Differences and Instructed Second Language Acquisition

The previous chapter covered some of the larger instructional and contextual issues that may influence the L2 acquisition process. The current chapter goes on to consider factors that vary across individual learners, and may therefore contribute to differences in L2 acquisition. Individual differences have been characterized as psychological traits that are relatively stable within a single individual but that vary across individuals (Dörnyei, 2005). The field of psychology has spent considerable time investigating a number of these differences, as has SLA research. Individual differences have been categorized in different ways in SLA, as can be seen in Table 10.1. Several categories, such as intelligence, language aptitude, and motivation, are consistent across all three taxonomies. Other individual differences, such as age, willingness to communicate, and learner beliefs appear in only one or two of the taxonomies. This chapter will not attempt to address all of these differences; instead, it will focus on several that have had particular influence within ISLA.

In terms of ISLA, it may also be helpful to think about individual differences in terms of those that are amenable to change and those that are not. Dörnyei (2005) indicates that individual differences are generally stable within individuals; however, there are some that are more easily manipulated, such as motivation, beliefs, and learning strategies; these individual differences have more potential to be influenced in the classroom. In contrast, other individual differences, such as aptitude and personality, are more or less fixed (Dörnyei & Skehan, 2003), and therefore the implication for ISLA is for teachers and learners to acknowledge and better understand these influences in the classroom rather than attempt to alter them. This chapter will explore the characteristics of these various individual differences and their relationship to ISLA.

TABLE 10.1

Taxonomies of individual differences in second language learning
(adapted from Ellis, 2008)

Robinson (2002)	Dörnyei (2005)	Ellis (2008)
1. Intelligence	1. Personality	1. Intelligence
2. Motivation	2. Language aptitude	2. Working memory
3. Anxiety	3. Motivation	3. Language aptitude
4. Language aptitude	4. Learning and	4. Learning style
5. Working memory	cognitive styles	5. Motivation
6. Age	5. Language learning	6. Anxiety
	strategies	7. Personality
	6. Other learner	8. Willingness to
	characteristics	communicate
	• anxiety	9. Learner beliefs
	• creativity	10. Learning strategies
	• willingness to	
	• communicate	
	• self-esteem	
	• learner beliefs	

THEORETICAL CONCERNS

Because of enormous amount of theory and research that each individual difference has generated, it is not possible to examine each topic in detail in this chapter. Rather, the purpose is to provide an overview of some of the main issues in each individual difference, beginning with those that have received the most attention for manipulation in the classroom.

Motivation

Motivation is often considered by teachers and learners to be one of the primary causes behind L2 learning in the classroom (Dörnyei, 2005), although not all researchers hypothesize a causal role for motivation in accounting for individual differences in L2 learning (e.g., Sparks, 2012). Nonetheless, many researchers and teachers are concerned with how to increase learner motivation in the classroom. Indeed considerable research has investigated its role in the classroom and its relationship to L2 acquisition. Motivation, put simply, is the stimulus that drives learners to initiate and sustain the L2 learning process (Dörnyei, 2005).

In earlier SLA research, motivation was considered to be a relatively stable trait. For example, Robert Gardner and his associates began investigating the socioeducational model of acquisition in the 1970s. One of the main ideas of this model is that integrativeness 'supports an individual's motivation to learn a second language, but that motivation is responsible for achievement in the second language' (Masgoret & Gardner, 2003, p. 124). Integrativeness is seen when learners identify strongly with the L2 culture and its speakers and want to become a part of that culture in some way. In addition, although not a central component of the socioeducational model, instrumental orientation, which is evidenced by learners' pragmatic reasons for studying the language such as passing a class or getting a job, has also been of interest to ISLA researchers. The socioeducational model was developed and researched primarily in bilingual contexts in Canada, where it has been applied at a societal level, and where integrating into the L2 culture is more possible. However, the generalizability of this construct has been questioned, particularly in relation to English as a lingua franca where the integrative aspect is largely absent. Nevertheless, the socioeducational model has had considerable and prolonged influence on research into the relationship between motivation and L2 learning (e.g., Masgoret & Gardner, 2003).

Another criticism of the socioeducational model is that it views motivation as a fairly stable and consistent characteristic. However, since the 1990s, motivation research has entered a process-oriented approach in which motivation is viewed as dynamic, fluid, and changing. Indeed, even within a single class or activity, motivation may increase, decrease, or change. From this perspective, Dörnyei and colleagues (e.g., Dörnyei, 2005; Dörnyei & Ottó, 1998) have characterized motivation as existing in three stages: preactional, actional, and postactional. These stages relate to the point in time that learners find themselves in relation to a specific task. The preactional stage, also described as choice motivation, involves the goals and intentions that learners have as they begin a task. The actional stage, or executive motivation, is that motivation that learners have as they are conducting the task; it is what keeps them going. Finally, the postactional stage, or motivational retrospection, involves looking back on the task, assessing it, and moving forward (Dörnyei, 2005).

Finally, a further expansion in motivation research is Dörnyei's (2005) development of the L2 Motivational Self System, which consists of the ideal self, the ought-to self, and L2 learning experience. The first two constructs have perhaps been the more influential. The concept of the ideal self proposes that motivation for L2 learning is enhanced if a learner views his or her ideal self as a person who speaks an L2. In contrast, the ought-to self refers to the feelings of obligation that learners might have about learning the L2. In other words, learning an L2 is something that they feel they should do.

While the theoretical concepts of motivation have changed over time, there has nevertheless been an enduring concern with how to increase learner motivation in the classroom. To that end, researchers have investigated the motivational strategies that might influence classroom learners, and Dörnyei and Csizér (1998) even proposed the following 10 commandments for motivating L2 learners, based on their survey of Hungarian EFL teachers.

Ten commandments for motivating language learners (Dörnyei & Csizér, 1998, p. 215):

1. Set a personal example with your own behaviour. ⊂ be engage / be into what you are doing
2. Create a pleasant, relaxed atmosphere in the classroom.
3. Present the tasks properly. − how clear / realistic setting expectation
4. Develop a good relationship with the learners.
5. Increase the learners' linguistic self-confidence. ← where they actually are
6. Make the language classes interesting.
7. Promote learner autonomy. − to what extent you can give them purpose − aethentic
8. Personalize the learning process. − liberty
9. Increase the learners' goal-orientedness. − to what extent we can facilitate
10. Familiarize learners with the target language culture. their own goal (meaningful for them)

While these motivational strategies are the result of a large-scale research project, and perhaps resonate with teachers and students, there has been concern that some strategies may be more applicable in some cultural contexts than in others. For example, Cheng and Dörnyei (2007), in a replication Dörnyei and Csizér's study in a Taiwanese context, found that many of the motivational strategies were similar across contexts. However, unlike the Hungarian context, the Taiwanese teachers did not view the promotion of learner autonomy as a particularly relevant motivational strategy. In addition, Taiwanese teachers placed more emphasis on the appreciation of effort in the learning process. These results suggest that some motivational strategies may be more or less culturally relevant.

Because of the importance of motivation in the classroom, recent research has examined the implementation of these motivational strategies in the classroom, and the results of several studies will be presented in the empirical evidence section.

Willingness to Communicate

A topic that is related to motivation and relatively new to individual differences research in SLA is that of willingness to communicate. Originally investigated in L1 communication research, willingness to communicate refers to the predisposition towards talkativeness that learners have in the classroom and also potentially outside the classroom; as such it is the behavioral intent that can result in actual communicative behavior (MacIntyre, Clément, Dörnyei, & Noels, 1998). According to MacIntyre, Burns, and Jessome (2011), willingness to communicate addresses multiple dimensions of learners' experiences, including psychological, linguistic, educational, and communicative. These dimensions are reflected in the conceptualization of willingness to communicate as a pyramid in which willingness to communicate and communicative behavior are seen as being supported by a number of layers, such as the immediate situation in which learners find themselves, the motivational propensities that they have, as well as the larger social context. The base layers of the pyramid are considered to be more stable and enduring qualities, like personality and the larger societal context, while influencing factors further up the pyramid are based more on the current situation and context. For example, in the L2 classroom, learners' willingness to communicate may be affected by the classroom interactional patterns, their interlocutors, as well as task type and topic (Cao, 2011). As such, willingness to communicate can be high at times, and low at others (MacIntyre et al., 2011).

Willingness to communicate is seen as particularly important in light of the current emphasis on interaction in the classroom because it is a predictor of frequency of communication. If learners are not willing to communicate, then they will not get some of the prime benefits of L2 instruction, according to recent interactionist approaches to ISLA.

Learning Strategies

Another individual difference that has received attention in ISLA research and has been viewed as open to instruction is learners' use of learning strategies. Oxford (2011) defines learning strategies as 'the learners' goal-directed actions for improving language proficiency or achievement, completing a task, or making learning more efficient, effective, and easier' (p. 167). Learners may have preferences for certain learning strategies, in part based on their personalities and learning styles; however, teachers may be able to help learners use their learning strategies more effectively. In addition, instruction may make learners aware of previously unknown strategies.

Oxford developed the Strategy Inventory of Language Learning (SILL), which has been very influential in the study of learning strategies. Through responding to a series of questions that reflect various types of learning strategies, learners can discover the learning strategies that they tend to rely on. Although the definitions and boundaries of learning strategies can be varied, there have been several categories that have generally been agreed upon (Dörnyei & Skehan, 2003).

'Cognitive strategies' are those that involve the use of the brain to manipulate or transform L2 input in order to better retain it. Memorization strategies such as the keyword technique, repetition or visualization are examples of this category.

'Metacognitive strategies' involve using higher order thinking to plan, analyze, monitor, and evaluate learning. For example, planning to use certain memorization techniques, or thinking about how well those techniques have worked are metacognitive strategies.

'Social strategies' are activities in which learners seek out other people to help them in their learning. For example, having conversations with native speakers, or practicing the language with fellow students are social strategies.

'Affective strategies' involve the emotional aspect of the learning process. These strategies help learners regulate their emotions in order to facilitate the learning process. Rewarding one's self for studying for a specific amount of time is an example of an affective strategy.

One issue pertaining to learning strategies is whether or not they should be taught in the classroom. Some researchers suggest that strategy instruction is worth the time because it helps learners become better strategy users. Others argue that class time is better spent providing learners with L2 input and opportunities to interact in the L2.

Learning Styles

Related to learning strategies are the learning styles that often underlie specific strategies. For example, if someone is an analytical learner, then cognitive strategies that analyze the constituent parts of the L2 input might be a strategy that this person uses. Several learning style dimensions have been identified, as seen in Table 10.2 (Dörnyei & Skehan, 2003).

Dörnyei and Skehan (2003) suggest that there are several reasons for the attractiveness of learning styles in ISLA research, particularly in comparison

TABLE 10.2

Learning styles (based on Dörnyei & Skehan, 2003, p. 605)

Cognitive	the preferred or habitual patterns of mental functioning
Executive	concerning the degree to which the person seeks order, organization, and closure, and manages his or her own learning process
Affective	concerning values, beliefs, and attitudes that influence what an individual pays attention to in a learning situation
Social	concerning the preferred extent of involvement with other people while learning
Physiological	concerning at least partly the person's anatomically-based sensory and perceptual tendencies
Behavioral	concerning the extent to which someone actively seeks to satisfy his or her learning preferences

to other individual differences such as language aptitude. First, each learning style has its own advantages and disadvantages, with the result that even though learners with differing learning styles may approach learning in different ways, a variety of styles will still result in effective L2 learning. In addition, different styles may be better for some aspects of L2 learning, while others might influence other areas. Finally, it is also thought that learning styles, and especially learning strategies that learners employ based on those styles, are not as invariable as aptitude, and thus even though there might be strong dispositions towards one style or another, there is some flexibility in when learners draw upon different styles and strategies.

Critics of learning strategies and learning styles argue that these terms have been used very broadly and that the categories proposed by different researchers are imprecise, and until further systematicity and precision develop in this area, these constructs will not allow rigorous empirical investigation and thus will have little influence in ISLA (Dörnyei & Skehan, 2003; Sparks, 2012).

Personality

Personality is another individual difference that is comparatively stable, but being aware of its effects in the classroom can be helpful. There are several components to personality. The big five model (Goldberg, 1993; McCrae & Costa, 2003) is a major theory of personality in psychology (Dörnyei, 2005), and it consists of the following five primary traits: (1) openness to experience; (2) conscientiousness; (3) agreeableness; (4) extraversion-introversion; and (5) neuroticism-emotional stability. The descriptors used for neuroticism in the big five model include anxious, insecure, self-conscious, and emotional (Dörnyei, 2005, p. 15).

In terms of ISLA, the main way that neuroticism has been examined is through research into anxiety. Dewaele (2013) describes neuroticism as a proxy for trait anxiety, which is seen as different from foreign language anxiety, such that people with high general anxiety may not necessarily have high levels of foreign language anxiety. Horwitz et al. (1986) define anxiety as 'the subjective feeling of tension, apprehension, nervousness, and worry associated with an arousal of the autonomic nervous system' (p. 125). When considering anxiety, a distinction is made between general anxiety and language learning anxiety (Sparks & Patton, 2013). In addition to language anxiety, Pae (2013) suggests that there might be anxiety related to specific L2 skills that is separate from general language anxiety. Speaking in the classroom, in particular, is considered to be a highly anxiety provoking activity (Dewaele, 2013; Pae, 2013). In general, anxiety may have a negative effect on L2 acquisition (Pae, 2013; Sparks & Patton, 2013).

Language Learning Aptitude

One individual difference that has seen considerable research in the past is language learning aptitude; however, for several years it fell out of favor, in large part because, although it was viewed as contributing to L2 acquisition, it was not seen as something that researchers and teachers could influence in any meaningful way (Dörnyei & Skehan, 2003; Li, 2013). If learners have poor language learning abilities, then there may be little that can be done to increase their abilities, although there may be compensatory strategies that learners can be taught to make up for low aptitude. However recently there has been increased attention to aptitude in ISLA research, in particular because there is interest in aptitude-treatment interaction, in which instruction is matched to learners' specific strengths in L2 learning (Ellis, 2005).

Although individuals have aptitude for a variety of cognitive and physical activities, language learning aptitude is seen as being distinct from other measures, such as general intelligence, as measured for example by IQ. Aptitude specific to language learning refers to the strengths that learners may have in relation to the cognitive processes that are involved in L2 learning (Robinson, 2005). Language aptitude is also considered to be a primarily innate, fairly stable trait that is not affected by training or instruction (Li, 2013). Moreover, language aptitude is considered to be one of the primary causal variables in L2 learning (Carroll, 1993; Granena, 2013).

Language aptitude has been identified as having several different components. Not all conceptualizations of language aptitude agree in every detail; nevertheless, there are some core components that are similar across views, based in large part on Carroll's (1981) categorization of language aptitude. Four aspects of language aptitude that are commonly referred to are phonemic coding ability, grammatical sensitivity, implicit learning ability, and memorization ability.

Phonemic coding ability refers to the ability that learners have to distinguish sounds in the input and to form and retain sound-symbol associations. Thus, it refers to learners' ability to discriminate between individual sounds, but also to listen to an incoming stream of sound, identify the phonological boundaries of words, and recall the meaning of the particular arrangement of sounds.

Grammatical sensitivity addresses the ability that learners have to recognize the grammatical functions of words in sentences, that is the skill that learners possess in identifying the grammatical roles that words play in the structure of a sentence. This ability does not consist of learners' knowledge of metalinguistic terminology, but rather their ability to recognize grammatical relationships in the input.

Implicit learning ability, also referred to as inductive learning ability, is learners' ability to infer the rules of a language based on the input that they are exposed to. In other words, without being taught specific, explicit grammatical rules, can learners recognize the grammatical patterns and relationships that are present in the input?

Memorization ability, or rote learning ability, characterizes learners' ability to make and retain sound-meaning associations: how good are learners at memorizing and remembering L2 words and other information?

One of the common instruments developed to measure language aptitude is the Modern Language Aptitude Test (MLAT), which consists of five parts that measure three dimensions of aptitude: phonetic coding ability, language analytic ability, and rote learning (memory) ability.

Although it may be the case that little can be done to increase learners' language aptitude, it is a possibility that different types or aspects of aptitude may be more helpful for L2 learning than others (Robinson, 2005). For example, Li (2013) suggests that grammatical sensitivity, also known as language analytic ability, may help with more implicit aspects of instruction because learners are better able to extract patterns and recognize things from the input.

Working Memory

One other aspect of aptitude that has become very popular in ISLA research is working memory. Unlike the aspects of language learning aptitude that relate specifically to language, working memory is not language specific although it is heavily implicated in the processing of language. Working memory has been described as a temporary storage system that allows individuals to hold and process information for a short period of time. Working memory is continually processing information as it comes in, and because it is a limited capacity system, the information either exits the working memory or gets transferred to long-term memory (Li, 2013; Williams, 2012). The exact makeup of the working memory system is debated, but the details are less important than the overall description for a survey such as this. See Baddeley (2007) or Williams (2012) for a fuller treatment of the specific components of working memory.

Working memory is viewed as especially important for L2 acquisition because of the role it plays in focusing attention on specific components of the input. With noticing and attention being key constructs in cognitive and interactionist approaches to SLA, a larger working memory allows learners to hold more information in that temporary storage facility, thereby facilitating the proposed mechanisms of language learning.

Working memory may be assessed in a variety of ways; however, in general such methods involve learners in retaining increasing amounts of information while involved in additional tasks. For example, Li (2013) used a listening span test in which learners were asked to judge the plausibility of sentences. The sentences were presented in sets, and at the end of each set, learners had to recall the final word of each sentence. As the test progressed the number of sentences in each set increased, thereby taxing the ability of the working memory to hold all of the elements.

EMPIRICAL EVIDENCE

Motivation

A considerable amount of effort has gone into motivation research, from a variety of different theoretical perspectives. One meta-analysis of studies from Gardner and his colleagues provides a nice overview of motivational research from the soicoeducational perspective. Masgoret and Gardner (2003) meta-analyzed 75 studies investigating the role of attitudes and motivation in L2 learning. They only looked at studies conducted within the framework of Gardner's socioeducational model, and these used the Attitude/Motivation Test Battery to collect the data. Of the 75 studies, only 9 were conducted outside of Canada. Their overall conclusion based on the analysis was that motivation had the greatest relationship with L2 achievement, although all of the five classes of variables that they investigated—attitudes toward the learning situation, integrativeness, motivation, integrative orientation, and instrumental orientation—were positively related to achievement in a second language. Finally, Masgoret and Gardner did not find any moderating effect for the availability of the L2 in the immediate environment, which they suggest counters claims that the socioeducational model is specific to bilingual contexts.

Although research into the nature of motivation is important from an SLA perspective, perhaps what is more important for instructed L2 learning are the ways in which teachers can influence learner motivation. A recent study on the links between teachers' motivational strategy use and learners' motivation was conducted by Guilloteaux and Dörnyei (2008). They examined 27 teachers and 1,381 junior high school students in South Korea. Data collection included classroom observations to assess teachers' use of motivational strategies, with an emphasis on teacher discourse, participation structure, and encouraging positive retrospective self-evaluation. Student motivation was measured through the use of a questionnaire. Results indicated a strong correlation between motivational strategies and student motivation, leading the researchers to call for more focused research on the effects of specific strategy domains.

In a similar study, Moskovsky et al. (2013) investigated the effects of 14 teachers' motivational strategy use on 300 Saudi learners' classroom behavior. The researchers exposed half of the learners to different motivational strategies over an eight-week period, while the other group received traditional instruction. Teachers were given training in implementing a variety of strategies based loosely on the motivational principles put forward by Dörnyei and Csizér (1998). Learners were given a motivation questionnaire with questions targeting both trait and state motivation at the beginning and end of the project. Their results indicated that there were significant increases in both kinds of motivation for the experimental group compared to the control group; however, situational state motivation showed a larger effect, suggesting that more general trait motivation may take longer to be influenced.

Willingness to Communicate

Because of the importance of interaction in the L2 classroom, it is important to understand what factors my make students more or less willing to communicate. In one such study, MacIntyre et al. (2011) investigated the journal entries of 100 junior high school students in a French immersion program in Canada. Passages within the journals were designated according to the amount of willingness to communicate that they indicating, ranging from least willing to most willing. MacIntyre et al. (2011) found that many situations prompted both willingness and unwillingness to communicate, and at times there were only subtle differences between the two. Students reported feeling most willing to communicate in class, as opposed to outside of class, and with their fellow students, rather than their teacher; however, strict guidelines to speak only in the target language sometimes made students less willing to communicate. In addition, interaction activities had the ability to increase willingness to communicate if they were conducted in ways that reaffirmed students' competence and autonomy. Furthermore, students indicated that the actions of other people had a significant effect on their willingness to communicate, sometimes increasing it and other times decreasing it. As such, MacIntyre et al., suggest that willingness to communicate is not just an internal individual difference but also one that is dialogic in nature, dependent on the relationship between interlocutors. Furthermore, results suggest that learners may experience both willingness and unwillingness to communicate at the same.

In another study, Cao (2011) empirically investigated the factors that may contribute to willingness to communicate. Cao employed a multiple-case study methodology over a 20-week period with six advanced-level students in an English for Academic Purposes class in New Zealand. Data collection involved classroom observations, stimulated recalls based upon those observations, and journal entries. To operationalize willingness to communicate, Cao examined the classroom interaction for instances of unforced learner participation. Cao found that a variety of factors, rather than one single factor, appeared to work together to influence willingness to communicate. These variables included: (a) individual ones such as personality, self-confidence and emotion; (b) linguistic ones such as L2 proficiency and reliance on L1; and

(c) environmental variables such as topic, interlocutor, and task type. Furthermore, the influence of each variable at a given point in the class waxed and waned.

Learning Strategies

Because of the potential usefulness of learning strategies for L2 learning and because of their teachability, numerous studies have investigated learners' use of them. In an overview study, Plonsky (2011) meta-analyzed 61 studies that investigated the effects of language strategy instruction on L2 learning. Overall, Plonsky found a small-to-medium effect for strategy instruction. In addition, he found effects for specific moderator variables. For example, the proficiency level of learners receiving strategy instruction was significant, with higher-proficiency learners being able to better employ new strategies. Plonsky also found that strategy instruction in second language contexts was more effective than in foreign language contexts, which he attributes in part to the greater opportunities that learners have to use learning strategies in second language contexts. Strategy training was also considerably more effective in laboratory settings than in classroom contexts. Finally, strategy instruction, especially for cognitive and metacognitive strategies, was found to be more effective when focusing on teaching one or two strategies over a longer period of time.

One specific study that found a positive effect for strategy instruction is Vandergrift and Tafaghodtari (2010), who investigated the effects of teaching metacognitive strategies for L2 listening. Over the course of a semester, two groups of French learners engaged in numerous listening activities, with one group receiving additional instruction on listening strategies. The strategies involved making predictions about the kinds of information learners might hear in the texts that they listened to. After discussing their predictions with their peers and then listening to the text multiple times, learners considered how accurate their predications had been. Learners in the control group also listened to the texts but did not do additional activities. Vandergrift and Tafaghodtari found that the strategy instruction group performed significantly better on listening tests at the end of the training period. In addition, less skilled listeners benefitted more from the training than did more skilled listeners.

In another study of listening strategy instruction, Cross (2009) investigated 15 advanced level Japanese learners of English. They were involved in a 10-week current affairs course based on materials from the BBC. One group received strategy instruction on 14 different strategies related to listening. These strategies included four metacognitive strategies, such as selective attention, seven cognitive strategies, such as detection and inferencing, and three social-affective strategies, including cooperation and self-motivation.

Both treatment and control groups went through a pedagogical cycle of pre-listening preparation, monitoring of comprehension, and evaluation of performance. Results indicated that both groups improved their listening abilities, but there was no advantage for the group that received strategy instruction. Cross suggests that the large number of strategies may have hindered the treatment group's ability to take advantage of the instruction. Furthermore, he notes that the three-stage pedagogical cycle may have been in large part responsible for the control group's improved performance.

Anxiety

Several studies have examined the effects of anxiety on L2 learning. For example, Révész (2011) investigated the performance of 43 advanced ESL learners on a series of simple and complex tasks. The purpose of the study was to assess the influence of task complexity on the accuracy and complexity of learners' language production, as well as the quality and quantity of interaction-driven learning opportunities, especially in the form of corrective feedback and language-related episodes. In addition, Révész used self-report questionnaires to examine the moderating effects of linguistic self-confidence, anxiety, and self-perceived communicative competence on learners' task performance. Results indicated that task complexity did affect learners' language production and interaction, with more accurate but less syntactically complex language being produced during complex tasks. In addition, complex tasks resulted in more language-related episodes. However, in contrast to expectations, no significant relationships among any of the individual difference scores and learners' accuracy and complexity were found. Révész suggests that the advanced proficiency level of the learners may have meant that they had developed compensation strategies to counteract any negative effects of individual differences such as high anxiety.

In another study of language anxiety, Y. Sheen (2008) investigated the effects of anxiety on learners' ability to benefit from corrective feedback. She had four groups of intermediate proficiency ESL learners, divided according to high and low anxiety, and presence or absence of recasts. English articles were the targeted structure. An anxiety questionnaire was used to measure learners' language anxiety. Sheen found that, overall, learners with low anxiety benefitted significantly more from recasts than did the high anxiety group. Sheen hypothesizes that anxiety interfered with learners' ability to process recasts, thereby rendering them ineffective. In addition, low anxiety learners also produced more modified output in response to recasts.

Another issue related to anxiety is the context in which it occurs. In particular, there is the suggestion that computer-mediated communication, especially in its written form, can reduce learners' anxiety related to producing language. In a study investigating this assumption, Baralt and Gurzynski-Weiss (2011) engaged 25 intermediate learners of Spanish at an American university in task-based interaction, both in a face-to-face context and through computer-mediated communication. Using a questionnaire, learners' state of anxiety was assessed twice, once during the middle of the interaction, and once at the end of the task. Contrary to their expectations, Baralt and Gurzynski-Weiss found no difference in learners' anxiety in the two modalities.

Language Learning Aptitude

Recent research has been concerned with the interaction of various aspects of language aptitude and different L2 instructional practices. For example, Li (2013) conducted a study that investigated the interaction between implicit and explicit types of corrective feedback and language analytic ability and working memory. Li involved 78 U.S. university learners of Chinese in dyadic interaction. One group received recasts on their errors of Chinese classifiers, while a second group received metalinguistic feedback, and a third group received no feedback. Li used the Words in Sentences subtest of the MLAT to measure language analytic ability and a listening span test to measure working memory. Li found that both implicit and explicit feedback were facilitative of learners' interlanguage development on Chinese classifiers. In addition, language analytic ability was associated with implicit feedback, while working memory was associated with the effects of explicit feedback. Li suggests that in the absence of metalinguistic feedback, language analytic ability helped learners notice linguistic problems and extract and generalize the syntactic regularities regarding classifier use from the recasts. Furthermore, the effects of metalinguistic feedback were enhanced by larger working memory capacity which enabled learners to better store and process the information that was provided.

In another study of aptitude abilities and recasts, Y. Sheen (2007) investigated the interaction between type of feedback (recasts versus metalinguistic feedback) and language aptitude; however, she found no correlation between the recast groups' gain scores and language analytic ability. Sheen suggests that because the feedback was implicit, learners were not aware of the target structure and thus did not use their analytic ability. However, in the metalinguistic group, a strong correlation was found between feedback and analytic ability, suggesting that learners with higher analytic ability were better able to benefit from the more explicit attention provided by the feedback.

PEDAGOGICAL IMPLICATIONS

It is clear that individual differences can impact the success of L2 acquisition; however, it is less clear the role that teachers have in influencing these factors.

In some cases, such as learning strategies, there is some evidence to suggest that instruction can be effective in increasing the quantity and quality of strategy use; however, the research results are far from conclusive, and in many cases, teachers may feel less inclined to use class time for activities other than language instruction.

In the case of other individual differences, such as motivation or anxiety, teachers may have some influence in improving these qualities for the classroom. For example, by employing motivational strategies such as those advocated by Dörnyei and Csizér, (1998), teachers may bring about a more positive atmosphere in the classroom, which may lead to an increase in motivation and a decrease in anxiety. Nevertheless, it may be difficult to completely overcome the effects of personality traits such as anxiety.

Finally, in terms of aptitude and working memory, there seems little that teachers can do except be aware of the workings of these factors. Recently, there has been an interest in ISLA in how different types of aptitude interact with different types of instruction (Robinson, 2005), and while such information may prove insightful from a theoretical perspective, the implications for pedagogy seem less clear. For example, Li's (2013) study found that corrective feedback in the form of recasts was more effective for learners with higher levels of language analytic ability, while metalinguistic feedback was more beneficial for learners with larger working memories. However, identifying learners with such aptitudes, while easy enough in a research context, is more difficult in the classroom. Even if identifying learners' aptitudes were easy, the question remains of how to put that information to use. Dividing learners according to ability may be impractical as well as unpopular. Thus, it would seem that one of the best methods of insuring that different types of aptitude are catered for is for teachers to employ a wide range of pedagogical activities, some of which may be more beneficial for some learners than for others.

ACTIVITIES

1. The following questions come from the motivation questionnaire used by Moskovsky et al. (2013) to measure Saudi students' state and trait motivation at the beginning and end of an eight-week treatment in which the teachers implemented motivational strategies. Learners had to indicate on a 7-point Likert scale how true or untrue these statements were for them. Half of the sentences were general, while half referred to the English course that the learners were taking. This difference can be seen in comparing Questions 5 and 6. What are the strengths and weaknesses of measuring motivation in this way? What other ways might there be to measure motivation in the L2 classroom, and what strengths and weaknesses would those methods have?

1. I am confident I will receive better grades if I try harder.
2. If I do well in my study, it will be because I try hard.
3. I enjoy learning very much.
4. I wouldn't study if I didn't have to.
5. Learning is a boring activity for me.
6. Thinking of learning English this semester, I feel that _____

   Learning English is a boring activity for me.
7. Thinking of my effort to learn English this semester, _____

   I have been working hard to learn English.
8. I haven't spent sufficient time working on my English homework.
9. In English classes this semester I feel confident that _____

   I can master hard learning tasks in English if I try.

2. Measuring Anxiety

Baralt and Gurzynski-Weiss (2011, p. 226) used the following questionnaire to measure learners' state of anxiety immediately after they finished a communicative task. What are the strengths and weaknesses of measuring motivation in this way? What other ways might there be to measure motivation in the L2 classroom, and what strengths and weaknesses would those methods have?

Instructions: Please circle if you strongly agree (SA), agree (A), neither agree nor disagree (N), disagree (D), or strongly disagree (SD) with each statement.

1. I was not bothered by my partner communicating quickly.
   SA   A   N   D   SD
2. I felt more anxious in class than completing the task.
   SA   A   N   D   SD
3. I got flustered when my partner communicated things I did not understand.
   SA   A   N   D   SD
4. I felt like I didn't have enough time to think before I had to respond.
   SA   A   N   D   SD
5. I felt rushed during the task.
   SA   A   N   D   SD
6. I felt confident in my ability to quickly learn new things in Spanish.
   SA   A   N   D   SD
7. I felt tense having to communicate with my partner.
   SA   A   N   D   SD
8. This task did not make me anxious.
   SA   A   N   D   SD

9. I was relaxed and comfortable completing the task.
SA   A   N   D   SD
10. This task made me less anxious than I feel in class.
SA   A   N   D   SD
11. I feel like I had enough time to complete the task.
SA   A   N   D   SD
12. The task was fun and enjoyable.
SA   A   N   D   SD
13. It did not bother me when I did not understand everything my partner was saying.
SA   A   N   D   SD
14. I enjoyed communicating with my partner during this task.
SA   A   N   D   SD
15. This task was stressful for me.
SA   A   N   D   SD

ADDITIONAL READINGS

Dörnyei, Z. (2001). *Motivational strategies in the language classroom.* Cambridge: Cambridge University Press.

Dörnyei, Z. (2005). *The psychology of the language learner: Individual differences in second language acquisition.* New York: Routledge.

Robinson, P. (2002). *Individual differences and instructed language learning.* Amsterdam: John Benjamins.

11

Conclusion

THE BASICS OF INSTRUCTED SECOND LANGUAGE ACQUISITION

Instructed SLA concerns any attempt to manipulate or intervene in the process of L2 acquisition. It is grounded in SLA theory and research, and it assumes that what we do in the classroom matters. Instruction can be beneficial, and one of the goals of ISLA theory and research is to investigate which interventions might be most helpful for L2 learning in the classroom. Another point is that the cognitive processes of learning are the same regardless of context—second language, foreign language, computer-assisted language learning, et cetera.

The Nature of L2 Knowledge

Learners have different types of L2 knowledge, which are available for use in different ways. Explicit knowledge is conscious knowledge that learners have, and it often consists of metalinguistic rules about the grammatical features of the L2. Much knowledge of vocabulary is also explicit, particularly in terms of form-meaning connections. Implicit knowledge is unconscious knowledge of the L2 that enables learners to use the language in spontaneous communication. Implicit knowledge applies to grammatical 'rules,' as well as some aspects of vocabulary such as collocations, multiword units, and frequency. Less research has considered how phonological and pragmatic knowledge are represented. Explicit instruction usually results in explicit knowledge. Implicit knowledge takes time and considerable exposure to develop. There is controversy regarding the idea that explicit knowledge can become implicit, although this is an important tenet of Skill Acquisition Theory, which suggests that learners typically begin with declarative knowledge and then through practice develop procedural knowledge, which can become fully automatized, meaning that learners can draw on it to produce language with relative ease. The goal of L2 instruction and learning is generally for learners to develop communicative competence, which requires implicit knowledge on their part.

Interaction in the Classroom

In response to excessive focus on explicit grammar instruction that did not result in learners with communicative competence, theorists have proposed that having learners participate in meaning-focused interaction in the classroom is a better way to develop their communicative abilities. Krashen's early Monitor Theory advocated the avoidance of grammar and the creation of input-rich environments in which learners were exposed to large amounts of comprehensible input. More recently the interaction approach has stressed the importance of learners engaging in negotiation for meaning in order to draw their attention to and potentially resolve problematic linguistic items. This combination of attention to language items during meaning-focused interaction is thought to bring together the optimal cognitive conditions for L2 acquisition. A pedagogical extension of the interaction approach is task-based teaching and learning, which proposes that tasks are the ideal way of providing learners with meaning-focused interaction in the classroom. Tasks consist of real-world types of activities that have non-linguistic goals as outcomes of the task. Learners are expected to rely primarily on their own linguistic resources, and attention to linguistic forms is kept to a minimum.

Focus on Form

There is general agreement that communication alone cannot help instructed learners achieve the desired levels of linguistic accuracy. Thus, focus on form extends the interaction approach by suggesting that attention to language might need to occur slightly more intentionally and explicitly than might happen if learners are left on their own during communicative tasks. Consequently, focus on form attempts to draw learners' attention to language structures within a larger communicative context, and one of its concerns is the most efficient and unobtrusive manner to bring this about. Input flood and input enhancement are two of the most implicit types focus on form, with the number of targeted linguistic forms being increased and highlighted in some way. While research has found some effects for these two methods, there is also evidence to suggest that they might not be the most effective in promoting L2 development. Another popular type of focus on form is the provision of corrective feedback during communicative interaction, which has been found to be frequently successful in for L2 learning.

The Acquisition of Grammar

In spite of the substantial emphasis on L2 learning through meaning-focused communication and interaction, there remains a concern for the role of explicit instruction in the acquisition of grammar. Explicit instruction consists of overt explanations of L2 grammatical patterns and rules, and it may involve practicing those rules in relatively decontextualized ways. However, there have been efforts to incorporate more emphasis on meaning within explicit instruction. In addition to more traditional types of explicit instruction, researchers have also investigated the effects of input-based approaches that emphasize the provision of structured input to make learners aware of strategies of L1 processing that are inefficient or inappropriate in the L2. After learners have been provided with this explicit information, they are given input that necessitates the use of more effective processing strategies. Another option within explicit instruction is the present, practice, and produce (PPP) method. Supported by skill acquisition theory, this method begins by developing learners' declarative knowledge and then provides them with increasingly less controlled opportunities to implement that knowledge. Although PPP has, in the past, been associated with more mechanical types of practice activities, there has been a recent emphasis on incorporating more meaning-focused types of activities. In sum, there are multiple options for more explicit types of grammar instruction, and scholars have found that while both implicit and explicit instruction can be beneficial for L2 learning, there is often an advantage for more explicit methods.

The Acquisition of Vocabulary

The acquisition of vocabulary has been a subject of intensive research in ISLA, with a primary focus on the acquisition of explicit form-meaning connections. However, there has also been consideration of the aspects of vocabulary knowledge that can potentially be implicit, such as knowledge of collocations, register, domain, and frequency. Vocabulary research has been concerned with developing both the breadth and depth of learners' vocabulary knowledge, and there has been emphasis on both receptive and productive knowledge. In terms of instructed vocabulary learning, there has been an emphasis on both incidental and intentional learning. Incidental learning occurs primarily through extensive reading, and while it has been found to be effective, it also takes considerable time for learners to acquire lexical items in this way. Focus on form and explicit instruction are also methods that can result in intentional learning. In particular, researchers suggest that engagement with lexical items, through numerous encounters in multiple contexts and through a variety of means, is optimal for facilitating acquisition.

The Acquisition of Pronunciation

Although less attention has been devoted to pronunciation acquisition, there is still a considerable amount of ISLA research in this area. In general, this research has investigated the effects of explicit instruction on learners' ability to perceive and produce L2 sounds, with evidence suggesting that such instruction can be beneficial. In addition, the integration of pronunciation into communicative activities holds some benefit as seen by studies of the effects of corrective feedback. One issue that is of considerable concern for pronunciation instruction is the goal that learners should aim to achieve. Although the goal of native-like pronunciation may be held by some individuals, researchers suggest that learners should strive for comprehensible L2 production rather than native-like accent.

The Acquisition of Pragmatics

Pragmatics is one of the last areas of language to be mastered in an L2. It is often not addressed in the classroom, and furthermore, learners often have limited exposure to L2 use outside of the classroom, with the consequence that learners often receive limited pragmatics instruction or input. Nevertheless, if pragmatics is addressed in the classroom, there is research suggesting that explicit instruction can be beneficial for learners. In particular, learners may need to be made aware of pragmatic differences between their L1 and L2. Finally, research suggests that getting learners involved in social interaction outside of the classroom can provide access to social situations that are difficult to replicate in the classroom. If learners are trained to go into such contexts with the intention of noticing the pragmatic norms, they may receive increased benefit from such opportunities.

Contexts of Instructed Second Language Acquisition

In addition to the traditional classroom, there are other contexts in which ISLA occurs. A distinction is made between foreign and second language contexts, based on whether the L2 is the language of the wider society that the learner is in. While the foreign versus second language distinction may have some utility, the differences between the two contexts may not be substantial. Another context that has been viewed as optimal for L2 learning is study abroad in which learners spend time in an L2-speaking environment. Although there are many linguistic advantages for study abroad, particularly in terms of oral proficiency, not all aspects of language may improve. Furthermore, learners may need to be made aware of the importance of social interaction for L2 learning and opportunities for them to engage with speakers in the host country should be fostered.

Other nontraditional contexts include immersion and content-based classes in which the primary goal is for learners to learn academic content through the L2. Acquisition of the L2 is also a goal, although teachers may vary in the degree to which they are trained in achieving this goal. Finally, the role of technology in current contexts for learning continues to increase, with the use of computer-mediated communication being of particular interest to ISLA researchers.

Individual Differences and Instructed Second Language Acquisition

Although the cognitive processes of learning are the same for all learners, there are individual differences that factor into the success or failure of the L2 learning enterprise. Motivation has been considered an important moderator variable in the effects of L2 instruction, and there is an increasing tendency to view motivation as more situated, fluid, and dynamic construct. Related to motivation is learners' willingness to communicate, an important variable in interactionist approaches to ISLA. If learners are reluctant to communicate in the classroom, then they may not experience the proposed acquisitional benefits for meaning-focused interaction. Learning strategies and learning styles are other individual variables that may influence learners' success, and while there has been some research investigating the effectiveness of teaching learners new strategies, the results are somewhat inconclusive. Finally, the role of aptitude in L2 learning has seen a resurgence of interest, as researchers become more interested in aptitude-treatment interaction and its implication for instruction.

OTHER OBSERVATIONS

In one sense, there is little that researchers, teachers, and learners can do to influence L2 acquisition. That is to say, the cognitive processes that learners undergo in L2 development appear to occur in the same way, regardless of the contexts in which learners find themselves, whether instructed or uninstructed. On the other hand, ISLA can do quite a lot to influence acquisition. In particular, the quality and quantity of input that learners receive, and the opportunities for interaction and output in the classroom, are potential advantages for L2 learning. In fact, the theories and research presented in the chapters of this book are quite positive about the efficacy of L2 instruction, while there is also the acknowledgment that instruction is not always effective in all contexts. The goal of ISLA is to ensure that these opportunities are maximized to enable learners to achieve the highest levels of success possible in their endeavor to learn a second language through classroom instruction.

FINAL COMMENTS

Many researchers have made recommendations regarding instruction in the L2 classroom. Rather than reinventing a list of my own, I would like to close with Rod Ellis's (2005, pp. 33–43) list of general principles of for successful instructed learning:

1. Instruction needs to ensure that learners develop both a rich repertoire of formulaic expressions and a rule-based competence.
2. Instruction needs to ensure that learners focus predominantly on meaning.
3. Instruction needs to ensure that learners also focus on form.
4. Instruction needs to be predominantly directed at developing implicit knowledge of the L2 while not neglecting explicit knowledge.
5. Instruction needs to take into account learners' 'built-in syllabus.'
6. Successful instructed language learning requires extensive L2 input.
7. Successful instructed language learning also requires opportunities for output.
8. The opportunity to interact in the L2 is central to developing L2 proficiency.
9. Instruction needs to take account of individual differences in learners.
10. In assessing learners' L2 proficiency it is important to examine free as well as controlled production.

References

Abraham, L. (2008). Computer-mediated glosses in second language reading comprehension and vocabulary learning: A meta-analysis. *Computer Assisted Language Learning, 21,* 199–226.

Adams, R. (2007). Do second language learners benefit from interacting with each other? In A. Mackey (Ed.), *Conversational interaction in second language acquisition* (pp. 30–51). Oxford: Oxford University Press.

Ahn, S. (2013). *L2 pragmatic development through conversational interaction: Heritage language background and explicitness of feedback.* (Unpublished doctoral dissertation). Michigan State University, East Lansing, MI.

Alderson, C., & Hudson, R. (2013). The metalinguistic knowledge of undergraduate students of English language or linguistics. *Language Awareness, 22,* 320–337.

Al-Homoud, F., & Schmitt, N. (2009). Extensive reading in a challenging environment: A comparison of extensive and intensive reading approaches in Saudi Arabia. *Language Teaching Research, 13,* 383–401.

Al-jasser, F. (2008). The effect of teaching English phonotactics on the lexical segmentation of English as a foreign language. *System, 36,* 94–106.

Andringa, S., de Glopper, K., & Hacquebord, H. (2011). Effect of explicit and implicit instruction on free written response task performance. *Language Learning, 61,* 868–903.

Baddeley, A. (2007). *Working memory, thought, and action.* Oxford: Oxford University Press.

Ballinger, S., & Lyster, R. (2011). Student and teacher oral language use in a two-way Spanish/English immersion school. *Language Teaching Research, 15,* 289–306.

Baralt, M., & Gurzynski-Weiss, L. (2011). Comparing learners' state anxiety during task-based interaction in computer-mediated and face-to-face communication. *Language Teaching Research, 15,* 201–229.

Bardovi-Harlig, K. (2000). *Tense and aspect in second language acquisition: Form, meaning, and use.* Oxford: Blackwell.

Bardovi-Harlig, K. (2013). Developing L2 pragmatics. *Language Learning, 1* (Suppl.), 68–86.

Bardovi-Harlig, K., & Vellenga, H. (2012). The effect of instruction on conventional expressions in L2 pragmatics. *System, 40,* 77–89.

Barraja-Rohan, A. (2011). Using conversation analysis in the second language classroom to teach interactional competence. *Language Teaching Research, 15,* 479–507.

Basturkmen, H., Loewen, S., & Ellis, R. (2002). Metalanguage in focus on form in the communicative classroom. *Language Awareness, 11,* 1–13.

Belz, J.A. (2007) The role of computer mediation in the instruction and development of L2 pragmatic competence. *Annual Review of Applied Linguistics, 27*, 45–75.

Belz, J.A., & Kinginger, C. (2003). Discourse options and the development of pragmatic competence by classroom learners of German: The case of address forms. *Language Learning, 53*, 591–647.

Bialystok, E. (1982). On the relationship between knowing and using forms. *Applied Linguistics, 3*, 181–206.

Bitchener, J. (2004). The Relationship between the negotiation of meaning and language learning: A longitudinal study. *Language Awareness, 13*, 81–95.

Blake, R. (2000). Computer mediated communication: A window on L2 Spanish interlanguage. *Language Learning & Technology, 4*, 120–136.

Blake, R. (2011). Current trends in online language learning. *Annual Review of Applied Linguistics, 31*, 19–35.

Boers, F., & Lindstromberg, S. (2009). *Optimizing a lexical approach to instructed second language acquisition.* New York: Palgrave Macmillan.

Boers, F., Lindstromberg, S., & Eyckmans, J. (2013). Is alliteration mnemonic without awareness-raising? *Language Awareness, 22*, 1–13.

Boers, F., Piquer Píriz, A., Stengers, H., & Eyckmans, J. (2009). Does pictorial elucidation foster recollection of idioms? *Language Teaching Research, 13*(4), 367–382.

Bouffard, L., & Sarkar, M. (2008). Training 8-year-old French immersion students in metalinguistic analysis: An innovation in form-focused pedagogy. *Language Awareness, 17*(1), 3–24.

Bowles, M. (2010). *The think aloud controversy in language acquisition research.* New York: Routledge.

Bowles, M. (2011). Measuring implicit and explicit linguistic knowledge: What can heritage language learners contribute? *Studies in Second Language Acquisition, 33*, 247–271.

Brinton, D.M., Snow, M.A., & Wesche, M. (2003). *Content-based second language instruction.* Ann Arbor: The University of Michigan Press.

Bueno-Alastuey, M. C. (2013). Interactional feedback in synchronous voice-based computer mediated communication: Effect of dyad. *System, 41*, 543–559.

Burnett, J. (2011). Two case studies of secondary language teaching: A critical look at the intersection of management and the local and social realities that shape our classrooms. *The Modern Language Journal, 95*, (Suppl.), 4–26.

Cammarata, L., & Tedick, D. (2012). Balancing content and language instruction: The experience of immersion teachers. *The Modern Language Journal, 96*, 251–269.

Canale, M., & Swain, M. (1980). Theoretical bases of communicative approaches to second language teaching and testing. *Applied Linguistics, 1*, 1–47.

Cao, Y. (2011). Investigating situational willingness to communicate within second language classrooms from an ecological perspective. *System, 39*, 468–479.

Carless, D. (2012). TBLT in EFL settings: Looking back and moving forward. In A. Shehadeh & C. Coombe (Eds.), *Task-based language teaching in foreign language contexts: Research and implementation* (pp. 346–358). Amsterdam: John Benjamins.

Carroll, J. (1981). Twenty-five years in foreign language aptitude. In K. Diller (Ed.), *Individual differences and universals in language learning aptitude* (pp. 83–118). Rowley, MA: Newbury House.

Carroll, J. (1993). *Human cognitive abilities: A survey of factor-analytic studies.* Cambridge: Cambridge University Press.

Chapelle, C. (2009). The relationship between second language acquisition theory and computer-assisted language learning. *The Modern Language Journal, 93*, 741–753.

Chaudron, C. (1988). *Second language classrooms: Research on teaching and learning.* Cambridge: Cambridge University Press.

Cheng, H., & Dörnyei, Z. (2007). The use of motivational strategies in language instruction: The case of EFL teaching in Taiwan. *Innovation in Language Learning and Teaching, 1,* 153–174.

Cobb, T. (2007). Computing the vocabulary demands of L2 reading. *Language Learning & Technology, 11,* 38–63.

Collentine, J. (2004). The effects of learning contexts on morphosyntactic and lexical development. *Studies in Second Language Acquisition, 26,* 227–248.

Collentine, J., & Freed, B. (2004). Learning context and its effects on second language acquisition: Introduction. *Studies in Second Language Acquisition, 26,* 153–171.

Coxhead, A. (2000). A new Academic Word List. *TESOL Quarterly, 34,* 213–238.

Cross, J. (2009). Effects of listening strategy instruction on news videotext comprehension. *Language Teaching Research, 13,* 151–176.

Dalton-Puffer, C. (2007). *Discourse in content and language integrated learning (CLIL) classrooms.* Philadelphia, PA: John Benjamins.

Davies, M. (2006). *A frequency dictionary of Spanish: Core vocabulary for learners.* New York: Routledge.

DeKeyser, R. (1998). Beyond focus on form: Cognitive perspective on learning and practicing second language grammar. In C. Doughty & J. Williams (Eds.), *Focus on form in classroom second language acquisition* (pp. 42–63). Cambridge: Cambridge University Press.

DeKeyser, R. (2007a). Conclusion: The future of practice. In R. DeKeyser (Ed.), *Practice in a second language: Perspectives from applied linguistics and cognitive psychology* (pp. 287–304). Cambridge: Cambridge University Press.

DeKeyser, R. (2007b). *Practice in a second language: Perspectives from applied linguistics and cognitive psychology.* Cambridge: Cambridge University Press.

DeKeyser, R. (2007c). Skill acquisition theory. In B. VanPatten & J. Williams (Eds.), *Theories in second language acquisition: An introduction* (pp. 97–113). Mahwah, NJ: Lawrence Erlbaum Associates.

DeKeyser, R. (2007d). Study abroad as foreign language practice. In R. DeKeyser (Ed.), *Practice in a second language: Perspectives from applied linguistics and cognitive psychology* (pp. 208–226). Cambridge: Cambridge University Press.

Derwing, T., & Munro, M. (2005). Second language accent and pronunciation teaching: A research-based approach. *TESOL Quarterly, 39,* 379–397.

Dewaele, J. (2013). The link between foreign language classroom anxiety and psychoticism, extraversion, and neuroticism among adult bi- and multilinguals. *The Modern Language Journal, 97*(3), 670–684.

Díaz-Campos, M. (2004). Context of learning in the acquisition of Spanish second language phonology. *Studies in Second Language Acquisition, 26,* 249–273.

Dilans, G. (2010). Corrective feedback and L2 vocabulary development: Prompts and recasts in the adult ESL classroom. *Canadian Modern Language Review/La Revue canadienne des langues vivantes, 66,* 787–815.

Dlaska, A., & Krekeler, C. (2013). The short-term effects of individual corrective feedback on L2 pronunciation. *System, 41,* 25–37.

Dörnyei, Z. (2001). *Motivational strategies in the language classroom.* Cambridge: Cambridge University Press.

Dörnyei, Z. (2005). *The psychology of the language learner: Individual differences in second language acquisition.* New York: Routledge.

Dörnyei, Z., & Csizér, K. (1998). Ten commandments for motivating language learners: Results of an empirical study. *Language Teaching Research, 2,* 203–229.

Dörnyei, Z., & Ottó, I. (1998). Motivation in action: A process model of L2 motivation. *Working Papers in Applied Linguistics (Thames Valley University, London), 4,* 43–69.

Dörnyei, Z., & Skehan, P. (2003). Individual differences in L2 learning. In C. Doughty & M. Long (Eds.), *The handbook of second language acquisition* (pp. 589–630). Malden, MA: Blackwell Publishing.

Doughty, C. (2003). Instructed SLA: Constraints, compensation, and enhancement. In C. Doughty & M. Long (Eds.), *The handbook of second language acquisition.* (pp. 256–310). Malden, MA: Blackwell Publishing.

Doughty, C., & Pica, T. (1986). 'Information gap' tasks: do they facilitate second language acquisition? *TESOL Quarterly, 20,* 305–325.

Doughty, C., & Williams, J. (Eds.). (1998). *Focus on from in classroom second language acquisition.* Cambridge: Cambridge University Press.

Du, H. (2013). The development of Chinese fluency during study abroad in China. *The Modern Language Journal, 97,* 131–143.

Eckerth, J. (2009). Negotiated interaction in the L2 classroom. *Language Teaching, 42,* 109–130.

Eckerth, J., & Tavakoli, P. (2012). The effects of word exposure frequency and elaboration of word processing on incidental L2 vocabulary acquisition through reading. *Language Teaching Research, 16,* 227–252.

Ellis, N.C. (2005). At the interface: Dynamic interactions of explicit and implicit language knowledge. *Studies in Second Language Acquisition, 27,* 305–352.

Ellis, N.C. (2007a). The Associative-Cognitive CREED. In B. VanPatten & J. Williams (Eds.), *Theories in second language acquisition: An Introduction* (pp. 77–96). Mahwah, NJ: Lawrence Erlbaum.

Ellis, N.C. (2007b). The weak interface, consciousness, and form-focused instruction: Mind the doors. In H. Nassaji & S. Fotos (Eds.), *Form-focused instruction and teacher education: Studies in honour of Rod Ellis* (pp. 17–34). Oxford: Oxford University Press.

Ellis, R. (1989). Are classroom and naturalistic acquisition the same? A study of the classroom acquisition of German word order rules. *Studies in Second Language Acquisition. 11,* 305–328.

Ellis, R. (1990). *Instructed second language acquisition.* Cambridge, MA: Basil Blackwell.

Ellis, R. (2001). Introduction: Investigating form-focused instruction. *Language Learning, 51,* (Suppl. 1), 1–46.

Ellis, R. (2003). *Task-based language learning and teaching.* Oxford: Oxford University Press.

Ellis, R. (2004). The definition and measurement of L2 explicit knowledge. *Language Learning, 54,* 227–275.

Ellis, R. (2005). *Instructed second language acquisition: A literature review.* Wellington: Ministry of Education, New Zealand.

Ellis, R. (2008). *The study of second language acquisition* (2nd ed.). Oxford: Oxford University Press.

Ellis, R. (2009). Implicit and explicit learning, knowledge and instruction. In R. Ellis, S. Loewen, C. Elder, R. Erlam, J. Philp, & H. Reinders (Eds.), *Implicit and explicit knowledge in second language learning, testing and teaching* (pp. 3–25). Bristol, UK: Multilingual Matters.

Ellis, R., Basturkmen, H., & Loewen, S. (2001a). Learner uptake in communicative ESL. *Language Learning, 51,* 281–318.

Ellis, R., Basturkmen, H., & Loewen, S. (2001b). Pre-emptive focus on form in the ESL classroom. *TESOL Quarterly, 35,* 407–432.

Ellis, R., Loewen, S., Elder, C., Erlam, R., Philp, J., & Reinders, H. (2009). *Implicit and explicit knowledge in second language learning, testing and teaching.* Bristol: Multilingual Matters.

Ellis, R., Loewen, S., & Erlam, R. (2006). Implicit and explicit corrective feedback and the acquisition of L2 grammar. *Studies in Second Language Acquisition, 28,* 339–368.

Farley, A., Ramonda, K., & Liu, X. (2012). The concreteness effect and the bilingual lexicon: The impact of visual stimuli attachment on meaning recall of abstract L2 words. *Language Teaching Research, 16,* 449–466.

Félix-Brasdefer, J.C. (2004). Interlanguage refusals: Linguistic politeness and length of residence in the target community. *Language Learning, 54,* 587–653.

Félix-Brasdefer, J.C. (2007). Pragmatic development in the Spanish as a FL classroom: A cross-sectional study of learner requests. *Intercultural Pragmatics, 4,* 253–286.

Félix-Brasdefer, J.C., & Cohen, A. (2012). Teaching pragmatics in the foreign language classroom: Grammar as a communicative resource. *Hispania, 95,* 650–669.

Fernández, C. (2008). Reexamining the role of explicit information in processing instruction. *Studies in Second Language Acquisition, 30,* 277–305.

Fernández Dobao, A. (2012). Collaborative writing tasks in the L2 classroom: Comparing group, pair, and individual work. *Journal of Second Language Writing, 21,* 40–58.

Fortune, T.W., & Tedick, D.J. (Eds.). (2008). *Pathways to multilingualism: Evolving perspectives on immersion education.* Clevedon, England: Multilingual Matters.

Foster, P. (1998). A classroom perspective on the negotiation of meaning. *Applied Linguistics, 19,* 1–23.

Foster, P. (2009). Task-based language learning research: Expecting too much or too little? *International Journal of Applied Linguistics, 19,* 247–263.

Freed, B.F., Segalowitz, N., & Dewey, D.D. (2004). Context of learning and second language fluency in French: Comparing regular classroom, study abroad, and intensive domestic immersion programs. *Studies in Second Language Acquisition, 26,* 275–301.

Garcia Mayo, M. (2005). Interactional strategies for interlanguage communication: Do they provide evidence for attention to form? In A. Housen & M. Pierrard (Eds.), *Investigations in instructed second language acquisition* (pp. 383–405). Berlin: Mouton de Gruyter.

Gass, S.M. (1989). Second and foreign language learning: Same, different or none of the above? In B. VanPatten & J.F. Lee (Eds.), *Second language acquisition/Foreign language learning* (pp. 34–44). Clevedon, UK: Multilingual Matters.

Gass, S. M. (1997). *Input, interaction and output in second language acquisition.* Mahwah, NJ: Lawrence Erlbaum.

Gass, S. M. & Mackey, A. (2007). Input, interaction, and output in second language acquisition. In B. VanPatten & J. Williams (Eds.), *Theories in second language acquisition: An introduction* (pp. 175–199). Mahwah, NJ: Lawrence Erlbaum.

Gass, S. M., Mackey, A., & Ross-Feldman, L. (2005). Task-based interactions in classroom and laboratory setting. *Language Learning, 55,* 575–611.

Gatbonton, E., & Segalowitz, N. (2005). Rethinking communicative language teaching: A focus on access to fluency. *The Canadian Modern Language Review/La Revue canadienne des language vivantes, 3,* 325–353.

Gatbonton, E., Trofimovich, P., & Magid, M. (2005). Learners' ethnic group affiliation and L2 pronunciation accuracy: A sociolinguistic investigation. *TESOL Quarterly, 39,* 489–511.

Goldberg, L. (1993). The structure of phenotypic personality traits. *American Psychologist*, 48, 26–34.

Granena, G. (2013). Individual differences in sequencing learning ability and second language acquisition in early childhood and adulthood. *Language Learning*, 63, 665–703.

Griggs, P. (2005). Assessment of the role of communication tasks in the development of second language oral production skills. In A. Housen & M. Pierrard (Eds.), *Investigations in instructed second language acquisition* (pp. 407–432). Berlin: Mouton de Gruyter.

Guilloteaux, M. J., & Dörnyei, Z. (2008). Motivating language learners: A classroom-oriented investigation of the effects of motivational strategies on student motivation. *TESOL Quarterly*, 42, 55–77.

Gurzynski-Weiss, L., & Baralt, M. (2013). Exploring learner perception and use of task-based interactional feedback in FTF and CMC modes. *Studies in Second Language Learning*, 36, 1–37.

Gutiérrez, X. (2013). Metalinguistic knowledge, metalingual knowledge and proficiency in L2 Spanish. *Language Awareness*, 22(2), 176–191.

Hamano-Bunce, D. (2011). Talk or chat? Chatroom and spoken interaction in a language classroom. *ELT Journal*, 65, 426–436.

Han, Z. (2008). On the role of meaning in focus on form. In Z. Han (Ed.), *Understanding second language process* (pp. 45–79). Clevedon, UK: Multilingual Matters.

Han, Z., & Finneran, R. (2013). Re-engaging the interface debate: Strong, weak, none, or all? *International Journal of Applied Linguistics*,

Han, Z., Park, E., & Combs, C. (2008). Textual enhancement of input: Issues and possibilities. *Applied Linguistics*, 29, 597–618.

Hansen Edwards, J., & Zampini, M. (2008). *Phonology and second language acquisition*. Amsterdam: John Benjamins.

Hanulíková, A., Dediu, D., Fang, Z, Banaková, J., & Huettig, F. (2012). Individual differences in the acquisition of complex L2 phonology: A training study. *Language Learning*, 62 (Suppl. 2), 79–109.

Hauser, E. (2005). Coding 'corrective recasts': The maintenance of meaning and more fundamental problems. *Applied Linguistics*, 26, 293–316.

Henry, H., Culman, H., & VanPatten, B. (2009). More on the effects of explicit information in instructed SLA: A partial replication and a response to Fernández (2008). *Studies in Second Language Acquisition*, 31, 559–575.

Henshaw, F. (2012). How effective are affective activities? Relative benefits of two types of structured input activities as part of a computer delivered lesson on the Spanish subjunctive. *Language Teaching Research*, 16, 393–414.

Hernández, T. (2011). Re-examining the role of explicit instruction and input flood on the acquisition of Spanish discourse markers. *Language Teaching Research*, 15, 159–182.

Horst, M. (2005). Learning L2 vocabulary through extensive reading: A measurement study. *Canadian Modern Language Review/La Revue canadienne des langues vivantes*, 61, 355–382.

Horst, M., Cobb, T., & Meara, P. (1998). Beyond a clockwork orange: Acquiring second language vocabulary through reading. *Reading in a Foreign Language*, 11, 207–223.

Horwitz, E. (2005). Classroom management for teachers of Japanese and other foreign languages. *Foreign Language Annals*, 38, 56–64.

Horwitz, E., Horwitz, M., & Cope, J. (1986). Foreign language classroom anxiety. *The Modern Language Journal*, 70, 125–132.

House, J. (1996). Developing pragmatic fluency in English as a foreign language: Routines and metapragmatic awareness. *Studies in Second Language Acquisition*, 18, 225–252.

Housen, A., & Pierrard, M. (2005). *Investigations in instructed second language acquisition*. Berlin: Mouton de Gruyter.

Howard, M. (2005). Second language acquisition in a study abroad context: A comparative investigation of the effects of study abroad and foreign language instruction on the L2 learner's grammatical development. In A. Housen & M. Pierrard (Eds.), *Investigations in instructed second language acquisition* (pp. 495–530). Berlin: Mouton de Gruyter.

Hulstijn, J. (2001). Intentional and incidental second language vocabulary learning: A reappraisal of elaboration, rehearsal and automaticity. In P. Robinson (Ed.), *Cognition and second language instruction* (pp. 258–286). New York: Cambridge University Press.

Hulstijn, J. (2002). Towards a unified account of the representation, processing and acquisition of second language knowledge. *Second Language Research, 18,* 193–223.

Hulstijn, J., & DeGraaf, R. (1994). Under what conditions does explicit knowledge of a second language facilitate the acquisition of implicit knowledge? A research proposal. In J. Hulstijn & R. Schmidt (Eds.), *Consciousness in Second Language Learning. AILA Review 11* (pp. 91–112). Amsterdam: John Benjamins.

Hummel, K. (2010). Translation and short-term L2 vocabulary retention: Hindrance or help? *Language Teaching Research, 14,* 61–74.

Huth, T. (2006). Negotiating structure and culture: L2 learners' realization of L2 compliment-response sequences in talk-in-interaction. *Journal of Pragmatics, 38,* 2025–2050.

Iwashita, N., & Li, H. (2012). Patterns of corrective feedback in a task-based EFL classroom setting in China. In A. Shehadeh & C. Coombe (Eds.), *Task-based language teaching in foreign language contexts: Research and implementation* (pp. 137–161). Amsterdam: John Benjamins.

Jenkins, J. (2002). A sociolinguistically based, empirically researched pronunciation syllabus for English as an International Language. *Applied Linguistics, 23,* 83–103.

Jenkins, J. (2004). Research in teaching pronunciation and intonation. *Annual Review of Applied Linguistics, 24,* 109–125.

Jeon, E., & Kaya, T. (2006). Effects of L2 instruction on interlanguage pragmatic development. In J. Norris & L. Ortega (Eds.), *Synthesizing research on language learning and teaching* (pp. 165–211). Philadelphia, PA: John Benjamins.

Jeon, K. (2007). Interaction-driven L2 learning: Characterizing linguistic development. In A. Mackey (Ed.), *Conversational interaction in second language acquisition* (pp. 379–403). Oxford: Oxford University Press.

Jin, L., & Cortazzi, M. (2011). Re-evaluating traditional approaches to second language teaching and learning. In E. Hinkel (Ed.), *Handbook of research in second language teaching and learning: Volume II* (pp. 558–575). New York: Routledge.

Kamiya, N., & Loewen, S. (2013). The influence of academic articles on an ESL teacher's stated beliefs. *Innovation in Language Learning and Teaching, 7,* 1–14.

Kasper, G., & Rose, K. (1999). Pragmatics and SLA. *Annual Review of Applied Linguistics, 19,* 81–104.

Kasper, G., & Rose, K. (2002). *Pragmatic development in a second language.* Oxford: Blackwell.

Keating, G. (2008). Task effectiveness and word learning in a second language: The involvement load hypothesis on trial. *Language Teaching Research, 12,* 365–386.

Keck, C., Iberri-Shea, N., Tracy-Ventura, N., & Wa-Mbaleka, S. (2006). Investigating the empirical link between task-based interaction and acquisition: A meta-analysis. In J. Norris and L. Ortega (Eds.), *Synthesizing research on language learning and teaching* (pp. 91–131). Philadelphia, PA: John Benjamins.

Kim, Y., & McDonough, K. (2008). The effect of interlocutor proficiency on the collaborative dialogue between Korean as a second language learners. *Language Teaching Research, 12,* 211–234.

Kinginger, C. (2011). Enhancing language learning in study abroad. *Annual Review of Applied Linguistics, 31,* 58–73.

Kissling, E. (2013). Teaching pronunciation: Is explicit phonetics instruction beneficial for FL learning? *The Modern Language Journal, 97*, 720–744.

Klapper, J., & Rees, J. (2003). Reviewing the case for explicit grammar instruction in the university foreign language learning context. *Language Teaching Research, 7*, 285–314.

Kong, S., & Hoare, P. (2011). Cognitive content engagement in content-based language teaching. *Language Teaching Research, 15*, 307–324.

Krashen, S. (1982). *Principles and practice in second language acquisition.* Oxford: Pergamon.

Krashen, S. (2003). *Explorations in language acquisition and use: The Taipei lectures.* Portsmouth, NH: Heinemann.

Kuiken, F., & Vedder, I. (2005). Noticing and the role of interaction in promoting language learning. In A. Housen & M. Pierrard (Eds.), *Investigations in instructed second language acquisition* (pp. 353–381). Berlin: Mouton de Gruyter.

Lantolf, J., & Thorne, S. (2007). Sociocultural theory and second language learning. In B. VanPatten & J. Williams (Eds.), *Theories in second language acquisition: An introduction* (pp. 201–224). Mahwah, NJ: Lawrence Erlbaum Associates.

Laufer, B. (1998). The development of passive and active vocabulary in a second language: Same of different? *Applied Linguistics, 19*, 255–271.

Laufer, B. (2005a). Focus on form in second language vocabulary learning. *EUROSLA Yearbook, 5*, 223–250.

Laufer, B. (2005b). Instructed second language vocabulary learning: The fault in the 'default hypothesis'. In A. Housen & M. Pierrard (Eds.), *Investigations in instructed second language acquisition* (pp. 311–329). Berlin: Mouton de Gruyter.

Laufer, B., & Girsai, N. (2008). Form-focused instruction in second language vocabulary learning: A case for contrastive analysis and translation. *Applied Linguistics, 29*(4), 694–716.

Laufer, B., & Hulstijn, J. (2001). Incidental vocabulary acquisition in a second language: The construct of tasked-induced involvement load. *Applied Linguistics, 22*, 1–26.

Laufer, B., & Paribakht, (1998). The relationship between passive and active vocabularies: Effects of language learning context. *Language Learning, 48*, 365–391.

Laufer, B., & Rozovski-Roitblat, B. (2011). Incidental vocabulary acquisition: The effects of task type, word occurrence and their combination. *Language Teaching Research, 15*, 391–411.

Lee, S., & Huang, H. (2008). Visual input enhancement and grammar learning: A meta-analytic review. *Studies in Second Language Acquisition, 30*, 307–331.

Lee, J., Jang, J., & Plonsky, L. (2014). *The effectiveness of second language pronunciation instruction: A meta-analysis.* Unpublished Manuscript.

Leeser, M. (2004). Learner proficiency and focus on form during collaborative dialogue. *Language Teaching Research, 8*, 55–81.

Leow, R. (2007). Input and the L2 classroom: An attentional perspective on receptive practice. In R. DeKeyser (Ed.), *Practice in a second language: Perspectives from applied linguistics and cognitive psychology* (pp. 21–50). Cambridge: Cambridge University Press.

Levis, J. (2005). Changing contexts and shifting paradigms in pronunciation teaching. *TESOL Quarterly, 39*, 369–377.

Levy, M. (2009). Technologies in use for second language learning. *The Modern Language Journal, 93*, 769–782.

Li, S. (2010). The effectiveness of corrective feedback in SLA: A meta-analysis. *Language Learning, 60*, 309–365.

Li, S. (2013). The interactions between the effects of implicit and explicit feedback and individual differences in language analytic ability and working memory. *The Modern Language Journal, 97,* 634–654.

Littlewood, W. (2011). Communicative language teaching: An expanding concept for a changing world. In E. Hinkel (Ed.), *Handbook of research in second language teaching and learning: Volume II* (pp. 541–557). New York: Routledge.

Llanes, A., & Muñoz, C. (2013). Age effects in a study abroad context: Children and adults studying abroad and at home. *Language Learning, 63,* 63–90.

Lockhart, R., & Craik, F. (1990). Levels of processing: A retrospective commentary on a framework for memory research. *Canadian Journal of Psychology, 44,* 87–112.

Loewen, S. (2003). Variation in frequency and characteristics of incidental focus on form. *Language Teaching Research, 7,* 315–345.

Loewen, S. (2004). Uptake in incidental focus on form in meaning-focused ESL lessons. *Language Learning, 54,* 153–187.

Loewen, S. (2005). Incidental focus on form and second language learning. *Studies in Second Language Acquisition, 27,* 361–386.

Loewen, S. (2011). Focus on form. In E. Hinkel (Ed.), *Handbook of research in second language teaching and learning* (Vol. 2, pp. 576–592). New York: Routledge.

Loewen, S. (2013). Instructed second language acquisition. In C. Chapelle (Ed.), *The encyclopedia of applied linguistics* (pp. 2716–2718). Malden, MA: Blackwell Publishing.

Loewen, S., & Erlam, R. (2006). Corrective feedback in the chatroom: An experimental study. *Computer Assisted Language Learning, 19,* 1–14.

Loewen, S., Erlam, R., & Ellis, R. (2009). The incidental acquisition of third person –*s* as implicit and explicit knowledge. In R. Ellis, S. Loewen, C. Elder, R. Erlam, J. Philp, & R. Reinders (Eds.), *Implicit and explicit knowledge in second language learning, testing and teaching* (pp. 262–280). Bristol, UK: Multilingual Matters.

Loewen, S., & Nabei, T. (2007). Measuring the effects of oral corrective feedback on L2 knowledge. In A. Mackey (Ed.), *Conversational interaction in second language acquisition* (pp. 361–378). Oxford: Oxford University Press.

Loewen, S., & Philp, J. (2006). Recasts in the adult English L2 classroom: Characteristics, explicitness, and effectiveness. *The Modern Language Journal, 90,* 536–556.

Loewen, S., & Reinders, H. (2011). *Key concepts in second language acquisition.* New York: Palgrave.

Long, M.H. (1983). Does second language instruction make a difference: A review of the research. *TESOL Quarterly, 15,* 359–382.

Long, M.H. (1991). Focus on form: A design feature in language teaching methodology. In K. de Bot, R. Ginsberg, & C. Kramsch (Eds.), *Foreign language research in cross-cultural perspective* (pp. 39–52). Amsterdam: John Benjamins.

Long, M. H. (1996). The role of the linguistic environment in second language acquisition. In W. Ritchie & T. Bhatia (Eds.), *Handbook of second language acquisition* (pp. 413–468). San Diego: Academic Press.

Long, M.H. (2007a). Age differences and the sensitive periods controversy in SLA. In M.H. Long (Ed.), *Problems in SLA* (pp. 43–74). Mahwah, NJ: Lawrence Erlbaum Associates.

Long, M.H. (2007b). Recasts in SLA: The story so far. In M.H. Long (Ed.), *Problems in SLA* (pp. 75–116). Mahwah, NJ: Lawrence Erlbaum.

Long, M.H., & Robinson, P. (1998). Focus on form: Theory, research, and practice. In C. Doughty & J. Williams (Eds.), *Focus on form in classroom second language acquisition* (pp. 16–42). Cambridge: Cambridge University Press.

Loschky, L., & Bley-Vroman, R. (1993). Grammar and task-based methodology. In G. Crookes & S. Gass (Eds.), *Tasks and language learning* (pp. 123–167). Clevedon, UK: Multilingual Matters.

Lyster, R. (1998a). Negotiation of form, recast, and explicit correction in relation to error types and learner repair in immersion classrooms. *Language Learning, 48*, 183–218.

Lyster, R. (1998b). Recasts, repetition and ambiguity in L2 classroom discourse. *Studies in Second Language Acquisition, 20*, 51–81.

Lyster, R. (2004). Differential effects of prompts and recast in form-focused instruction. *Studies in Second Language Acquisition, 26*, 399–432.

Lyster, R. (2007). *Learning and teaching languages through content: A counterbalanced approach*. Amsterdam: John Benjamins.

Lyster, R., & Ballinger, S. (2011). Content-based language teaching: Convergent concerns across divergent contexts. *Language Teaching Research, 15*(3), 279–288.

Lyster, R., & Izquierdo, J. (2009). Prompts versus recasts in dyadic interaction. *Language Learning, 59*, 453–498.

Lyster, R., & Mori, J. (2006). Interactional feedback and instructional counterbalance. *Studies in Second Language Acquisition, 28*, 269–300.

Lyster, R., & Ranta, L. (1997). Corrective feedback and learner uptake: Negotiation of form in communicative classrooms. *Studies in Second Language Acquisition, 19*, 37–66.

Lyster, R., & Ranta, L. (2007). A cognitive approach to improving immersion students' oral language abilities: The Awareness-Practice-Feedback sequence. In R. DeKeyser (Ed.), *Practice in a second language: Perspectives from applied linguistics and cognitive psychology* (pp. 141–160). Cambridge: Cambridge University Press.

Lyster, R., & Saito, K. (2010). Oral feedback in classroom SLA: A meta-analysis. *Studies in Second Language Acquisition, 32*, 265–302.

Macaro, E., & Masterman, L. (2006). Does intensive explicit grammar instruction make all the difference? *Language Teaching Research, 10*, 297–327.

MacIntyre, P., Burns, C., & Jessome, A. (2011). Ambivalence about communicating in a second language: A qualitative study of French immersion students' willingness to communicate. *Modern Language Journal, 95*, 81–96.

MacIntyre, P., Clément, R., Dörnyei, Z., & Noels, K. (1998). Conceptualizing willingness to communicate in a L2: A situated model of confidence and affiliation. *Modern Language Journal, 82*, 545–562.

Mackey, A. (1999). Input, interaction and second language development: An empirical study of question formation in ESL. *Studies in Second Language Acquisition, 21*, 557–587.

Mackey, A. (2006). Feedback, noticing and instructed second language learning. *Applied Linguistics, 27*, 405–430.

Mackey, A. (2007). *Conversational interaction in second language acquisition: A series of empirical studies*. Oxford: Oxford University Press.

Mackey, A., & Gass, S. M. (2012). *Research methods in second language acquisition: A practical guide*. Malden, MA: Wiley Blackwell.

Mackey, A., Gass, S., & McDonough, K. (2000). How do learners perceive interactional feedback? *Studies in Second Language Acquisition, 22*, 471–497.

Mackey, A., & Goo, J. (2007). Interaction research in SLA: A meta-analysis and research synthesis. In A. Mackey (Ed.), *Conversational interaction in second language acquisition: A series of empirical studies* (pp. 407–452). Oxford: Oxford University Press.

Masgoret, A.-M., & Gardner, R.C. (2003). Attitudes, motivation, and second language learning: A meta-analysis of studies conducted by Gardner and associates. *Language Learning, 53*, 123–163.

McConachy, T. (2013). Exploring the meta-pragmatic realm in English language teaching. *Language Awareness, 22*(2), 100–110.

McCrae, R., & Costa, P. (2003). *Personality in adulthood: A five-factor theory perspective* (2nd ed.). New York: Guilford Press.

Mora, J., & Valls-Ferrer, M. (2012). Oral fluency, accuracy and complexity in formal instruction and study abroad learning contexts. *TESOL Quarterly, 46*, 610–641.

Moskovsky, C., Alrabai, F., Paolini, S., & Ratcheva, S. (2013). The effects of teachers' motivation strategies on learners' motivation: A controlled investigation of second language acquisition. *Language Learning, 63*, 34–62.

Moyer, A. (1999). Ultimate attainment in L2 phonology: The critical factors of age, motivation, and instruction. *Studies in Second Language Acquisition, 21*, 81–108.

Moyer, A. (2011). An investigation of experience in L2 phonology: Does quality matter more than quantity? *The Canadian Modern Language Review/ La revue canadienne des langues vivantes, 67*, 191–216.

Muranoi, H. (2007). Output practice in the L2 classroom. In R. DeKeyser (Ed.), *Practice in a second language: Perspectives from applied linguistics and cognitive psychology* (pp. 51–84). Cambridge: Cambridge University Press.

Nassaji, H., & Fotos, S. (2004). Current developments in research on the teaching of grammar. *Annual Review of Applied Linguistics, 24*, 126–145.

Nassaji, H., & Fotos, S. (2007). Issues in form-focused instruction and teacher education. In H. Nassaji & S. Fotos (Eds.), *Form-focused instruction and teacher education: Studies in honour of Rod Ellis* (pp. 7–15). Oxford: Oxford University Press.

Nassaji, H., & Fotos, S. (2011). *Teaching grammar in second language classrooms: Integrating form-focused instruction in communicative contexts.* New York: Routledge.

Nation, I. S. P. (2001). *Learning vocabulary in another language.* Cambridge: Cambridge University Press.

Nation, I. S. P., (2011). Second language speaking. In E. Hinkel (Ed.), *Handbook of research in second language teaching and learning, Vol. II* (pp. 445–454). New York: Routledge.

Naughton, D. (2006). Cooperative strategy training and oral interaction: Enhancing small group communication in the language classroom. *The Modern Language Journal, 90*, 169–184.

Nguyen, T. (2013). Instructional effects on the acquisition of modifies in constructive criticism by EFL learners. *System, 22*, 76–94.

Nobuyoshi, J., & Ellis, R. (1993). Focused communication tasks. *ELT Journal, 47*, 203–210.

Norris, J., & Ortega, L. (2000). Effectiveness of L2 instruction: A research synthesis and quantitative meta-analysis. *Language Learning, 50*, 417–528.

O'Dowd, R. (2011). Online foreign language interaction: Moving from the periphery to the core of foreign language education? *Language Teaching, 44*, 368–380.

Ortega, L. (2007). Second language learning explained? SLA across nine contemporary theories. In B. VanPatten & J. Williams (Eds.), *Theories in second language acquisition: An introduction* (pp. 225–250). Mahwah, NJ: Lawrence Erlbaum Associates.

Ortega, L. (2013). SLA for the 21st century: Disciplinary progress, transdisciplinary relevance, and the bi/multilingual turn. *Language Learning, 63*, (Suppl. 1), 1–24.

Oxford, R. (2011). Strategies for learning a second or foreign language. *Language Teaching, 44*, 167–180.

Pae, T. (2013). Skill-based L2 anxieties revisited: Their intra-relations and their inter-relations with general foreign language anxiety. *Applied Linguistics, 34*(2), 232–252.

Panova, I., & Lyster, R. (2002). Patterns of corrective feedback and uptake in an adult ESL classroom. *TESOL Quarterly, 36*, 573–595.

Pasfield-Neofitou, S. (2012). *Online communication in a second language: Social interaction, language use, and learning Japanese.* Bristol: Multilingual Matters.

Pearson, L. (2006). Patterns of development in Spanish L2 pragmatic acquisition: An analysis of novice learners' production of directives. *Modern Language Journal, 90,* 473–495.

Peterson, M. (2006). Learner interaction management in an avatar and chat-based virtual world. *Computer Assisted Language Learning, 19,* 79–103.

Philp, J., Walter, S., & Basturkmen, H. (2010). Peer interaction in the foreign language classroom: What factors foster a focus on form? *Language Awareness, 19,* 261–279.

Pica, T. (1994). Research on negotiation: What does it reveal about second-language learning conditions, processes and outcomes? *Language Learning, 44,* 493–527.

Pica, T., & Doughty, C. (1985). The role of group work in classroom second language acquisition. *Studies in Second Language Acquisition, 7,* 233–248.

Pica, T., Kanagy, R., & Falodun, J. (1993). Choosing and using communication tasks for second language instruction. In G. Crookes & S. M. Gass (Eds.), *Tasks and language learning* (pp. 9–34). Clevedon, UK: Multilingual Matters.

Pienemann, M. (1998). *Language processing and second language development: Processability theory.* Amsterdam: John Benjamins.

Pienemann, M. (2007). Processability theory. In B. VanPatten & J. Williams (Eds.), *Theories in second language acquisition: An introduction* (pp. 137–154). Mahwah, NJ: Lawrence Erlbaum Associates.

Plonsky, L. (2011). The effectiveness of second language strategy instruction: A meta-analysis. *Language Learning, 61,* 993–1038.

Plonsky, L. (2013). Study quality in SLA: An assessment of designs, analyses, and reporting practices in quantitative L2 research. *Studies in Second Language Acquisition, 35,* 655–687.

Plonsky, L., & Gass, S. (2011). Quantitative research methods, study quality, and outcomes: The case of interaction research. *Language Learning, 61*(2), 325–366.

Polio, C. (2012). The acquisition of second language writing. In S. Gass & A. Mackey (Eds.), *The Routledge handbook of second language acquisition* (pp. 319–334). New York: Routledge.

Qian, D. D., & Schedl, M. (2004). Evaluation of an in-depth vocabulary knowledge measure for assessing reading performance. *Language Testing, 21,* 28–52.

Qin, J. (2008). The effect of processing instruction and dictogloss tasks on acquisition of the English passive voice. *Language Teaching Research, 12,* 61–82.

Ranta, L., & Meckelborg, A. (2013). How much exposure to English do international students really get?: Measuring language use in a naturalistic setting. *The Canadian Modern Language Review/ La Revue Canadienne Des Langues Vivantes, 69,* 1–33.

Rebuschat, P. (2013). Measuring implicit and explicit knowledge in second language research. *Language Learning, 63,* 595–626.

Rebuschat, P., & Williams, J. (2012). Implicit and explicit knowledge in second language acquisition. *Applied Psycholinguistics, 33,* 829–856.

Reinders, H., & Ellis, R. (2009). The effects of two types of input on intake and the acquisition of implicit and explicit knowledge. In R. Ellis, S. Loewen, C. Elder, R. Erlam, J. Philp, & R. Reinders, (Eds.), *Implicit and explicit knowledge in second language learning, testing and teaching* (pp. 281–302). Bristol: Multilingual Matters.

Révész, A. (2011). Task complexity, focus on L2 constructions, and individual differences: A classroom-based study. *The Modern Language Journal, 95* (Suppl.), 162–181.

Richards, J. (2007). Materials development and research: towards a form-focused perspective. In H. Nassaji & S. Fotos (Eds.), *Form-focused instruction and teacher education: Studies in honour of Rod Ellis* (pp. 147–160). Oxford: Oxford University Press.

Robinson, P. (1995). Attention, memory, and the "noticing" hypothesis. *Language Learning, 45*, 283–331.

Robinson, P. (2002). *Individual differences and instructed language learning.* Amsterdam: John Benjamins.

Robinson, P. (2005). Aptitude and second language acquisition. *Annual Review of Applied Linguistics, 25*, 46–73.

Rose, K. (2005). On the effects of instruction in second language pragmatics. *System, 33*, 385–399.

Rose, K., & Kasper, G. (2001). *Pragmatics in language teaching.* Cambridge: Cambridge University Press.

Rott, S. (1999). The effect of exposure frequency on intermediate language learners' incidental vocabulary acquisition and retention through reading. *Studies in Second Language Acquisition, 21*, 589–619.

Russell, J., & Spada, N. (2006). The effectiveness of corrective feedback for the acquisition of L2 grammar: A meta-analysis of the research. In J. Norris & L. Ortega (Eds.), *Synthesizing research on language learning and teaching* (pp. 133–164). Amsterdam: John Benjamins.

Saito, K. (2011). Examining the role of explicit phonetic instruction in native-like and comprehensible pronunciation development: An instructed SLA approach to L2 phonology. *Language Awareness, 20*, 45–59.

Saito, K. (2013a). Reexamining effects of form-focused instruction on L2 pronunciation development: The role of explicit phonetic information. *Studies in Second Language Acquisition, 35*, 1–29.

Saito, K. (2013b). The acquisitional value of recasts in instructed second language speech learning: Teaching the perception and production of English /ɹ/ to adult Japanese learners. *Language Learning, 63*, 499–529.

Saito, K., & Lyster, R. (2012). Effects of form-focused instruction and corrective feedback on L2 pronunciation development of /ʔ/ by Japanese learners of English. *Language Learning, 62*, 595–633.

Sato, M. (2013). Beliefs about peer interaction and peer corrective feedback: Efficacy of classroom intervention. *The Modern Language Journal, 97*, 611–633.

Sato, M., & Ballinger, S. (2012). Raising language awareness in peer interaction: A cross-context, cross-methodology examination. *Language Awareness, 21*, 157–179.

Sauro, S. (2011). SCMC for SLA: A research synthesis. *CALICO Journal, 28*, 369–391.

Scheffler, P. (2012). Theories pass. Learners and teachers remain. *Applied Linguistics, 33*, 603–607.

Scheffler, P., & Cincała, M. (2010). Explicit grammar rules and L2 acquisition. *ELT Journal, 65*, 13–23.

Schmidt, R. (1990). The role of consciousness in second language learning. *Applied Linguistics, 11*, 129–158.

Schmidt, R. (1995). *Attention and awareness in foreign language learning.* Honolulu: University of Hawai'i Press.

Schmidt, R. (2001). Attention. In P. Robinson (Ed.), *Cognition and second language instruction* (pp. 3–32). Cambridge: Cambridge University Press.

Schmidt, R., & Frota, S. (1996). Developing basic conversational ability in a second language: A case study of an adult learner. In R. Day (Ed.), *Talking to learn: Conversations in second language acquisition* (pp. 237–326). Rowley, MA: Newbury House.

Schmitt, N. (2008). Review article: Instructed second language vocabulary learning. *Language Teaching Research, 12,* 329–363.

Segalowitz, N. (2003). Automaticity and second languages. In C. Doughty & M. Long (Eds.), *The handbook of second language acquisition* (pp. 382–408). Malden, MA: Blackwell Publishing.

Selinker, L. (1972). Interlanguage. *International Review of Applied Linguistics, 10,* 209–231.

Sharwood Smith, M. (1991). Speaking to many minds: On the relevance of different types of language information for the L2 learner. *Second Language Research, 72,* 118–132.

Sharwood Smith, M. (1993). Input enhancement in instructed SLA. *Studies in Second Language Acquisition, 15,* 165–179.

Sheen, R. (2005). Focus on forms as a means of improving accurate oral production. In A. Housen & M. Pierrard (Eds.), *Investigations in instructed second language acquisition* (pp. 271–310). Berlin: Mouton de Gruyter.

Sheen, Y. (2004). Corrective feedback and learner uptake in communicative classrooms across instructional settings. *Language Teaching Research, 8*(3), 263–300.

Sheen, Y. (2006). Exploring the relationship between characteristics of recasts and learner uptake. *Language Teaching Research, 10,* 361–392.

Sheen, Y. (2007). The effects of corrective feedback, language aptitude, and learner attitudes on the acquisition of English articles. In A. Mackey (Ed.), *Conversational interaction in second language acquisition* (pp. 301–322). Oxford: Oxford University Press.

Sheen, Y. (2008). Recasts, language anxiety, modified output, and L2 learning. *Language Learning, 58,* 835–874.

Shehadeh, A. (2012). Broadening the perspective of task-based language teaching scholarship: The contribution of research in foreign language contexts. In A. Shehadeh & C. Coombe (Eds.), *Task-based language teaching in foreign language contexts: Research and implementation* (pp. 1–20). Amsterdam: John Benjamins.

Shehadah, A., & Coombe, C. (2012). *Task-based language teaching in foreign language contexts: Research and implementation.* Amsterdam: John Benjamins.

Shen, H. (2010). Imagery and verbal coding approaches in Chinese vocabulary instruction. *Language Teaching Research, 14,* 485–499.

Shintani, N. (2011). A comparative study of the effects of input-based and production-based instruction on vocabulary acquisition by young EFL learners. *Language Teaching Research, 15*(2), 137–158.

Shintani, N. (2012). Input-based tasks and the acquisition of vocabulary and grammar: A process-product study. *Language Teaching Research, 16*(2), 253–279.

Shintani, N. (2013). The effect of focus on form and focus on forms instruction on the acquisition of productive knowledge of L2 vocabulary by young beginning-level learners. *TESOL Quarterly, 47,* 36–62.

Shintani, N., Li, S., & Ellis, R. (2013). Comprehension-based versus production-based grammar instruction: A meta-analysis of comparative studies. *Language Learning, 63,* 296–329.

Simard, D. (2009). Differential effects of textual enhancement formats on intake. *System, 37,* 124–135.

Skehan, P., Bei, X., Qian, L., & Wang, Z. (2012). The task is not enough: Processing approaches to task-based performance. *Language Teaching Research, 16,* 170–187.

Smith, B. (2009). The relationship between scrolling, negotiation, and self-initiated self-repair in a SCMC environment. *CALICO Journal, 26,* 231–45.

Smith, B., & Sauro, S. (2009). Interruptions in chat. *Computer Assisted Language Learning, 22,* 229–247.

Sonbul, S., & Schmitt, N. (2013). Explicit and implicit lexical knowledge: Acquisition of collocations under different input conditions. *Language Learning, 63,* 121–159.

Spada, N., & Tomita, Y. (2010). Interactions between type of instruction and type of language feature: A meta-analysis. *Language Learning, 60,* 263–308.

Sparks, R. (2012). Individual differences in L2 learning and long-term L1-L2 relationships. *Language Learning, 62* (Suppl. 2), 5–27.

Sparks, R., & Patton, J. (2013). Relationship of L1 skills and L2 aptitude to L2 anxiety on the Foreign Language Classroom Anxiety Scale. *Language Learning, 63,* 870–895.

Squire, L. (2009) Memory and brain systems: 1969–2009. *The Journal of Neuroscience, 29,* 12711–12716.

Stafford, C., Bowden, H. W., & Sanz, C. (2012). Optimizing language instruction: Matters of explicitness, practice and cue learning. *Language Learning, 62,* 741–768.

Storch, N. (2001). How collaborative is pair work? ESL tertiary students composing in pairs. *Language Teaching Research, 5,* 29–53.

Storch, N. (2002). Patterns of interaction in ESL pair work. *Language Learning, 52,* 119–158.

Storch, N., & Aldosari, A. (2010). Learners' use of first language (Arabic) in pair work in an EFL class. *Language Teaching Research, 14,* 355–375.

Storch, N., & Aldosari, A. (2013). Pairing learners in pair work activity. *Language Teaching Research, 17,* 31–48.

Swain, M. (1995). Three functions of output in second language learning. In G. Cook & B. Seidlhofer (Eds.), *Principles and practice in applied linguistics* (pp. 125–144). Oxford: Oxford University Press.

Swain, M. (2005). The output hypothesis: Theory and research. In E. Hinkel (Ed.), *Handbook of research in second language teaching and learning* (pp. 471–483). Mahwah, NJ: Lawrence Erlbaum Associates.

Swain, M., & Lapkin, S. (1995). Problems in output and the cognitive processes they generate: A step towards second language learning. *Applied Linguistics, 16,* 371–391.

Swain, M., & Lapkin, S. (2001). Focus on from through collaborative dialogue: Exploring task effects. In M. Bygate, P. Skehan, & M. Swain (Eds.), *Researching pedagogic tasks, second language learning, teaching and testing* (pp. 99–118). Harlow, UK: Longman.

Swan, M. (2005). Legislation by hypothesis: The case of task-based instruction. *Applied Linguistics, 26,* 376–401.

Taguchi, N. (2006). Analysis of appropriateness in a speech act of request in L2 English. *Pragmatics, 16,* 513–533.

Taguchi, N. (2011). Teaching pragmatics: Trends and issues. *Annual Review of Applied Linguistics, 31,* 289–310.

Taguchi, N. (2013). Production of routines in L2 English: Effect of proficiency and study-abroad experience. *System, 41,* 109–121.

Takahashi, S. (2010). Assessing learnability in second language pragmatics. In A. Trosborg (Ed.), *Handbook of pragmatics: Vol. VII* (pp. 391–421). Berlin: Mouton De Gruyter.

Takimoto, M. (2006). The effects of explicit feedback on the development of pragmatic proficiency. *Language Teaching Research, 10,* 393–418.

Tan, M. (2011). Mathematics and science teachers' beliefs and practices regarding the teaching of language in content learning. *Language Teaching Research, 15,* 325–342.

Thorne, S., Black, R., & Sykes, J. (2009). Second language use, socialization, and learning in internet interest communities and online gaming. *The Modern Language Journal, 93,* 802–821.

Tian, L., & Macaro, E. (2012). Comparing the effect of teacher codeswitching with English-only explanations on the vocabulary acquisition of Chinese university students: A lexical focus-on-form study. *Language Teaching Research, 16,* 367–391.

Tomita, Y., & Spada, N. (2013). Form-focused instruction and learner investment in L2 communication. *The Modern Language Journal, 97,* 591–610.

Tomlin, R., & Villa, V. (1994). Attention in cognitive science and second language acquisition. *Studies in Second Language Acquisition, 16,* 183–203.

Trahey, M. & White, L. (1993). Positive evidence and preemption in the second language classroom. *Studies in Second Language Acquisition, 15,* 181–204.

Trofimovich, P. & Gatbonton, E. (2006). Repetition and focus on form in L2 Spanish word processing: Implications for pronunciation instruction. *The Modern Language Journal, 90,* 519–535.

Truscott, J. (1999). What's wrong with oral grammar correction? *The Canadian Modern Language Review, 55,* 437–456.

Ur, P. (2011). Grammar teaching: Research, theory, and practice. In E. Hinkel (Ed.), *Handbook of research in second language teaching and learning: Volume II* (pp. 507–522). New York: Routledge.

Valeo, A. (2013). Language awareness in a content-based language programme. *Language Awareness, 22,* 126–145.

Van den Branden, K., Bygate, M., & Norris, J. (Eds.). (2009). *Task-based language teaching: A reader.* Amsterdam: John Benjamins.

Vandergrift, L., & Tafaghodtari, M. (2010) Teaching L2 learners how to listen does make a difference: An empirical study. *Language Learning, 60,* 470–497.

VanPatten, B. (1990). Attending to form and content in the input. *Studies in Second Language Acquisition, 12,* 287–301.

VanPatten, B. (2002). Processing instruction: An update. *Language Learning, 52,* 755–803.

VanPatten, B. (2004). *Processing instruction: Theory, research, and commentary.* Mahwah, NJ: Lawrence Erlbaum Associates.

VanPatten, B. (2005). Input processing in adult second language acquisition. In B. VanPatten & J. Williams (Eds.), *Theories in second language acquisition: An introduction* (pp. 115–135). Mahwah, NJ: Lawrence Erlbaum.

VanPatten, B. (2007). Input processing in adult second language acquisition. In B. VanPatten & J. Williams (Eds.), *Theories in second language acquisition: An introduction* (pp. 115–136). Mahwah, NJ: Lawrence Erlbaum Associates.

VanPatten, B., & Williams, J. (2007). Early theories in second language acquisition. In B. VanPatten & J. Williams (Eds.), *Theories in second language acquisition: An introduction* (pp. 17–35). Mahwah, NJ: Lawrence Erlbaum Associates.

Venkatagiri, H.S., & Levis, J.M. (2007). Phonological awareness and speech comprehensibility: An exploratory study. *Language Awareness, 16,* 263–277.

Webb, S. (2008). Receptive and productive vocabulary size. *Studies in Second Language Acquisition, 30,* 79–95.

Webb, S. (2010). Pre-learning low-frequency vocabulary in second language television programs. *Language Teaching Research, 14,* 501–515.

White, L. (2007). Linguistic theory, universal grammar, and second language acquisition. In B. VanPatten & J. Williams (Eds.), *Theories in second language acquisition: An introduction* (pp. 37–55). Mahwah, NJ: Lawrence Erlbaum Associates.

Wilkinson, S. (2002). The omnipresent classroom during summer study abroad: American students in conversation with their French hosts. *The Modern Language Journal, 86,* 157–173.

Williams, J. (1999). Learner-generated attention to form. *Language Learning, 49*, 583–625.

Williams, J. (2005). Form-focused instruction. In E. Hinkel (Ed.), *Handbook of research in second language teaching and learning* (pp. 671–691). Mahwah, NJ: Lawrence Erlbaum Associates.

Williams, J.N. (2012). Working memory and SLA. In S. Gass & A. Mackey (Eds.), *The Routledge handbook of second language acquisition* (pp. 427–441). New York: Routledge.

Wray, A. (2000). Formulaic sequences in second language teaching: Principles and practice. *Applied Linguistics, 21*, 463–489.

Wright, T. (2005). *Classroom management in language education.* New York: Palgrave Macmillan.

Yanguas, Í. (2010). Oral computer-mediated interaction between L2 learners: It's about time. *Language Learning & Technology, 14*, 72–93.

Yilmaz, Y. (2011). Task effects on focus on form in synchronous computer-mediated communication. *The Modern Language Journal, 95*, 115–132.

Yun, J. (2011). The effects of hypertext glosses on L2 vocabulary acquisition: A meta-analysis. *Computer Assisted Language Learning, 24*, 39–58.

Zyzik, E., & Polio, C. (2008). Incidental focus on form in a university Spanish literature courses. *The Modern Language Journal, 92*, 53–70.

Index

anxiety: in L2 learning 174–5; measurement of 177–8

aptitude and L2 language learning 15, 118, 162, 169–70, 175–6, 183

Associative-Cognitive CREED 9

attentional resources 60

audiolingualism 11, 90, 115, 121

automatization 27, 84

Autonomous Induction Theory 8

behaviorist theories 38, 90, 115

bilingualism 3, 31, 51, 92, 149–50, 164, 171

clarification request 42, 65

classrooms: EFL 48, 51; ESL 33, 49, 70, 137; interaction in 180; management of 11; second language acquisition in 2; see also instructed second language acquisition (ISLA); instructional contexts of ISLA; second language (L2) classroom interaction

CMC see computer-mediated communication

cognitive linguistic systems 19–20

cognitive processes 1, 6–7, 9, 145, 179, 183

collocations 32, 33, 96, 97, 98, 100, 107, 109, 179, 181

communicative competence 12, 15, 18, 19, 21, 24, 25, 28, 35, 38, 39, 52, 53, 54, 57, 62, 69, 78, 80, 102, 109, 115, 120, 128, 148, 172, 174, 180

communicative language learning 14, 15, 16, 47–54

communicative language interaction see communicative language learning

competence: communicative 12, 15, 18, 19, 21, 24, 25, 28, 35, 38, 39, 52, 53, 54, 57, 62, 69, 78, 80, 102, 109, 115, 120, 128, 148, 172, 174, 180; discourse 19; linguistic 19, 57; pragmatic 129, 139, 148; rule-based 184; sociolinguistic 19; strategic 19

complement sequences 137–8

comprehensibility 118, 122, 123, 124, 126

comprehensible input hypothesis 41

comprehensible output hypothesis 43

comprehension check 42

computer-assisted language learning (CALL) 151–3, 158–9, 183

computer-mediated communication (CMC) 46–7, 49, 54, 69

computer-mediated glosses 104–5

Concept-Oriented Approach 8

confirmation check 42

connectionist theories 9

consciousness-raising tasks 81

Content and Language Integrated Learning (CLIL) 149–51; see also immersion programs

content-based instruction (CBI) 15, 149–51, 183; see also immersion programs

contexts: characteristics of 46–7; influence of 48–9; of L2 acquisition 182–3; social 128, 133, 144, 146–7, 153, 182; *see also* instructional contexts of ISLA
contrastive analysis 115, 116
conversation analysis techniques 53
conversational interaction *see* communicative language learning/ interaction
critical period hypothesis 115, 118
criticism modifiers 138, 140–1
cultural awareness 146; *see also* pragmatics

development: of communicative competence 24, 39, 53–4, 102; of declarative knowledge 53, 130; of English negation 79; of English question 41; of explicit knowledge 31–2, 34, 120; of fluency 155–6; grammar 52, 78–9, 92; of implicit knowledge 25–6, 32–5, 38–9, 53, 86, 120, 131; interlanguage 175; morphosyntactic 119; of motivation 164; of pragmatics knowledge 131–2, 134, 135–7; of procedural knowledge 53, 120, 130; second language (L2) 1–4, 7, 9, 10, 12, 14, 15, 41, 43, 47, 50, 52, 61, 65, 69, 70, 73, 75, 84–5, 87, 88, 92, 117, 123, 125, 148–9, 150, 180, 183
dictogloss activities 51, 68, 85, 88
discourse competence 19
downgraders 137, 140–1
dual coding 108

engagement 6, 99, 103, 152–3, 181
English, as international language 118
English Academic Word List 97
English as a Foreign Language (EFL) classrooms 48, 51
English as a Second Language (ESL) classrooms 33, 49, 70, 137
English negotiation, developmental stages of 79
explicit information 23, 70, 71, 82, 83, 88–9, 90, 93, 124–6, 134, 138, 140, 181

explicit instruction 54, 61, 70–1, 84, 85–6, 90–1, 93, 109, 179; compared to implicit 93; direct 80; and grammar 15, 181; and pragmatics acquisition 134–5, 137–9; and pronunciation acquisition 121, 123–6, 182; resulting in explicit knowledge 31–2; and vocabulary acquisition 102–3, 107–8, 109; *see also* explicit information; explicit knowledge; explicit learning; instruction
explicit knowledge 86, 92, 179; measurement of 28–30; oral narrative test 35–6; about pragmatics 130–1; and pronunciation 119–20; resulting from explicit instruction 31–2; about vocabulary 31–2, 95, 99–100; *see also* explicit information; explicit instruction; explicit learning; knowledge
explicit learning 20–1, 24–6; and the interface hypothesis 26–8; *see also* explicit information; explicit instruction; explicit knowledge; learning

feedback: beneficial results of 50, 51; corrective 10, 34, 40, 59, 62, 64, 65, 72, 73, 106, 121, 122–3, 125, 126, 154, 158, 159, 180, 182; examples of corrective 74–5; metalinguistic 65–6, 85; phonological 69
first language (L1) 3, 8, 20; use of in classroom interaction 46, 48, 52
First Noun Principle 13
focus on form 16, 91, 109; corrective feedback 72; effect of on L2 acquisition 69; examples of 64–6; features of 57–60; input enhancement 71; input flood 70–1; lexical 102; negative evidence 62; noticing of forms 60–2, 68–9; occurrence of 66–7; occurrence of language-related episodes 67–8; pedagogical implications 72–4; and pragmatics instruction 134; and pronunciation acquisition 121, 122–3, 125; summary 180; teachers' statements 160–1; types of 62–4; and vocabulary

acquisition 103, 104–7; *see also* instruction, content-based

focus on forms 58, 81, 91; consciousness-raising tasks 81

focus on meaning 44, 45, 58, 60, 121

foreign literature classes, university level 157

form, attention to 58; *see also* focus on form; focus on forms; form-meaning mapping

form-meaning mapping 96

formulaic chunks 97

fossilization 7, 79

gaming environments, online 153

gender roles 148

generativist perspective 8

goals: communicative 73; of computer-assisted learning 152; of immersion programs 160; of ISLA 44, 179, 183; for L2 instruction 15, 34–5, 135, 151; for L2 study 12, 34–5, 98; linguistic 73; non-linguistic 153, 180; of pragmatics 129; of pronunciation learning 117–18, 126; of study abroad 147; of tasks 44–5, 164; for vocabulary size 98–9

grammar (morpho-syntax) 1, 3; aspects of 76–8; assessment of 30; developmental stages of 79; in at-home contexts 159; prescriptive vs. descriptive 76–7; relation to pragmatics 132; rule-based vs. item-based 78; *see also* grammar acquisition; grammar instruction; grammar rules

grammar acquisition 76; and CALL 152; consciousness-raising tasks 81; developmental sequences 78–9; empirical evidence 86–92; input-based instruction 81–3, 85–6, 87–90; instruction and 79–86; issues in 78–9; output-based instruction 84–5; Present, Practice, Produce (PPP) 83–4, 90–2; summary 181; *see also* grammar; grammar instruction; grammar rules

grammar instruction 11, 15, 16, 25, 50, 60, 79–81; comprehension-based 14; explicit instruction 80; grammar translation 80; present, practice, produce (PPP) 80; production-based 1; *see also* grammar; grammar acquisition; grammar rules

grammar rules 25, 26, 54, 63, 76, 85; value of 18–19; *see also* grammar

grammaticality judgment test 36–7

halo effect 46

homework 104, 109–10

hypertext glosses 105

idioms 97, 108

immersion programs 15, 43, 143–4, 149–51, 157–8, 159–60, 183. *See also* study abroad programs

implicit instruction 30–2, 61, 90–1; compared to explicit 93; implicit knowledge resulting from 33–5; *see also* implicit knowledge; implicit learning; instruction

implicit knowledge 38, 53, 86, 90, 92, 93, 179; of grammar 31; measurement of 28–30; about pragmatics 130–1; and pronunciation 119–20; resulting from explicit instruction 32–3; resulting from implicit instruction 33–4; about vocabulary 95, 99–100, 104; *see also* implicit learning; knowledge

implicit learning 20–1, 24–6; and the interface hypothesis 26–8; *see also* implicit knowledge; learning

incidental learning 63, 109, 181; vs. intentional learning 100–1; and vocabulary acquisition 103–4

individual differences in second language (L2) learning 162; anxiety 174–5; empirical evidence 171–5; foreign language vs. second language contexts 144–5; language learning aptitude 169–70, 175, 183; learning strategies 166–7, 173–4, 183; learning styles 167–8, 183; motivation 163–5, 171–2, 183; pedagogical implications 175–6; personality 168; summary 183; taxonomies of 163; theoretical concerns

163–71; willingness to communicate 165–6, 172–3, 183; working memory 170–1

information: explicit 23, 70, 71, 82, 83, 88–9, 90, 93, 124–6, 134, 138, 140, 181; metapragmatic 135, 138

input: comprehensible 41; positive vs. negative evidence 40; *see also* input enhancement; input flood

input enhancement 63–4, 71, 180

input flood 63, 70–1, 180

Input Hypothesis 41, 80

Input Processing Theory 9, 13–14, 82, 121

instructed second language acquisition (ISLA) 1, 7; defined and described 2–7; general principles for success 184; goal of 183; instructed nature of 4; scope of 14–16; *see also* instructional context of ISLA; second language acquisition (SLA)

instruction: communicative 39, 52; comprehension-based 87–8; content-based 149, 157–8 (*see also* focus on form); general principles for successful 184; input-based 81–3, 87–90, 92; optimization of 1; output-based 84–5; pragmatics 15; processing 6, 82–3, 88–90, 92; production-based 87–8; types of 5; *see also* explicit instruction; grammar instruction; implicit instruction; instructional contexts of ISLA; learning; second language (L2) instruction; vocabulary instruction

instructional contexts of ISLA: at-home (traditional classroom) 143–5; computer-assisted language learning (CALL) 151–3, 158–9, 183; content-based instruction 157–8; empirical evidence 153–9; foreign language vs. second language 144–5, 153–4; immersion 143–4, 149–51, 157–8, 159–60, 183; pedagogical implications 159–60; study abroad 143–4, 146–9, 154–7, 182; summary 182–3; theoretical concerns 144–53

intelligent CALL (iCALL) 152; *see also* computer-assisted language learning (CALL)

intelligibility principle 117–18

intentional learning 109, 181

Interaction Approach 9, 13, 15, 39, 180, 183; on input, interaction, and output 43

interactive tasks 10, 50–1, 69, 73; and CALL 153

intercultural understanding 146

interface hypothesis 23, 26–8, 31

interlanguage 70, 78, 119, 139, 175

interlocutor, characteristics of 45–6, 48

Involvement Load Hypothesis 101–2, 105–6

item-learning, vs. rule-learning 22–3

knowledge: breadth of 98–9; declarative 27; depth of 98–100; linguistic 19–20; phonological 179; pragmalinguistic 129; pragmatics 130–1, 179; procedural 27, 38, 53, 179; *see also* explicit knowledge; implicit knowledge; second language knowledge; vocabulary knowledge

Krashen, Stephen 3, 12–13, 38, 41, 80, 180

language: anxiety about producing 109, 175; aptitude for learning 15, 118, 162, 169–70, 175–6, 183; aspects of 76; attention to 74, 100, 102, 160, 180; cognitive processing of 9; components of 3; and declarative memory 20; exposure to 2, 23, 133–4, 147; first 3, 8, 20, 46, 48, 52; foreign vs. second 144–5, 153–4, 182; forms of 13, 40, 48, 54, 62, 70, 73; morphosyntactic and lexical components of 18, 43; natural learning process for 13; segmental components of 121; semantic processing of 43; in social contexts 3; sounds (pronunciation) of 116; spontaneous use of 20, 26, 39, 179–80; use of to communicate 18–19, 25, 57, 128, 143; *see also* grammar; pragmatics; pronunciation; second language (L2) acquisition; second language (L2) instruction;

second language (L2) knowledge; second
   language (L2) learning; vocabulary
language minority students 150
language-related episodes (LREs) 66, 67–8
learners: engagement of 6, 99, 103, 152–3,
   181; see also individual differences in
   second language (L2) learning; students
learning: vs. acquisition 3; incidental 63,
   103–4, 181; incidental vs. intentional
   100–1; intentional 109, 181; item- vs.
   rule- 22–3; phonological 15; rule 22–3,
   25; second language (SL) 1–2; task-based
   15, 43–5, 147; see also explicit learning;
   implicit learning; learning conditions;
   learning strategies; learning styles
learning conditions, manipulation of 5–6;
   see also instructional contexts of ISLA
learning strategies, and L2 language
   learning 166–7, 173–4, 183
learning styles, and L2 language learning
   167–8, 183
learning-acquisition hypothesis 38–9
lexical downgraders 137, 140–1
lexical items 96–7, 99, 109, 129, 181
lexis 3, 19, 69
linguistic competence 19, 57
linguistic knowledge 19–20
linguistic rules 19
literature classes, university level 157
Long, Michael H. 13, 14

meaning-focused interaction 59, 183
memorization 22–3, 145, 166–7, 169–70;
   see also memory
memory 20–1, 97, 170; declarative vs.
   nondeclarative 20; long-term 61; short-
   term 61; working 16, 61, 163, 170–1, 175,
   176; see also memorization
metalinguistics: explanations 157; rules
   179; task knowledge 33; terminology 85
metapragmatic information 135, 138
Monitor Model of SLA 3, 12–13, 38–9, 180
morphemes 77, 129, 130
morphology 14, 76–7, 96–7; see also
   grammar; grammar instruction;
   morphosyntax

morphosyntax 60, 63, 69, 129; see also
   morphology; syntax
motivation: as factor in L2 learning
   15, 163–5, 171–2, 183; motivation
   questionnaire 176–7
Motivational Self System 164
multiword units 97, 109, 179

natural order hypothesis 12–13
naturalistic L2 acquisition 4, 6
negative evidence 40, 62
negotiation for meaning 40, 41–2, 49, 51,
   53, 121
noticing: effects of focus on form on
   68–9; of the gap 62; importance of
   60–2
Noticing Hypothesis 60–1

online gaming environments 153
oral fluency 147, 154, 157, 159
oral proficiency 182
Oral Proficiency Interview 156
orthographic forms 96, 99
output 42–3; modified 53, 62, 72; practice
   135; role of in interaction 51
output-based instruction 83, 84–5, 87

pair dynamics 46, 48, 52–3, 121
pedagogical implications: of explicit vs.
   implicit instruction 34–5; of focus on
   form 72–5; of grammar acquisition
   92–3; of individual differences in L2
   learning 175–6; of instructional contexts
   of ISLA 159–60; of interaction in the
   second language classroom 52–4; of
   pragmatics acquisition 139; of the
   nature of second language acquisition
   34–5; regarding pronunciation 126
pedagogy, second language 11; see also
   pedagogical implications
peer interaction 46, 53, 73
personality, and L2 learning 168; see
   also individual differences in second
   language (L2) learning
phonemes 24, 60, 116–17, 120, 125, 157
phonetic transcriptions 121

phonology 23–4, 116; phonological forms 96, 99; phonological knowledge 179; phonological learning 15; phonological resources 129; *see also* pronunciation; pronunciation acquisition

phrasal downgraders 137, 140–1

politeness strategies 158

positive evidence 40, 64, 86

practice 14, 19, 22, 25, 27, 32, 53, 73, 121, 125–6, 134–8, 147, 153, 158, 179, 181; *see also* Present, Practice, Produce (PPP)

pragmalinguistics 129–30, 135

pragmatic competence 129, 139, 148

pragmatics 3, 24, 60, 182; aspects of 129–30; *see also* pragmatics acquisition; pragmatics instruction; pragmatics knowledge

pragmatics acquisition 3, 128; empirical evidence 135–9; explicit instruction 134–5, 137–9; and exposure 136–7; instruction and 133–5; issues in 130–3 ; L1 transfer 132; pedagogical implications 139; perception vs. production 132–3; social values and 133; summary 182

pragmatics instruction 15

pragmatics knowledge 179; developmental stages 131–2; implicit and explicit 130–1, 179

Present, Practice, Produce (PPP) 83–4, 90–2

procedural knowledge 27, 38, 53, 179

Processability Theory 8–9, 78–9

processing instruction 6, 82–3, 88–90, 92

proficiency pairing 48; *see also* pair dynamics

prompts 72

pronunciation 3, 15,23, 60, 68, 96; aspects of 116; and CALL 153; in study abroad contexts 157; *see also* phonology; pronunciation acquisition

pronunciation acquisition 115; age and aptitude 118; and audiolinguistic drills 115; by repetition 121; and contrastive analysis 115, 116; empirical evidence 122–6; explicit instruction 121, 123–6;

explicit and implicit pronunciation knowledge 119–20; focus on form 121, 122–3; goals of 117–18; instruction and 121–2; issues in 116–20; pedagogical implications 126; perception vs. production 116–17; and social identity 118–19; summary 182; and technology 121–2; *see also* phonology; pronunciation

psycholinguistic processes 1

recasts 64–5, 72

repetitive drills 11, 38, 115, 121

role plays 136, 139–41

rule learning 25; vs. item-learning 22–3

rule-based competence 184

Schmidt's Noticing Hypothesis *see* Noticing Hypothesis

second language acquisition (SLA) 1, 3–4; vs. learning, 3; measurement of 69; naturalistic 4, 6; research methodology 10–11; social aspects of 1; theory of 7–8; *see also* grammar acquisition; instructed second language acquisition (ISLA); pragmatics acquisition; pronunciation acquisition; vocabulary acquisition

second language (L2) classroom interaction 38–39, 54; components of 39–43; contextual characteristics of 46–7; effects of 50–2; factors 47–50; interlocutor characteristics 45–6; pedagogical implications 52–4; task-based 52; task characteristics 44–5, 47; variables affecting 44–7

second language (L2) instruction: effectiveness of 12–14; goals of 14–15, 18–20; Loewen's taxonomy of 58, 80; pragmatics 15; and vocabulary acquisition 15, 50, 60, 100–3; *see also* explicit instruction; grammar instruction; implicit instruction; instruction

second language (L2) knowledge: acquisition of 24–8; declarative and procedural 21–4; explicit and implicit 20–1; measurement of 28–30; nature of 179–80; *see also* explicit knowledge; implicit knowledge; knowledge; pragmatics knowledge; vocabulary knowledge

second language (L2) learning 1, 2; *see also* individual differences in second language (L2) learning; learning; second language (L2) classroom interaction

second language (L2) pedagogy 11; *see also* second language (L2) classroom interaction; pedagogical implications

second language (L2) reading courses 18

segmentals 116, 124

semantics 68, 69, 99

Silent Way 11

single coding 108

Skill Acquisition Theory 9, 13, 14, 21–2, 27, 121, 179

social contexts 128, 133, 144, 146–7, 153, 182; and CALL 153; *see also* pragmatics; sociopragmatics

Sociocultural Theory 9

sociolinguistic competence 19

sociopragmatics 129–30, 135

speech acts 130

spelling 23, 68, 96

strategic competence 19

students: acquisition of language by 1–9, 13–14, 19; contexts of instruction for 143, 145, 154, 156–7; EFL 48, 51; ESL 33, 49, 70, 137; and focus on form 59–60, 65, 67, 70, 73, 91; and grammar acquisition 79, 91–2; goals of 11–12, 18, 19–20, 26, 34; in immersion programs 146, 147, 150, 156, 158; interactional behaviors of 52–3; language-minority 150; learning strategies of 166–7; learning styles of 73, 157; motivation of 165, 171; and negotiation of meaning 19; and pragmatics 130, 135, 136, 137, 138; preference for explicit instruction by 54; and pronunciation 120; social identity of 52; in study abroad programs 4, 148, 155, 156–7; and vocabulary acquisition 103, 105, 106, 107; willingness of to communicate 172–3; *see also* learners

study abroad programs 143–4, 146–9, 154–7, 182; mixed effects of 156; no effects of 156–7; positive effects of 154–6; *see also* immersion programs

Suggestopedia 11

suprasegmentals 116; *see also* segmentals

syntax 76; *see also* grammar; grammar instruction; morphosyntax

task characteristics 44–5

task-based interaction 15, 43–5, 52, 145

teachability hypothesis 78–9

teachers: and content-based literature courses 160–1; and focus on form 73, 74; goals of 35; and grammar instruction 24–6, 78–9, 80; and immersion programs 147, 149, 150, 151, 154, 157, 158, 159–60; and ISLA 2, 4, 8, 12–13, 16, 18, 34, 40, 41, 43, 45, 52–4, 60, 63, 145, 162; and the manipulation of learning conditions 6; and pragmatics 128, 130, 132, 133, 139; and Processability Theory 9; and pronunciation 116–18, 126; role of 175–6, 183; and Sociocultural Theory 9; and student aptitude 169, 176; and student learning strategies 166, 175–6; and student motivation 163, 165, 171; use of corrective feedback by 154

teaching *see* instruction; teachers

technology: effect of on interaction 46–7, 49; and pragmatics 139; and pronunciation acquisition 121–2; *see also* computer-assisted language learning (CALL); intelligent CALL (iCALL)

think-aloud protocols 10

Total Physical Response (TPR) 11

Universal Grammar (UG) Theory 8, 9

virtual worlds, L2 interaction in 158–9

vocabulary (lexis) 3; aspects of 96–8; assessment of 30; and CALL 153; *see also* vocabulary acquisition; vocabulary instruction; vocabulary knowledge

vocabulary acquisition 23, 95–6; breadth of knowledge 98–9; depth of knowledge test 110–12; through contrastive analysis 102, 107; depth of knowledge 98–100; through dual coding 108; empirical evidence 103–8; through engagement 103; through extensive reading 100–1, 104, 109; form-meaning mapping 96; in first language 101; frequency of exposure 99; pedagogical implications 108–10; summary 181; theoretical concerns 96–103; through translation 102–3, 107–8

vocabulary instruction 15, 50, 60, 100–3
vocabulary knowledge: active vs. passive 99; in at-home contexts 159; as explicit knowledge 179; frequency of word use 98; implicit and explicit 99–100; receptive and productive 99; and relation to pragmatics 132; social setting 97–8; test of levels 112–13; test of levels 112–13

written fluency 154